Media Industries

Perspectives on an Evolving Field

Edited by Amelia Arsenault and Alisa Perren

Media Industries seeks quality research articles for consideration in the publication of upcoming issues. We accept submissions on a rolling basis.

We invite contributions that range across the full spectrum of media industries, including film, television, internet, radio, music, publishing, electronic games, advertising, and mobile communications. Submissions may explore these industries individually or examine inter-medial relations between industrial sectors. We encourage both contemporary and historical studies, and are especially interested in contributions that draw attention to global and international perspectives.

Media Industries is furthermore committed to the exploration of innovative methodologies, imaginative theoretical approaches, and new research directions.

Launched in 2014, *Media Industries* is a peer-reviewed, multi-media, open-access online journal that supports critical studies of media industries and institutions worldwide. We seek to take advantage of the online format by encouraging inclusion of multimedia elements and hyperlinks within the submitted article as well as utilizing a fully online submission process through our website: http://www.mediaindustriesjournal.org.

Articles should be between 5,000 and 7,000 words; word count includes image captions and endnotes, but does not include the bibliography. Full guidelines can be found on our submission page. If you have any questions, please contact the journal at mediaindjournal@gmail.com.

To keep up-to-date with our publications and news, follow us on social media via Twitter @mediaindjournal and on Facebook.

ACKNOWLEDGEMENTS

The essays included in this volume represent the hard work of Media Industries' esteemed editorial board. All 36 essays first appeared in article form in the three introductory issues of the first volume of the journal. As they represent cutting-edge perspectives on the state of the field, many of our colleagues requested that we publish them as a collection.

We would like to acknowledge our editorial board, not only for the considered and diverse pieces that they contributed to this volume, but also for their patience, as our team navigated the exciting, but often unexpectedly challenging process of launching an open-access, not-for profit, peer-reviewed journal from scratch. We would also like to recognize the work of the Editorial Collective, the group of scholars and institutions that not only provided editorial feedback for these articles but whose collective brain power gave birth to Media Industries. They include:

Amelia Arsenault, Georgia State University
Stuart Cunningham, Queensland University of Technology
Michael Curtin, University of California, Santa Barbara
Elizabeth Evans, University Nottingham
Terry Flew, Queensland University of Technology
Anthony Fung, The Chinese University of Hong Kong
Jennifer Holt, University of California, Santa Barbara
Paul McDonald, University of Nottingham
Brian McNair, Queensland University of Technology
Alisa Perren, University of Texas at Austin
Kevin Sanson, Queensland University of Technology

Media Industries is a free, open-access, not-for-profit journal. This endeavor is made possible by the financial and institutional support of our member institutions: The Chinese University of Hong Kong; Georgia State University, Atlanta; Queensland University of Technology; University of California, Santa Barbara; University of Nottingham; and University of Texas at Austin.

We would like to make a particular note of appreciation to the current chair of the GSU Department of Communication, Greg Lisby, as well as to the former chair, David Cheshier. In addition, we extend our thanks to UT-Austin's Moody College of Communication Dean Rod Hart and Radio-Television-Film Department Chair, Paul Stekler. Our departments have wholeheartedly backed the journal, providing graduate research assistance, course releases, and financial support. Without such support, Media Industries – and thus this collection – would not be possible.

Creating an online journal that holds to the highest publication standards – while operating on a shoestring budget – is certainly a challenge. This challenge has been made significantly easier by our amazing team of graduate research assistants. Without them, there would be no journal and no volume. Graduate Student Journal Managers Charlotte Howell (2012 – 2014) and Laura Felschow (2014 -), along with website and logo designer and general tech guru, Kyle Wrather, are deserving of particular recognition for their work.

We would also like to thank the many staff members who have provided support for the journal including: AJ Bunyard, Char Burke, Gloria Holder, and Michelle Monk at UT-Austin and Nedda Ahmed and Jani Faison at GSU. Our colleagues have also provided invaluable advice and support. In particular, we would like to thank: Caroline Frick, Kathy Fuller-Seeley, Shanti Kumar, Tom Schatz, and Ethan Tussey.

Last, but not least, we would like to thank our partners in life, Shawn Powers and Cully Hamner, who have provided emotional support to us through this exciting albeit time-consuming adventure.

CONTENTS

Introduction: Welcome to the Media Industries   1
Media Industries Editorial Collective

1. Dirt Research for Media Industries   5
   Charles Acland

2. Work in the Media   13
   Mark Deuze

3. Media Policy Research and the Media
   Industries   19
   Des Freedman

4. The Value of Ethnography   25
   Tejaswini Ganti

5. On Comparison   33
   Nitin Govil

6. Media Programming in the Era of Big Data   41
   Timothy Havens

7. The Menace of Instrumentalism in Media
   Industries Research and Education   49
   David Hesmondalgh

8. Transnational TV: What Do We Mean by
   "Coproduction" Anymore?   57
   Michele Hilmes

9. The Film Festival as an Industry Node   65
   Dina Iordanova

10. Placing International Media Production   73
    Aphra Kerr

11. The Industrialization and Globalization of   81
    China's Musical Theater
    Shin Dong Kim

12. Media Industries in Revolutionary Times   89
    Marwan M. Kraidy

13. Media Industries in India: An Emerging   97
    Regional Framework
    Shanti Kumar

14. Assembling a Toolkit   107
    Amanda Lotz

15. Welcome to the Unregulated Wild, Wild,   113
    Digital West
    Denise Mann

16. Media Industries and the Ecological Crisis   121
    Richard Maxwell

17. Media Work, Management, and Greed: 127
    A New Agenda?
    Vicki Mayer

18. "Invisible Work" in the Indian Media Industries 133
    Ranjani Mazumdar

19. The Discourse on Media is Dominated by   141
    Reactionary Cant
    Toby Miller

20. On Automation in Media Industries: Integrating   155
    Algorithmic Media Production into Media
    Industries Scholarship
    Philip M. Napoli

21. "It's TV's Fault I Am This Way": Learning   163
    From Love-Hating the Media Industries
    Phil Oppenheim

22. Politically Charged Media Sites: The "Right,"   171
    the "Left," and the Self in Research
    Yeidy Rivero

23. Film Studies, Cultural Studies, and Media   177
    Industries Studies
    Thomas Schatz

24. Navigating the Two Worlds of Research   185
    James Schwoch

25. Advertising, the Media, and Globalization   189
    John Sinclair

26. Selling Television: Addressing Transformations   197
    in the International Distribution of Television
    Content
    Jeanette Steemers

27. Global, Regional, Transnational, Translocal   205
    Joe Straubhaar

28. There Is No Music Industry   215
    Jonathan Sterne

29. Globalization through the Eyes of Runners: 223
    Student Interns as Ethnographers on Runaway
    Productions in Prague
    Petr Szczepanik

30. Where in the World is *Orphan Black*? Change   231
    and Continuity in Global TV Production and
    Distribution
    Serra Tinic

31. The Case for Studying In-Store Media   239
    Joseph Turow

32. Industry Proximity   249
    Patrick Vonderau

33. TV, Digital, and Social: A Debate   257
    Jing Wang

34. Learning from the History of the Field   267
    Janet Wasko

35. The Ramifications of Media Globalization   273
    in the Global South for the Study of Media
    Industries
    Herman Wasserman

36. Home is Where Hollywood Isn't: Recasting   281
    East Asian Film Industries
    Emilie Yueh_yu Yeh

    Contributors   288

    About Media Industries   299

Introduction

Welcome to Media Industries

MEDIA INDUSTRIES EDITORIAL COLLECTIVE

Media industry studies has grown substantially since the 1980s as scholars have sought to understand the significance of dramatic transformations in the media landscape. In a historical sense, it was not so long ago that media industries largely comprised tightly regulated institutions in service of a national imaginary. To the extent that their operations crossed borders, their activities were kept under the watchful eye of national guardians. In only a short time we have witnessed the growth and consolidation of huge transnational conglomerates and media infrastructures in virtually every corner of the globe. Relentless pressure from corporate enterprises and financial markets sparked waves of innovation that have profoundly transformed the ways in which media are produced, regulated, distributed, marketed, and consumed. These developments extended the reach of dominant players while simultaneously ushering in a period of unruly innovation that has fostered niche production, DIY creativity, and novel networks of cultural flows. Such interconnected trends have afforded unprecedented circulation for products springing from the margins and opened doors to new modes of exchange that were unimaginable even ten years ago.

These transformations in the media industries have invigorated the scholarly pursuit of new conceptual approaches and innovative methodologies. What was once an area largely characterized by historical, management, quantitative, and political economic studies has become a burgeoning and fully articulated subfield that transcends disciplines and academic societies. Media industry studies has evolved into a truly global endeavor characterized by the proliferation of research sites and a surging expansion of industry-centered programs around the world. The subfield now welcomes discursive, ethnographic, and conjunctural analysis along with investigations of labor practices, networks of production, urban and economic geography, genealogies of media policy and ownership, and the politics of difference in institutional settings and sites of circulation.

Despite this marked growth, it is nevertheless remarkable that media industry studies still lacks a journal specifically dedicated to this rich and diverse literature. With this in mind, members of the *Media Industries* editorial collective began conversations about the possibility of launching such a publication: one that could be as innovative and transformative as the industries it studies. We therefore committed ourselves to a timely, open-access format that would embrace the potential of the online world while honoring the traditions of judicious peer review under the leadership of an esteemed editorial board. We considered this balance between innovation and scholarly tradition to be essential because we wanted our authors to feel comfortable that their scholarship would be widely available online and yet as presentable to tenure and merit review committees as other leading media studies journals.

Media Industries is therefore a peer-reviewed, open-access, online journal promoting critical studies of media industries, institutions, and policies worldwide. We invite contributions that examine the full spectrum of media industries, including but not limited to film, television, internet, radio, music, publishing, gaming, advertising, animation, merchandising, and mobile communications. Submissions may explore these industries individually or examine intermedial relations between industrial sectors through a diverse array of theoretical and methodological approaches ranging from media law and policy to labor studies, from cultural studies to political economy, and everywhere in between. We encourage contemporary and historical studies and are especially interested in contributions that draw attention to global and international perspectives that produce genuinely insightful comparative studies. The journal is furthermore dedicated to the exploration of inventive methodologies, imaginative theoretical approaches, creative uses of the online publishing format, and new research directions.

The ambitious scope outlined above made it clear to us that ongoing operations would require many hands and perspectives. While traditionally journals are operated by one or two managing editors, *Media Industries* represents an international collaboration among six universities on four different continents: Chinese University of Hong Kong; Georgia State University; the University of California, Santa Barbara; the University of Nottingham; the University of Texas at Austin; and Queensland University of Technology.

The journal's administrative and editorial processes are managed by leading faculty—what we have termed "the editorial collective"—from these institutions. We paired this editorial collective with an editorial board that also spans the globe. We hope that the geographic and theoretical diversity of our leadership as well as the open-access platform will attract submissions and readers from around the world.

Given our genesis and the mission outlined above, we decided to devote the first three issues of *Media Industries* to short essays contributed by our editorial board. In these commentaries—which will be published over the next several months—individual board members offer a range of perspectives on the history, current status, and future prospects for media industry studies. Some essays focus on key issues, some on theoretical concerns, and others on methodology. This diversity aims both to represent the richness of this area of study and to invite a genuine variety of contributions for upcoming issues.

We're now open for business, so please send us your submissions, which will be peer reviewed by members of our editorial collective and editorial board. We expect the journal to remain a dynamic entity that will continue to evolve in response to industry and academic trends as well as the world of online publishing. We thus invite our readers to email us with any ideas or suggestions, and we encourage contributors to fully exploit the creative capacities of the internet by including multimedia elements, audiovisual material, and hyperlinks in their submissions. We look forward to your submissions and your engagement with what we believe to be one of the most exciting endeavors in academic publishing.

Sincerely,

The Editorial Collective

Amelia Arsenault, Georgia State University

Stuart Cunningham, Queensland University of Technology

Michael Curtin, University of California, Santa Barbara

Terry Flew, Queensland University of Technology

Anthony Fung, The Chinese University of Hong Kong

Jennifer Holt, University of California, Santa Barbara

Paul McDonald, University of Nottingham

Brian McNair, Queensland University of Technology

Alisa Perren, University of Texas at Austin

Kevin Sanson, University of California, Santa Barbara

1.

Dirt Research For Media Industries

CHARLES ACLAND

As the research ferment that falls under the general heading of
"media industries" continues to expand, it is curious how taken for
granted that domain can appear to be. But what are these "media
industries" of which we speak? One thinks of large-scale
coordinated production and distribution activity oriented toward
commercial cultural production. The plural "industries" mirrors the
plural "media," and together as a term immediately reference the
big culture businesses of motion pictures, broadcasting, music,
publishing, cable, and social media. Even the industry studies of
subcultural, micro-organizational, and non-dominant media
activities still, by and large, articulate to these grand domains.
Unlike the more singularly inflected "culture industry" defined by
Adorno and company,[1] where an array of productive mechanisms
coordinate to produce mass capitalist societies and subjects, "media
industries" tries to capture more asynchronous endeavors, ones that
might in fact be in competition with one another. Nonetheless, with
the settlement of transmedia as a major shared conceptual umbrella,
"media industries" today has come to reference a field with a
degree of coherence, one into which "convergence" smuggles an
idea of symbiosis among media forms. In this way, we write and
think about media corporations, producers of media commodities,
and harvesters of profit from expressive and communicative
materials as sharing core features, agendas, audiences, practices,
and technologies. As a result, the appreciation of variance and
multiplicity in media is dampened.

The work of maintaining plurality and provisionality in our critical
engagements produces another demand. As someone who has
insisted on the necessity of understanding the multiplicity of the
film industry, and of seeing it as entwined with a range of media
and other businesses, I still confront the frustrating need to
reference something called "the film industry," with all the implied

5

coherence I want to refute. The plural in writing can come across as a forced and clunky stylistic demand, one that draws inordinate attention to itself and slows down progress to the point one actually wishes to make. It's the writerly equivalent of trudging in rain boots on a sunny day.

But there it is. We just seem to know what we are talking about when we evoke "media industry" in its singular or plural form, and it suggests a coherence that may in fact be lacking. Of course, media industries produce far more than media commodities. First, study of publicly funded and mandated cultural institutions is one of the more underdeveloped domains of American media industries research. Additionally, as the major contributions of cultural theory instruct us, cultural enterprises of all sorts produce audiences, fans, artists, conversations, understandings, spaces, occasions, moods, communities, differences, divisions, myths, falsehoods, and so on. The more regularized patterns of activity settle provisionally into cultural formations, consisting of localized waves of activity, styles, and priorities. Cultural formations are provisional features of cultural life. They bear a degree of informality that makes identifying them challenging. But they provoke and can act as agents of change. Though these are just some general components of cultural production, and there are many others, to ignore them would seriously wound our ability to respond to, and comment upon in a meaningful fashion, the conditions of our time.

Media industries have long been exemplars of post-Fordist, "disorganized" capitalism, with their flexible operations, short-term contract labor, and high geographic mobility. The media industries are, in many ways, the neoliberal vanguard of advanced digital capitalism. The concomitant massification of large media-focused corporations and the multiplication of small media businesses is a situation that has given fuel to the tales of start-up Davids slinging killer apps at generally receptive old media Goliaths, and being rewarded with unimaginable riches. Indeed, Malcolm Gladwell's newest bestseller is yet another contribution to the mythological advantages of being disadvantaged.[2] This ideological mystification, clouding the concrete production of material advantage with the foggy reverie of magical bastion-storming, resonates with a broad embrace of individual, promotional, and aspirational narratives of success. Gina Neff's *Venture Labor* offers detailed myth-busting about these narratives, documenting the actual precarious work conditions in the high-tech industry.[3]

We are in the midst of the full flourishing of the enterprise society, which Michel Foucault identified as a truly distinctive feature of neoliberal society, more so than tropes of spectacle or supermarket.[4] Nowhere is this more apparent than in the media industries. The thrill of the fast buck made on the virtual capitalization of personal data, which characterizes many of the most visible digital media start-ups in recent years, has sparked a new celebration of "idols of production." Leo Lowenthal coined this characteristic in 1944, noting that it had been overtaken as a theme of popular biographical articles by "idols of consumption."[5] Well, the attention paid to Jobs, Zuckerberg, Gates, and others of that moneyed ilk suggests that those idols of production, though of a decidedly twenty-first century digital kind, have returned. The difference this time around is that enthusiasm for YouTube, Facebook, Google, LinkedIn, and Twitter springs from the possibility that their wares will engender some other new enterprise that in turn will rocket to riches. The social media wonder is that they provide platforms — the software infrastructure — for success elsewhere. Social media have leveraged a new tycoon culture; namely, a limitless promise of more tycoons. Parts of the media industries are converging to become an *enterprise industry*.

I present these claims, partial as they are, to mark some of the cultural dimensions that might be overlooked by research more closely attentive to strictly defined industrial operations and organizations. But even on a narrowly industrial terrain, there are forces and histories that often remain untapped in analysis. Currently, the most prominent scholarly approaches on the critical scene are production culture studies focusing on media work contexts, political economic analysis prioritizing ownership and commodities, and policy studies attending to regulatory structures. To unsettle our view of what we study when we study "media industries," the innovations of economist and historian Harold Innis can be instructive. In the 1930s and 1940s, Innis proposed that a study of the resource-based infrastructure of major industrial sectors was essential to any full accounting and understanding of economic life. This deep infrastructural analysis involved comparative historical study through archival research that ran the gamut of documentation, including secondary historical accounts, government papers, corporate records, and ephemera. Additionally, Innis insisted upon extensive field research, and in a self-deprecating manner called himself a "dirt economist." By "dirt" research, Innis meant a form of witnessing and experiencing the sites, routes, venues, and operations of industrial production, refinement, and transport. To do this, he travelled extraordinary distances through remote regions, doing so by rail, boat, and canoe. This "dirt" research was not conventional ethnographic writing, but rather a form of attentiveness to the minute and localized aspects of extraction, transportation, refinement, and distribution stages of the economy, whether at moments of ascension, prosperity, or decline.[6]

Innis's "dirt" research helps us expand the boundaries of media industries studies to encompass some of the foundational resource requirements and implications of the production and distribution of media works. If we follow the traces of industrial impacts backward, we end up at the level of minerals, the manufacture of basic materials, and the resource economies that underlie the production and circulation of goods. So much of Innis's work on the history of communication focused on paper, its manufacture, its distinction from other writing materials like papyrus and manuscript, and its role in constructing monopolies of economy and knowledge. Today, he would say our media environment requires an economic history of plastic, microchips, processing units, and electrical power.

Via Innis, we've had a way to understand that the newspaper and book trade was also a lumber and railroad industry. A model of economic depth would, for example, capture film as a chemical and electronics industry, radio as a physics industry, television as a mining industry, and the Internet as an electricity industry. No media industry operates without an elaborate distribution network specifically designed for a medium's particular technological contours, which means that the speed of travel for goods and materials plays prominently in the state of industrial endeavors. In fact, this is a defining characteristic for a media industry: Of all the possible forms of mediation one might imagine, it is this distributive feature that typifies highly developed industrialization of a medium. At one level, media commodities are but a surface manifestation of a deep structure of materials and their movement.

Our analytical capabilities would be impoverished if they only charted the topsoil and ignored the geological layers beneath. Pursuing the dirt and depth of cultural economies should not dissolve medium specificity, but should help us conceptualize and understand the full systemic entwinement of our media objects with resource economies. This opens up the historical contingencies of industrial expansion, such that a media industry can only develop in a relative fashion with the resource industries it relies upon.[7]

As I read so much invigorating and inspiring work that operates in the orbit of media industries research, some of it veers into the cozy territory occupied by Paul Lazarsfeld's definition of *administrative research*, "carried through in the service of some kind of administrative agency of public or private character."[8] Some accounts of industrial relations and activities inadvertently naturalize "the industry" as a timeless and essential beast. Yes, media industries are crucial points of focus for our critical imagination if only due to their dominant presence in daily life. But we must continue to seek wider epistemological frames for investigating, and keeping tabs on, the enterprises that spring from the pool of media activities and ambitions, frames that trouble us to see the dirt and depth of economic systems and the shifting tendencies in cultural formations that result.

---

1 Horkheimer, Max, and Theodor W. Adorno, *Dialectic of Enlightenment: Philosophical Fragments*, (1944; reprint, Stanford, CA: Stanford University Press, 2002).

2 Malcolm Gladwell, *David and Goliath: Underdogs, Misfits, and the Art of Battling Giants* (New York: Little, Brown and Company, 2013).

3 Gina Neff, *Venture Labor: Work and the Burden of Risk in Innovation Industries* (Cambridge: MIT Press, 2012).

4 Michel Foucault, *The Birth of Biopolitics: Lectures at the Collège de France, 1978-1979* (New York: Picador, 2008), 251.

5 Leo Lowenthal, "The Triumph of Mass Idols," in *Literature, Popular Culture, and Society* (Englewood Cliffs, NJ: Prentice-Hall, 1961 [1944]), 109-136.

6 The fullest account of this aspect of Innis's work appears in the recent release William J. Buxton, ed., *Harold Innis and*

the North: Appraisals and Contestations (Montreal/Kingston: McGill-Queen's University Press, 2013).

7 The work of Lisa Parks and Nicole Starosielski is offering such advances, e.g. *Signal Traffic: Critical Studies of Media Infrastructures* (Urbana: University of Illinois Press, forthcoming).

8 Paul Lazarsfeld, "Remarks on Administrative and Critical Communication Research," *Studies in Philosophy and Social Science* 9, no. 1 (1941): 8.

Bibliography

Buxton, William J., editor. *Harold Innis and the North: Appraisals and Contestations.* Montreal/Kingston: McGill-Queen's University Press, 2013.

Foucault, Michel. *The Birth of Biopolitics: Lectures at the Collège de France, 1978-1979.* New York: Picador, 2008.

Gladwell, Malcolm. *David and Goliath: Underdogs, Misfits, and the Art of Battling Giants.* New York: Little, Brown and Company, 2013.

Horkheimer, Max, and Theodor W. Adorno. *Dialectic of Enlightenment: Philosophical Fragments.* 1944: reprint, ,Stanford, CA: Stanford University Press, 2002.

Lazarsfeld, Paul. "Remarks on Administrative and Critical Communication Research." *Studies in Philosophy and Social Science* 9, no. 1 (1941): 2-16.

Lowenthal, Leo. "The Triumph of Mass Idols." In *Literature, Popular Culture, and Society.* Englewood Cliffs, NJ: Prentice-Hall, 1961 [1944], 109-136.

Neff, Gina. *Venture Labor: Work and the Burden of Risk in Innovation Industries.* Cambridge: MIT Press, 2012.

Parks, Lisa and Nicole Starosielski. *Signal Traffic: Critical Studies of Media Infrastuctures*. Urbana: University of Illinois Press, forthcoming.

2.

Work in the Media

MARK DEUZE

People spend more time with media today than at any previous point in history. The number of media channels, forms, genres, devices, applications, and formats is multiplying—more media are produced every year, and we spend more of our time concurrently exposed to media. At the same time, the news about work in the media is less than optimistic. Reports about continuing layoffs across all media industries—most notably, film and television entertainment, journalism, digital game development, and advertising—are paramount. This suggests a paradox: as people engage with media in an increasingly immersive, always-on, almost instantaneous, and interconnected way, the very people whose livelihood and sense of professional identity depend on delivering media content and experiences seem to be at a loss on how to come up with survival strategies—in terms of business models, effective regulatory practices (for example regarding copyrights and universal access provisions), and perhaps, most specifically, the organization of entrepreneurial working conditions that would support and sustain the creative process needed to meet the demands of a global market saturated with media.

The well-documented precarious nature of employment across the media industries—I respectfully refer to the published work of editorial board members of *Media Industries*—does not seem to scare off students choosing careers in the creative industries. Schools, departments, and programs in media, communication, journalism, and related disciplines are continually overflowing. To some extent, it is problematic that we tend to advertise our programs with unquestioned statistics demonstrating that a majority of alumni secured jobs in the media, often using a handful of high-profile alumni-turned-media-professionals to suggest that enrolled students are on their way to becoming just as successful. What we neglect to tell incoming students is that the majority of "jobs" these

13

alumni have are based on temporary contracts (if contracted at all), that these stars generally did not get to where they are now based on any predictable or stable career trajectory, and that even if they enjoy some kind of stardom, their environment tends to consider them only as good as the last project they completed. I am not suggesting that we should discourage students from pursuing what they are passionate about; I am just highlighting the ways that, despite our best intentions, media scholars contribute to the mythical status of media professions.

Beyond the popularity of degree programs and careers related to the media industries, it must be said that the developments affecting media industries and professions are not unique. Across the manufacturing, service, and creative industries, a new world of work is taking shape that seems to be premised on individual rather than industry-level responsibility, requires a high degree of skillset flexibility, and implicitly expects portfolio careerism. Media industries are notable in this context for their long history of manifesting these broader trends, and in some instances serving as an inspiration for management developments in other economic sectors. Moreover, media industries are unique with regard to the powerful link between work and self-realization that is generally evident in motivations to pursue creative careers. This individualization of work (in terms of motivations and careers) makes media professionals both easier and harder to manage: easier, because they are less likely to engage in collective action and bargaining, and harder because managing a more or less temporary network of fragmented individuals can be quite costly and complicated.

As students and scholars of media industries, we have tended to respond to these trends either by altogether ignoring the labor context of media production — considering the relative "youth" of what only recently has been conceptualized as media production studies — or by both celebrating and condemning the ways in which media work is organized. Celebratory accounts tend to emphasize the value of entrepreneurship, self-actualization, creativity, and freedom expected of a career in the media, whereas critical perspectives highlight media work's (self-) exploitative, impermanent, and insecure nature. In fairness, most of the literature on the organization of labor in media industries tends to at least

14

recognize both perspectives at work. Similarly, both our teaching and studying of media industries should always be mindful of both pleasurable and precarious elements that make up the lived experience of media work.

The key challenge moving forward, as I see it, is not so much settling normative debates about the quality of media work or the power imbalances present throughout media industries. We have an opportunity to better prepare students and to articulate a more complex view of media industries by looking at the ways in which media professionals navigate and negotiate the ecosystem in which they are drawn—neither as individuals nor as contracted and salaried employees of small or large companies but as more or less stable collectives moving through the field of work.

Media workers develop all kinds of tactics and strategies to counter the precarity embedded in their work styles. For example, they informally self-organize into groups or teams that tend to move from project to project together for a certain period of time. These so-called semi-permanent work groups (SPWG) benefit both employer and employee, as the first can outsource the hiring and firing of team members to those in charge of specific aspects of the production process (such as team leads in game development, magazine editors, or assistant directors in film and television), whereas employees can secure future employment through their (largely informal) personal networks.[1] These SPWGs are not without power, as the creative talent of their—generally informal— leaders can be an essential element in the production process, allowing them to make certain demands. SPWGs are not just teams of individuals: the definition must be extended to include local or global networks of firms and companies, as well as temporary lineups of the interests of consumers and producers in specific user-producer communities (such as in the case of citizen journalism projects) or contexts (as in discussion forums related to television shows or computer games). To this list one could add start-ups—a typical feature in media industries such as advertising agencies and film production houses since at least the 1980s, and increasingly common in the news and mobile games industries.

Beyond specific organizational forms, an additional focus of study should be the ways in which media professionals collectively organize in order to reduce the precarity intrinsic to their careers.

An example of this is a *Broodfonds*, or "bread fund," defined on Wikipedia as a Dutch organization that helps independent entrepreneurs provide sick leave. Professionals who choose to participate can join or form a group of similar people and pay a regular amount each month; if a member falls sick, he or she is paid from the group's account to provide for primary needs. Other examples are organized networks beyond the scope of institutions, such as trade unions, including but not limited to online communities (often through Facebook and LinkedIn) documenting best and worst practices of employers in specific media sectors; professional associations of particular subgroups in media work (such as online journalists and below-the-line workers in film and television); and even social groups through which media workers gather to exchange information (and "war stories") during and after work. Such social groups include atelier-style work environments, after-hours bars, specific teams at sport clubs and events, and so on.

My point is that beyond individual agency, creative autonomy, and self-realization, the experience of an active, critical yet supportive peer community is a key motivation to work in media industries. Because of precarity, the ongoing fragmentation of media companies, and the project-based nature of much media work, participation in somewhat stable peer communities is anything but guaranteed. It is clear that media professionals find all kinds of ways of reconstituting themselves as collectives, and perhaps it is there that what it means to work in the media is articulated most precisely. That intentional collectives catalyze the nature of media work raises numerous challenges for the researcher: how to find such places and people, how to procure and maintain access, how to develop ways to document this kind of research, and how to validate and report it effectively (to media scholars and students, as well as professionals). It must be clear that to study the way media industries do what they do is an exciting, emerging, and challenging endeavor. Beyond an understandable fixation on individuals and stars in production studies research and teaching, I would advocate a renewed focus on the social, communal, and collaborative aspects that make up much of the lived experience of media work today, because I feel it is there where instances of empowerment and agency for media professionals can most often be found.

1 Helen Blair, Nigel Culkin, and Keith Randle, "From London to Los Angeles: A Comparison of Local Labour Market Processes in the US and UK Film Industries," *International Journal of Human Resource Management* 14 (2003): 619–33.

Bibliography

Blair, Helen, Nigel Culkin, and Keith Randle. "From London to Los Angeles: A Comparison of Local Labour Market Processes in the US and UK Film Industries." *International Journal of Human Resource Management* 14 (2003): 619–33.

3.

Media Policy Research and the Media Industries

DES FREEDMAN

How the media industries "work" is connected to how they are structured in relation to the various policy frameworks to which they are exposed. In order to fathom the dynamics of these industries, therefore, one of our tasks is to research media policy environments and pressures. And yet there is a problem, based in part on reputation and in part on conception. All too often, media *policy* research is viewed as not just a poor relative of more exciting media industries research but rather the boring next-door neighbor who spends too long at your house, convinced that he has lots of interesting things to say while everyone else makes polite excuses and tries to usher him out.

There is good reason for this. Both media policy and media policy research are frequently reduced to the drawing up of rules and regulations, of laws and liabilities, rather than the setting of boundaries within which these interventions are devised and implemented. Furthermore, media policy lacks the participatory edge of other areas of media production and consumption: it does not have fans or celebrities or the seductive powers of actors and special effects; it lacks exoticism and is "marginal" only to the extent that it appears to be indifferent to everyday life; it lacks transparency and accessibility; and it marginalizes agency. Of course there are media policy "actors" but they are remote and "expert": civil servants, ministers, special advisers, lobbyists, moguls, executives, technologists, entrepreneurs, and the odd academic. Media policy has a particularly pragmatic and positivist character and is understood (and often researched) in terms of political bargaining processes rather than creative practice. Policies exist on pieces of paper, they are written in arcane parliamentary language, and they are to be applied and expected to achieve measurable effects. They are tangible, rational, necessary prescriptions for a healthy media ecology.

Most of the time media policy *appears* to work this way and most of the time, many (though certainly not all) media policy researchers are implicated in this process. We provide the evidence, turn up at the seminars, produce the submissions, and bid for the research projects. We participate in a system over which we have little control but a great desire to make work better—more efficiently, more rationally and, perhaps, more democratically.

What is the problem with this approach? First, this account of policy reminds me of Stephen Lukes's description of the first "face" of power which is all about the visible jostling for advantage in any bargaining process.[1] Think back to Robert Dahl's study of the political system of New Haven, Connecticut, *Who Governs?*,[2] where politics is dominated by coalitions, rival groups of actors and interests, none of whom could be said to exercise complete control. This is a form of pluralist politics that, according to Dahl, is notable for its "dispersion of political resources," the "disappearance of elite rule," and the emergence of polyarchy, which Dahl saw ultimately as a benign mode of democratic politics.[3]

But this is not how I understand media policy, which I see not simply as conflictual, but rather a fundamentally distorted process where rival interests interact in unequal conditions in order to shape the dynamics of the media environment and to lay the preconditions for the production, circulation, and consumption of media goods. This means that we need to look at ideologies as well as institutions, power as well as paperwork, elites as well as evidence. As Matthias Kunzler argues, we need a "force of ideas approach" to think about the values espoused by leading actors in the policy process and how these then have an impact on the design and institutionalization of different approaches to the media world.[4] Given the domination of neoliberal conceptions of market value and private property together with the tensions apparent across the world in relation to issues of media ownership, surveillance, freedom of expression, and representation, I hardly need to spell out that there is a lot more to media policymaking than the happy pluralism with which it is often associated by those "inside the circle," particularly in places like the US and the UK.

It also means that it is vital *not* to insulate questions of policy from those of content and creative practice and from the spaces of media

---

institutions and flows. The artificial separation between policy and media production and consumption weakens our understanding of media industries. The aesthetic strategies, creative endeavors, and forms of resistance that may or may not be present in popular, everyday communication are critically related to the wider structural contexts of media environments in which certain types of behavior and certain political preferences are rewarded or marginalized. The ability to not only talk "truth to power" but to represent the voices of ordinary people, to speak in dialect, to open up conversations that others do not want to open up, to reflect the way a society is headed—all these are constrained by the policy choices debated and enacted in any contemporary mediated society. Media policy matters so much precisely because it relates to an increasingly central part of the way in which governments everywhere seek to legitimize themselves—through management and control of the means of communication—and in which citizens seek to navigate the world in which we live.

Of course, media policy is not simply about elite news management but about wider processes of social reproduction seen as the terms on which society represents itself and holds itself accountable. It is about who is allowed to speak on social media, in the press, on television, and how the conversations are structured. Media policy shapes and is shaped by contextual factors: Are media industries designed to make money for advertisers, to massage the ego of a particular administration, or to help produce informed, active, independently-minded citizens? What are the connections between state elites and media elites? What are the labor and speech conditions under which media professionals are able to work? Media policies help to structure these outcomes and we should not allow its research orientation to be reduced, as it often is, either to administrative procedure or to technological multiple choice.

We need, therefore, to treat media policy a bit more like a production study, to investigate as Mayer et al. put it, "the complexity of routines and rituals, the routines of seemingly complex processes, the economic and political forces that shape roles, technologies, and the distribution of resources according to cultural and demographic differences."[5] Above all, we need to engage with questions of power in terms of the distribution of resources that are concentrated inside the media and the struggles for the redistribution of those resources.

My second thought is about what happens when media policy breaks out of its institutional location—when it moves from the private dining and meeting rooms, from the palaces and parliaments, into public arenas and, sometimes even, onto the streets. This has happened in a whole number of places in recent years, including in Mexico City with the Yo Soy 132 movement protesting the duopoly of Televisa and TV Azteca; in Athens following the shutdown of the Greek public service broadcaster; in Istanbul where protestors gathered outside private TV stations complaining about the refusal by mainstream TV to cover the attacks on peaceful demonstrators in Taksim Gezi Park; and in the US, where there were protests in at least twelve cities against the takeover of local newspapers by the politically and socially conservative Koch Brothers.

Perhaps these protests were simply responses to undesirable media policies: bad ones, misguided ones, or "nonexistent" ones.[6] But I want to argue that these protests constitute a central element of the policy process: the public contestation of the terms on which policies are conceptualized and debated. This is what I call public participation in the policy process, even though it is usually bad-tempered, not within the guidelines of the usual methods for taking part, not couched in particularly parliamentary language, and sometimes not even using the language of media policy at all. Nevertheless, this is living, breathing media policy and it should be taken just as seriously as the formal submissions to a parliamentary select committee. More significantly for this journal, these protests matter because they ask fundamental questions about the conditions under which creative practices take place (or are prevented from taking place).

In these circumstances, we need an approach to media policy that is ideological as opposed to administrative, political as opposed to partisan, interested as opposed to disinterested, and committed to principles of social justice rather than serving the interests of either state or private elites in their pursuit of "efficiencies" and control. When we consider how best to respond to controversies concerning ownership, net neutrality, press freedom, copyright, labor relations—all of them phenomena that condition the dynamics and the possibilities of the media industries—we need to think of policy as both an empirical fact and an ideological tool. Indeed, media policy in particular is becoming increasingly contested as the resources needed to govern and control media are becoming increasingly intertwined with processes of mediation.

If media policy is to be made meaningful, inclusive, and democratic, then it will have to be dragged, kicking and screaming, from the corridors of power and into the public domain. The same goes for media policy research that can illuminate the wider mechanisms of power that underpin the performance and possibilities of media industries. We need a research agenda for the media industries that examines not just performative routines and creative rituals, not just the allocation of resources and the mechanisms of representation, but the power relations that are brought to bear in shaping the policy contexts that underlie these phenomena. If we do so, perhaps more people will then invite us 'round to dinner.

---

1 Steven Lukes, *Power: A Radical View* (Basingstoke: Palgrave Macmillan, 2005 [1974]).
2 Robert Dahl, *Who Governs? Democracy and Power in an American City* (London: Yale University Press, 2005 [1961]).
3 Dahl, *Who Governs?*, 85-86.
4 Matthias Kunzler, "'It's the Idea, Stupid!' How Ideas Challenge Broadcasting Liberalization," in *Trends in Communication Policy Research*, eds. Natascha Just and Manuel Puppis (Bristol: Intellect, 2012), 57.
5 Vicki Mayer, Miranda Banks, and John Thornton Caldwell, "Introduction: Production Studies: Roots and Routes," in *Production Studies: Cultural Studies of Media Industries*, eds. Vicki Mayer, Miranda Banks, and John Thornton Caldwell (New York: Routledge, 2009), 4.
6 Des Freedman, "Media Policy Silences: The Hidden Face of Communications Decision-making," *International Journal of Press/Politics* 15, no. 3 (2010): 344-61.

Bibliography

Dahl, Robert. *Who Governs? Democracy and Power in an American City*. London: Yale University Press, 2005 [1961].

Freedman, Des. "Media Policy Silences: The Hidden Face of Communications Decision-making." *International Journal of Press/Politics* 15, no. 3 (2010): 344-61.

Kunzler, Matthias. "'It's the Idea, Stupid!' How Ideas Challenge Broadcasting Liberalization." In *Trends in Communication Policy Research*, edited by Natascha Just and Manuel Puppis 55-74. Bristol: Intellect, 2012.

Lukes, Steven. *Power: A Radical View*. Basingstoke: Palgrave Macmillan, 2005 [1974].

Mayer, Vicki, Miranda Banks, and John Thornton Caldwell, "Introduction: Production Studies: Roots and Routes." In *Production Studies: Cultural Studies of Media Industries*, edited by Vicki Mayer, Miranda Banks, and John Thornton Caldwell. 1-12. New York: Routledge, 2009.

4.

The Value of Ethnography

TEJASWINI GANTI

Imagine a media-making context where most contracts are oral, nothing is written down, nearly everyone is related, and no one knows exactly how much money a film has made. What sort of media industry is that? Actually, a very successful one – one that has been captivating and entertaining audiences throughout the globe for more than six decades. I am referring to the Hindi-language film industry located in Mumbai, an industry that is now more commonly referred to as "Bollywood" both within India and globally. Although aesthetically, culturally, and structurally distinct from Hollywood, the Hindi film industry is as prolific and powerful in its production and circulation of narratives and images; as globally ambitious in terms of seeking new markets; and as driven by commercial imperatives. As an anthropologist whose research site is the Hindi film industry and whose main methodological approach to the study of media industries is long-term ethnographic fieldwork, in this essay I want to highlight the utility of ethnography as a method that enables us to address questions of practice, social relations, and subjectivity – issues critical to understanding media industries, but mostly inaccessible from a conventional cultural industry approach. An ethnographic approach to media industries can help us to accomplish three important goals: to diversify the study of media industries; to take into account contestations over status and other forms of cultural and symbolic capital that characterize the "field" of media production;[1] and to be able to critically examine discourses and quantitative data generated by media industries.

While it has become a truism that audiences and the practices of media consumption are diverse, scholars and lay people alike frequently assume that the processes of media production – mainly due to the technological properties of film and television – are somehow the same all over the world. An ethnographic approach to media production is important for understanding how differently media are produced, and for countering the ethnocentrism of much of the scholarship on media industries that is mainly based on the study of North American and Western European media institutions and corporate capitalism. Critically, the commercial nature of a media industry does not render its structure or organization transparent. For example, while the Hindi film industry is a commercially driven, blockbuster-oriented industry, its structures of financing and distribution, sites of power, organization of labor, and overall work culture are quite distinct from media industries located in the US. In contrast to Hollywood, the Hindi film industry is highly decentralized, has been financed primarily by entrepreneurial capital, organized along social and kin networks, and until the early 2000s was governed by oral rather than written contracts. Yet, even with its fragmented, decentralized, and informal nature, the Hindi film industry has been producing big-budget films that are as globally ubiquitous and commercially successful as those produced by integrated media conglomerates funded by corporate capital. Hence, within the field of media industry studies, we must expand our understanding of what an "industry" is and not presume certain organizational structures, division of labor, or financial arrangements from the outset. In fact, a productive avenue of inquiry would be to examine what structures, representations, and practices help to constitute a media industry as an "industry." For example, the Indian state granted "industry status" to filmmaking only in 1998, so one of the questions I explore in my research is the value and impact of that state recognition.

Ethnography grounds the study of media in a specific time and space and offers insights into the processes, possibilities, and constraints of media production that are not apparent from close readings of media texts or analysis of macro-level data about media institutions and commercial outcomes. A focus on the processes and practices of production allows us to look beyond the instances of "success" — those films or shows that do get completed and distributed in some manner — since many films or television shows do not progress beyond a conceptualization or pilot stage, and some are abandoned halfway. Such "failures" also add to our knowledge, offering productive insights and possibilities for theorizing about cinema and other media forms.[2] Additionally, in contexts of financial secrecy and the willful absence of record keeping, ethnography offers insights into the production process that exhortations to simply "follow the money," i.e., to trace the broad contours of capital investment and ownership, could not achieve.[3]

Ethnography, however, is not just about interviewing people, but is centrally about paying attention to what Malinowski referred to as the "imponderabilia of everyday life," which is best achieved through long-term, sustained participant-observation.[4] Spending time observing the daily life at the sites of media production provides an important contextual frame with which to understand media producers' self-representations and discourses about their practice. Paying attention to what people do in addition to what they say illuminates both norms and expectations of what constitutes appropriate or acceptable practice. A short-term or "parachuting" approach to research can make one miss or ignore important features of the production culture of a media industry because they may initially seem irrelevant to the "real work" of production. For example, throughout my fieldwork over the last two decades, I have consistently observed Hindi filmmakers lamenting the quality of filmmaking, bemoaning the lack of discipline and professionalism among their peers, and presenting themselves in the forefront of trying to organize and professionalize the industry. Rather than dismissing such attitudes as trivial or superfluous, I chose to examine what sort of work they were doing as these attitudes constituted such a significant part of the everyday life of film production in Mumbai. I realized that these sentiments and discourses operate as a form of "boundary-work," the industry's ideological efforts to define legitimate membership and practice.[5] In a fragmented, decentralized industry marked by an abundance of producers, high rates of commercial failure, and historically high costs of capital, distinctions posited between genuine and illegitimate filmmakers have been significant for the process of raising finance. Thus, boundary-work is a discursive strategy that has significant material implications within the Hindi film industry.[6] What sorts of formal and informal boundary-work practices exist in other media industries and what role do they play in shaping access to various forms of capital and resources?

An ethnographic approach to media production also enables us to incorporate questions of subjectivity and social relations into the analysis of mainstream mass media production. Studies of large-scale, commercially oriented media industries have neglected issues of individual subjectivity and social relations among cultural producers—a longstanding legacy of the Frankfurt School's "culture industry" approach to the analysis of mass media.[7] Analyses of subjectivity—in terms of affect, perceptions, thoughts, sentiments, and desires that constitute the basis of agency—and the complex production of meaning have more often been the concern of scholars studying media audiences, or indigenous, oppositional, minority media practitioners. In order to understand the complexities of media production, it is necessary to examine producers' sentiments and subjectivities in conjunction with questions of political economy. For example, I realized during my research that Hindi filmmakers were extremely concerned with issues of prestige, status, and cultural legitimacy. These concerns manifested most strongly in their highly disdainful attitudes toward the majority of their audiences in India, so much so that once certain structural changes around distribution and exhibition came into place, the driving commercial logic of the Hindi film industry for the first decade of the millennium was characterized by an inverse relationship between the numbers of viewers and the amount of revenue; in other words, rather than trying to expand their market, filmmakers were trying to make more money from fewer people.[8]

Regarding media industries as populated by agents grounded in specific social, historical, and interpretive locations reminds us to be wary of reproducing industry discourses about success and other assessments of popularity. As scholars, we need to be cautious with how we deal with the barrage of statistics and aggregate figures generated by media industries. Numbers should not be taken as objective realities, but as postulates put forward to make certain assertions or claims about our social world.[9] For example, media scholars have long pointed out that audiences for large-scale culture industries such as television are literally unknowable.[10] I would argue that the same conclusions could be applied to film audiences as well. Box-office receipts merely quantify the act of purchasing a ticket, which at the most measures awareness and interest in a film, but not the more complex processes of reception. Box-office data does not yield information about viewers' intentions, perceptions, experiences, likes, or dislikes; in fact, displeasure with a film once it has been viewed in a theater can never really be quantified, since the action of purchasing a ticket gets registered and interpreted as audience approval. While box-office outcome at best can be understood as an index of a commercial transaction, media producers frequently interpret it as an indexical expression of social identity, subjectivity, and affect. Industry categories, however, should not be our analytical categories; instead, we should ask, what stories are media industries trying to tell, or what claims are media producers making, through their use of quantitative data? Otherwise, we fall into the trap of replicating the discourses of the very industries that we are attempting to analyze. Thus, one challenge that we face as scholars of media industries is to not jump too quickly to extrapolate from media consumption to subjectivity or vice versa. Furthermore, how do we theorize about affect and engagement with visual media that does not replicate or mirror what media producers are asserting?

Viewing mainstream filmmakers as complex beings who seek and make meaning through their work helps to "break up the 'massness' of the media,"[11] and reminds us that for-profit media-making are neither simple acts of conscious manipulation nor unthinking, mechanical ones, but rather social practices undertaken by complex subjects with diverse interests and motivations.

1 Pierre Bourdieu, *The Field of Cultural Production* (New York: Columbia University Press, 1993).
2 Tejaswini Ganti, "And Yet My Heart Is Still Indian: The Bombay Film Industry and the (H)Indianization of Hollywood," in *Media Worlds: Anthropology on New Terrain*, ed. Faye D. Ginsburg et al. (Berkeley: University of California Press, 2002), 283.
3 Tejaswini Ganti, *Producing Bollywood: Inside the Contemporary Hindi Film Industry* (Durham: Duke University Press, 2012), 22.
4 Bronislaw Malinowski, *Argonauts of the Western Pacific* (Prospect Heights: Waveland Press, 1984), 20.
5 Thomas Gieryn, "Boundary-Work and the Demarcation of Science from Non-Science: Strains and Interests in

Professional Ideologies of Scientists," *American Sociological Review* 48, no. 6 (1983): 781.

6 Tejaswini Ganti, "Sentiments of Disdain and Practices of Distinction: Boundary-Work, Subjectivity, and Value in the Hindi Film Industry," *The Anthropological Quarterly* 85, no. 1 (2012): 7.

7 Mark Banks, *The Politics of Cultural Work* (New York: Palgrave MacMillan, 2007), 28.

8 Tejaswini Ganti, *Producing Bollywood: Inside the Contemporary Hindi Film Industry* (Durham: Duke University Press, 2012), 346.

9 Mary Poovey, *A History of the Modern Fact* (Chicago: University of Chicago, 1998), xii.

10 Ien Ang, *Desperately Seeking the Audience* (London: Routledge, 1991); John Hartley, "Invisible Fictions: Television Audiences, Paeodocracy, Pleasure," *Textual Practice* 1, no. 2 (1987): 121-38.

11 Faye Ginsburg, "Culture/Media: A (Mild) Polemic," *Anthropology Today* 10, no. 2 (1994): 12.

Bibliography

Ang, Ien. *Desperately Seeking the Audience*. London: Routledge, 1991.

Banks, Mark. *The Politics of Cultural Work*. New York: Palgrave MacMillan, 2007.

Bourdieu, Pierre. *The Field of Cultural Production*. New York: Columbia University Press, 1993.

Ganti, Tejaswini. "Sentiments of Disdain and Practices of Distinction: Boundary-Work, Subjectivity, and Value in the Hindi Film Industry." *The Anthropological Quarterly* 85, no. 1 (2012): 5-43.

Ganti, Tejaswini. *Producing Bollywood: Inside the Contemporary Hindi Film Industry*. Durham: Duke University Press, 2012.

Ganti, Tejaswini. "And Yet My Heart Is Still Indian: The Bombay Film Industry and the (H)Indianization of Hollywood." In *Media Worlds: Anthropology on New Terrain,* edited by Faye D. Ginsburg, Lila Abu-Lughod, and Brian Larkin, 281-300. Berkeley: University of California Press, 2002.

Gieryn, Thomas. "Boundary-Work and the Demarcation of Science from Non-Science: Strains and Interests in Professional Ideologies of Scientists." *American Sociological Review* 48, no. 6 (1983): 781-95.

Ginsburg, Faye. "Culture/Media: A (Mild) Polemic." *Anthropology Today* 10, no. 2 (1994): 5-15.

Hartley, John. "Invisible Fictions: Television Audiences, Paeodocracy, Pleasure." *Textual Practice* 1, no. 2 (1987): 121-38.

Malinowski, Bronislaw. *Argonauts of the Western Pacific.* Prospect Heights: Waveland Press, 1984.

Poovey, Mary. *A History of the Modern Fact.* Chicago: University of Chicago, 1998.

5.

On Comparison

NITIN GOVIL

We are now at the close of a fascinating century of encounter between Hollywood and Bombay cinema. Throughout this history, the two global media industries have circled each other in a dance of difference and similarity: in one moment, facing each other as Manichean opposites; at another, joined at the hip like kindred formations. Because of this history, it has become somewhat commonplace to claim that Bombay cinema and Hollywood are studies in contrast. Yet contemporary press and trade accounts seem to have boiled down these interindustry encounters to a core budgetary logic.

For example, *The Hollywood Reporter* recently featured an interview about interindustry relations with one of Hindi cinema's biggest stars, Shahrukh Khan. His recently-released film *Chennai Express* (2013) is a coproduction between Khan's media company, Red Chillies Entertainment, and Disney-UTV. With its US$454 million acquisition of the Indian media and entertainment company UTV in 2012, Disney's entry into locally branded Indian film content represents a relatively rare instance of its involvement in non-Hollywood production. Commenting on the Red Chillies and UTV-Disney tie-in, Khan notes that:

> I think that it's fantastic that the Hollywood studios are here. At first the studios wanted to popularize Hollywood films here but our cinema is deeply rooted in Indian culture. So it's good to see them producing Indian films. We also learn a lot from the experience of working with an international studio . . . it's a sign of changing times and will benefit Indian films to go international faster.[1]

Given the recent proliferation of financial alignments between Bombay cinema and Hollywood, global press accounts comparing India and the United States are dominated by stories of rising profits and media mergers. Part of the enthusiasm in such comparisons is that they deal with a perceived inversion of power relations in the international media economy, with Hollywood toppled from its position of global mastery. Not only are affinities between Hollywood and Bombay cinema taken as a sign of Indian media achievement, but these proliferating economic connections also testify to a globally relevant India.

While I acknowledge the realignment of financial arrangements and the social forces that have "reoriented" world trade flows,[2] I remain skeptical of the economic logic of such contemporary comparisons. As a preliminary attempt at suggesting alternatives, I've thought that rather than taking media industries as predetermined and stable formations, we might think about the provisional forms, sites, and practices that media industries comprise. This would involve thinking about the social, textual, political, and cultural infrastructures and interactions assembled under the semiotic sign of "industry." This would mean that we begin with a dynamic sense of industries as social and textual arrangements, sites of enactment and other dramaturgies of interaction, reflection, and reflexivity. When it comes to Hollywood-Bombay cinema encounters, such a fluid conception of industry might help enliven comparative methods by suggesting that the term *industry* itself creates a certain frame of reference within which to compare media practices dispersed in space and time. But how can we get around the fact that comparison deals in the "boundary work" of differentiation? In demarcating its object of inquiry, doesn't comparative work simply redraw the lines that figure industry? Before we move along to looking at the possibilities and limits of comparison in greater detail, it might be useful to think broadly about methods and disciplines.

Comparison is a widely used type of scholarly analysis informing methodology, theory, and practice in the humanities and social sciences. Comparison is central to both empirical and interpretive work. As a medium of measurement in both quantitative and qualitative methods, comparison regularizes difference within standard frameworks — in other words, comparison is a form of framing. This suggests stasis, but comparative methods are also dynamic because they organize claims and engage contrasts. At the same time, comparison tends toward objectification by formalizing phenomena in the process of analysis, creating trajectories of proximity and distance, networks of affinity and dissimilarity, and taxonomies of features both shared and exceptional. But comparison is also a tremendously broad enterprise. Susan Friedman has usefully described a number of imperatives to comparison, from the cognitive (comparison is integral to analogical and figural thinking) to the sociocultural (comparison is a way of organizing human behavior and social relations) and the ethicopolitical (comparison can either revivify or reject the "romance" of the universal and the singular).[3]

In our field, thinking critically about comparison means that we engage the multiple dimensions of comparativity produced across disciplinary cultures. This means understanding comparison as a kind of "travelling concept," Mieke Bal's term for the movement of meanings between disciplines, scholars, and histories, with "processes of differing assessed before, during, and after each 'trip.[4]'"

Thinking archeologically about media, for example, Katherine Hayles suggests that a comparative media studies can provide a "rubric" for the study of print and digital productions in way that is historical, formal, procedural, and material. The multiple ways in which to approach and theorize media transitions help ward off teleologies of technological development.[5] In a more sociological vein, Daniel Hallin and Paulo Mancini suggest that a comparative approach to media demystifies assumptions about the universality of media practices while making possible certain structural similarities that link media systems to one another.[6] The focus here is analytic precision in the drawing of models in the generation of concepts and theories in the vein of Weberian ideal types. Both the archeological and sociological approaches to comparative media represented by Hayles, Hallin, and Mancini are united by a project of clarification while preserving the possibilities of more experimental and speculative forms of comparison. Capturing this contradiction with a focus on media structures, Sonia Livingstone calls the comparative study of cross-national media industries an "apparent impossibility and an urgent necessity."[7]

Yet, comparison can also breed contempt, especially when one considers this cross-national history and its institutionalization. Postwar intellectual formations like area studies used comparison to justify Cold War mentalities, focusing on the regional and the national as a geopolitical unit.[8] The institutionalization of comparison in modernization theory forged a policy alignment between university and state interests. Comparison's role in this disciplinary history was to frame the national as an index of psychological, social, and cultural disposition. In this way, the national was a "modular" form, capable of registering difference through a common discourse.[9]

Modernization theory activated such national distinctions to organize media industries in hierarchies according to their development. Even in oppositional disciplinary cultures like political economy, which seek to address structural inequalities and the management and redistribution of resources, the national serves as a site to aggregate data and situate power. This national aggregation generates the tropes of economic magnitude that dominate accounts of media transit. After all, despite the rhetoric and texture of media encounter, scholarly legitimacy is often granted only to those comparative accounts that demonstrate definitive, measurable, and spectacular market impact. For example, in his study of the international development of film industries prior to World War II, Gerben Bakker excludes Japanese, Indian, and Hong Kong industries on the grounds that "since 1945 they have become quite successful relative to Europe, but before that they were internationally insignificant."[10] Similarly, Manuel Castells suggests that the Indian film industries have "evolved largely independently from the global network of media networks," and only now, because of state and market subsidy, are more enumerated "structures of collaboration" between Indian and American media industries proliferating.[11] To follow Bakker's rationalization, we needn't be interested in Hollywood's investment in India, which, in the mid-1990s, made about as much money as it did in Israel and less than it did in Poland. To follow Castells, we should prioritize Hollywood's history in India by focusing on Hollywood's encouragement of recent corporatization initiatives in Indian film. Yet, for all their analytical clarity, approaches taken by Bakker and Castells risk missing the ephemeral points of contact that seep into and slip beyond official histories and formal political economies.

Comparison remains a vital and energetic way to study media industries in global and local contexts. For those of us interested in working on media industries, our task is not to refuse comparison but to compare differently: to figure a politics and practice of relation that is transformative rather than taxonomic. In this way, we might gesture beyond comparison to what Rey Chow calls "entanglement," encounters figured "through disparity rather than equivalence." By disrupting frames of classification, entanglements signal a "derangement in the organization of knowledge caused by unprecedented adjacency and comparability or parity."[12]

Of course, we must account for the cultural forms that organize media industries in different ways.[13] But we must also understand industry comparisons in terms of the "occasions" toward which they are oriented and intended.[14] In addition to this "occasionality" of comparison, we might also—to follow Rita Felski and Susan Friedman's formulation—engage media industries as "*agents* as well as *objects* of comparison."[15] If media industries are "forms of comparative thinking," then perhaps comparison is at the root of their materiality as well as our scholarship.

[1] Quoted in Nyay Bhushan, "Bollywood Star Shah Rukh Khan: 'It's Good to See Hollywood Producing Films,'" *Hollywood Reporter*, July 26, 2013.

[2] See Andre Gunder Frank, *ReOrient: Global Economy in the Asian Age* (Berkeley: University of California Press, 1998) and Michael Curtin and Hemant Shah, eds., *Reorienting Global Communication: Indian and Chinese Media beyond Borders* (Urbana-Champaign: University of Illinois Press, 2010).

[3] Susan Stanford Friedman, "Why Not Compare?" *PMLA* 126, no. 3 (2011): 753–62.

[4] Mieke Bal, *Traveling Concepts in the Humanities: A Rough Guide* (Toronto: University of Toronto Press, 2002), 24.

[5] N. Katherine Hayles, *How We Think: Digital Media and Contemporary Technogenesis* (Chicago: University of Chicago Press, 2012).

[6] Daniel C. Hallin and Paolo Mancini, *Comparative Media Systems: Three Models of Media and Politics* (New York: Cambridge University Press, 2004).

[7] Sonia Livingstone, "On the Challenges of Cross-National Comparative Media Research," *European Journal of Communication* 18, no. 4 (2003): 477–500.

[8] For an assessment of this history and the possibilities of recuperation in the work of comparative scholars like Benedict Anderson, see H. D. Harootunian, "Ghostly Comparisons: Anderson's Telescope," *Diacritics* 29, no. 4 (1999): 135–49.

[9] For a critique of the "modular" form of the national, see Partha Chatterjee, *Nationalist Thought and the Colonial World: A Derivative Discourse* (Tokyo: Zed Books, 1986). For a sense of how these modular forms have been "refortified" under contemporary neoliberal regimes, see Manu Goswami, "Rethinking the Modular Form: Toward a Sociohistorical Conception of Nationalism," *Comparative Studies in Society and History* 44, no. 4 (2002): 770–99.

[10] Gerben Bakker, *Entertainment Industrialized: The Emergence of the International Film Industry, 1890–1940* (Cambridge: Cambridge University Press, 2008), 4.

[11] Manuel Castells, *Communication Power* (New York: Oxford University Press, 2009), 92.

[12] Rey Chow, *Entanglements, or Transmedial Thinking of Capture* (Durham, NC: Duke University Press, 2012), 11.

[13] Paul Willemen, "For a Comparative Film Studies," *Inter-Asia Cultural Studies* 6, no. 1 (2005): 103.

[14] For more on the concepts of "occasion" and "occasionality," rooted in arts and aesthetics, see Hans-Georg Gadamer, *Truth and Method*, trans. Joel Weinsheimer and Donald G. Marshall (London: Bloomsbury, 1989). For an extension of "occasion" into novelistic genres and the literary marketplace—what he calls "the practical circumstances governing the composition and reception of a piece of speech or writing"—see Ian Hunter, "Providence and Profit: Speculations in the Genre Market," *Southern Review* 22, no. 3 (1989): 211–23. Similarly, in his discussion of media texts and spectators, Toby Miller suggests that occasionality "details the conditions under which a text is made, circulated, received, interpreted, and criticized . . . a life remade again

and again by institutions, discourses, and practices of distribution and reception." See Toby Miller and Robert Stam, *A Companion to Film Theory* (Malden, MA: Blackwell, 1999), 4.

[15] Rita Felski and Susan Friedman, "Introduction," *New Literary History* 40, no. 3 (2009): v–ix.

Bibliography

Bakker, Gerben. *Entertainment Industrialized: The Emergence of the International Film Industry, 1890–1940.* Cambridge: Cambridge University Press, 2008.

Bal, Mieke. *Traveling Concepts in the Humanities: A Rough Guide.* Toronto: University of Toronto Press, 2002.

Bhushan, Nyay. "Bollywood Star Shah Rukh Khan: 'It's Good to See Hollywood Producing Films.'" *Hollywood Reporter*, July 26, 2013.

Castells, Manuel. *Communication Power.* New York: Oxford University Press, 2009.

Chatterjee, Partha. *Nationalist Thought and the Colonial World: A Derivative Discourse.* Tokyo: Zed Books, 1986.

Chow, Rey. *Entanglements, or Transmedial Thinking of Capture.* Durham, NC: Duke University Press, 2012.

Curtin, Michael, and Hemant Shah, eds. *Reorienting Global Communication: Indian and Chinese Media Beyond Borders.* Urbana-Champaign: University of Illinois Press, 2010.

Felski, Rita, and Susan Friedman. "Introduction." *New Literary History* 40, no. 3 (2009): v–ix.

Frank, Andre Gunder. *ReOrient: Global Economy in the Asian Age.* Berkeley: University of California Press, 1998.

Friedman, Susan Stanford. "Why Not Compare?" *PMLA* 126, no. 3 (2011): 753–62.

Gadamer, Hans-Georg. *Truth and Method.* Translated by Joel Weinsheimer and Donald G. Marshall. London: Bloomsbury, 1989.

Goswami, Manu. "Rethinking the Modular Form: Toward a Sociohistorical Conception of Nationalism." *Comparative Studies in Society and History* 44, no. 4 (2002): 770–99.

Hallin, Daniel C., and Paolo Mancini. *Comparative Media Systems: Three Models of Media and Politics.* New York: Cambridge University Press, 2004.

Harootunian, H. D. "Ghostly Comparisons: Anderson's Telescope," *Diacritics* 29, no. 4 (1999): 135–49.

Hayles, N. Katherine. *How We Think: Digital Media and Contemporary Technogenesis.* Chicago: University of Chicago Press, 2012.

Hunter, Ian. "Providence and Profit: Speculations in the Genre Market." *Southern Review* 22, no. 3 (1989): 211–23.

Livingstone, Sonia. "On the Challenges of Cross-National Comparative Media Research." *European Journal of Communication* 18, no. 4 (2003): 477–500.

Miller, Toby, and Robert Stam. *A Companion to Film Theory.* Malden, MA: Blackwell, 1999.

Willemen, Paul. "For a Comparative Film Studies." *Inter-Asia Cultural Studies* 6, no. 1 (2005): 98–112

6.

Media Programming in the Era of Big Data

TIMOTHY HAVENS

Media industries research and education are booming. Since hitting a low point of fashionability in the postmodernist and post-Marxist 1990s, media production and media industries research has bounced back.[1] The most powerful enclaves of social science — business schools and the economists who often work there — are now paying more attention to the media industries than ever before. Media industries are also a major object of interest for geographers and urban studies analysts concerned with the potential regenerative effects of creative or cultural industries. Those interested in the way that new information technologies have "democratized" cultural production have given an analytical prominence to media industries that they haven't enjoyed for decades. Cultural studies of media production have revivified the intellectual agenda and brought new and talented researchers to the field.

Much of this new wave of research is frustratingly amnesiac about the valuable research that preceded the twenty-first century boom, for example in political economy of media or in sociology of culture. Indeed, researchers working within particular traditions at times seem deaf and blind to developments in other fields that also deal with media production. But these problems might in themselves partly be a result of the abundance of media industry studies. This isn't just a matter of laziness or a busy schedule; it's getting harder to keep track of everything.

There is an even greater danger for media industries scholarship and teaching: the menace of instrumentalism. Most media industries research takes place outside universities. Much of it is concerned with quantifying the characteristics and behaviors of audiences, and analyzing change. Much of it is futurological, predicting trends and providing perspectives that might inform the strategy of firms. It is often commissioned or bought by media companies from hundreds of marketing and forecasting firms.

And it is usually extremely expensive and closed to public access. University libraries often cannot afford it, let alone ordinary citizens. Some university researchers compete with such organizations to carry out commissioned research.

Most university research on media industries has not been of this instrumentalist kind. Much of it would claim to be *critical*: of concentration and conglomeration, of international inequality, of poor and unequal labor conditions, of organizational dynamics that lead to content that fails adequately to provide public knowledge or rich aesthetic experiences. However, the pressures towards instrumentalism are growing.

What might we mean by *critical*? In one of the earliest and most famous contributions to media studies, Paul Lazarsfeld distinguished between critical and administrative communication research.[2] Lazarsfeld, a major figure in twentieth-century social research, is often cast as villain in a research melodrama, playing the black-hatted positivist against the heroic figures of Theodor Adorno and C. Wright Mills (both of whom he provided with research jobs).[3] Generations of media educators, who have understandably wanted their students to be questioning rather than compliant subjects, used the distinction as a means to explain the value of critique.

Lazarsfeld, his essay, and the critical/administrative distinction, are more complex than the caricatures make out. The core of his essay considered three objections to administrative research. One, from government and businesses, was against the way in which careful empirical work might produce conclusions that were too qualified and complex to be of practical use. Another, from publicly minded sociologists, was that administrative research is too often directed towards rather small issues, and research should instead be oriented to solving major social problems. A third was that the media are much more complex and diffuse in their influence than administrative research, with its focus on specific aims and problems, had been willing to recognize or able to address.

This objection, which had been articulated by a group of fellow German émigrés associated with "critical theory," notably Max Horkheimer and Theodor Adorno, was the main focus of

Lazarsfeld's attention in his essay. Critical research, explained Lazarsfeld, required that "the general role of our media of communication in the present social system should be studied." Lazarsfeld was by no means hostile to this viewpoint. Much of his essay was about how insights from critical research (those produced by his colleague Adorno) might enrich empirically oriented communication research, and how empirical work might inform critical theory.[4]

We should be suspicious, then, of simplified and Manichean (good versus evil) distinctions between critical and administrative research. Yet some kind of distinction between knowledge that serves more general flourishing and emancipation, and that which does not, seems fundamental to any debate about the value and purpose of research, including media industries research. Arguably, research and education oriented primarily to boosting the dividends of shareholders or the salaries of individuals might be less about such flourishing and emancipation than other types.[5] Such a conception seems to underpin the perspective of Lazarsfeld, pragmatist though he was.

In addressing such issues, and in many other ways, media industries research and education would benefit from a greater engagement with social theory. As Andrew Sayer has explained,[6] philosophical reconstructions of critical social science often emphasize four elements: the identification of problems (false beliefs, suffering, unmet needs, etc.); identification of the causes or sources of those problems, such as forms of domination; negative appraisals of those sources; and approval of actions which reduce or remove those sources. Such a critical social science is most likely to be cogent, coherent, and effective when it addresses normative questions of good and bad, right and wrong, rather than dismissing explicit ethical discourse as Enlightenment will-to-power (as many postmodernists have), or as an unscientific failure to bracket questions of value (as many positivists do).

And media industries research informed by a critical social science perspective would involve *explanation* as well as *evaluation*. Often both are missing from research that aspires to be, or merely "feels," critical. Some "critical" researchers seem to think that the first stage of critical social science, the identification of problems, is moot, because, in their view, social media and other features of the digital world will resolve most problems anyway. In the work of some other researchers, it is conceptually far from clear what the problems, sources, and alternatives are meant to be.

In a twenty-first century context where universities are increasingly encouraged to service the requirements of governments and businesses, and to find alternative sources of funding beyond student fees and public research money, the specter of instrumentalism looms larger than ever over *all* research. Few would doubt that recent times have seen an erosion of the Humboldtian vision of the university as a free space centered on the Enlightenment goal that knowledge should ultimately serve social emancipation. That vision and that goal were always compromised by domination and privilege. But their erosion is deeply problematic. A number of factors have contributed to this decline. Attacks on elitism and paternalism have been appropriated and have served to undermine the legitimacy of universities and of (in the broadest sense) scientific knowledge. In an era when private businesses are often dubiously presented as more efficient than public organizations, universities are being pushed in the direction of marketization, promotionalism, and instrumentalism. In an effort to protect research funding in the social sciences and humanities, research councils have increasingly been influenced by the agendas of their political paymasters.[7]

Another push in the direction of instrumentalism is the pressure for academic researchers to accumulate professional capital. Only a saint would have no interest in success; but as Craig Calhoun has pointed out, to the extent that researchers involve themselves in such accumulation they are

> encouraged to accept commonplace understandings of the world. To challenge these too deeply would be to court detachment from those whose "purchase" of their products enables them to accumulate capital...In the spirit of professionalism they betray the calling truly and openly to explore the world.[8]

When many university managers and workers today have an uncertain grasp of the value of the autonomy of their own institutions, it is hardly surprising that others struggle to affirm the legitimacy of those institutions, or appreciate their potential social and cultural contributions.

These problems take a specific form when it comes to media industries research. Many media professionals share a more general distrust of "fusty" academics. Some adopt robust entrepreneurial attitudes and are not shy in saying that academics should be willing to provide directly useful services to them — preferably for free, or subsidized by the public purse. Because the media industries themselves are major producers of knowledge, ideas, and commentary, arguably professionals from these industries are even more inclined to question the value of autonomous research oriented towards emancipation than those working in other sectors. After all, such professionals are in competition with universities. This makes genuine and open collaboration between media workers and academics all the more valuable, and there undoubtedly should be a place for such collaboration alongside independent research. Media professionals who have an understanding of the value of autonomous, independent research can be a joy to work with. But collaborative research still needs to be judged by scientific principles of rigor, originality, and significance, rather than on the basis of whether it contributes to economic prosperity within a particular company, country, or region.

A separate but related problem for media industries research is instrumentalism among students. Many look to media industries education for an entry into what appears to be a desirable form of work.

Given the difficulties for teachers, inside and outside universities, in articulating the value of knowledge and learning, it is hardly surprising that some students seek vocationalist forms of education, and underappreciate open inquiry. Some of these students seem to seek a certain notion of a business school approach to media industries, based on the secrets of media management.

I strongly believe it is possible to give students exposure to media production practices, and an understanding of media management, while emphasizing that media degrees might also have a higher purpose: to provide symbol makers and creative managers with an education that encourages them to live good lives, and to contribute to the flourishing of their fellow citizens. Our main purpose as teachers, and as researchers, should not be to help young people accumulate educational and cultural capital, or to provide training so that the media industries don't have to. It should be to build and share critical understandings of how media industries shape public knowledge and aesthetic experience. To achieve this will mean confronting the menace of instrumentalism.

---

1 See David Hesmondhalgh, "Politics, Theory and Method in Media Industries Research," in *Media Industries: History, Theory, Method*, eds. Jennifer Holt and Alisa Perren (Malden, MA and Oxford: Wiley-Blackwell, 2009), 245-55; David Hesmondhalgh, *The Cultural Industries*, 3rd edition (London and Los Angeles: Sage Publications, 2013), chap. 1.

2 Paul Felix Lazarsfeld, "Remarks on Administrative and Critical Communications Research," *Studies in Philosophy and Social Science* 9 (1941): 2-16.

3 C. Wright Mills' later dismissal of Lazarsfeld's "abstracted empiricism" in *The Sociological Imagination* (New York: Oxford University Press, 1959) cemented Lazarsfeld's role as the bad guy in the critical-versus-administrative soap opera. See Jonathan Sterne's essay "C. Wright Mills, The Bureau for Applied Social Research, and the Meaning of Critical Scholarship," *Cultural Studies/Critical Methodologies* 5(1) (2005): 65-94.

4 Lazarsfeld's essay leaves major problems concerning administrative research untouched: how to fund research, and how funding might affect research.

5 Of course this makes all knowledge "instrumental" in the broadest sense: The term "instrumentalist" is intended here to draw attention to "bad" instrumentality that favours the flourishing of the few over the many, and/or inhibits collective flourishing.

6 Andrew Sayer, *Realism and Social Science* (London: Sage, 2000), 159.

7 See Allison Hearn, "'Through the Looking Glass': The Promotional University 2.0," in *Blowing Up the Brand*, eds. Melissa Aronczyk and Devon Powers (New York: Peter Lang, 2010), 195-218.

8 Craig Calhoun, *Critical Social Theory* (Oxford: Blackwell, 1995), 2.

Bibliography

Calhoun, Craig. *Critical Social Theory*. Oxford: Blackwell, 1995.

Hearn, Allison. "'Through the Looking Glass': The Promotional University 2.0." In *Blowing Up the Brand*, edited by Melissa Aronczyk and Devon Powers, 195-218. New York: Peter Lang, 2010.

Hesmondhalgh, David. "Politics, Theory and Method in Media Industries Research." In *Media Industries: History, Theory, Method*, edited by Jennifer Holt and Alisa Perren, 245-255. Malden, MA and Oxford: Wiley-Blackwell, 2009.

Hesmondhalgh, David. *The Cultural Industries*, 3rd edition. London and Los Angeles: Sage Publications, 2013.

Lazarsfeld, Paul. "Remarks on Administrative and Critical Communications Research." *Studies in Philosophy and Social Science* 9 (1941): 2-16.

Mills, C. Wright. *The Sociological Imagination*. New York: Oxford University Press, 1959.

Sayer, Andrew. *Realism and Social Science*. London: Sage, 2000.

Sterne, Jonathan. "C. Wright Mills, The Bureau for Applied Social Research, and the Meaning of Critical Scholarship." *Cultural Studies/Critical Methodologies* 5(1) (2005): 65-94.

7.

The Menace of Instrumentalism in Media Industries Research and Education

DAVID HESMONDALGH

Media industries research and education are booming. Since hitting a low point of fashionability in the postmodernist and post-Marxist 1990s, media production and media industries research has bounced back.[1] The most powerful enclaves of social science — business schools and the economists who often work there — are now paying more attention to the media industries than ever before. Media industries are also a major object of interest for geographers and urban studies analysts concerned with the potential regenerative effects of creative or cultural industries. Those interested in the way that new information technologies have "democratized" cultural production have given an analytical prominence to media industries that they haven't enjoyed for decades. Cultural studies of media production have revivified the intellectual agenda and brought new and talented researchers to the field.

Much of this new wave of research is frustratingly amnesiac about the valuable research that preceded the twenty-first century boom, for example in political economy of media or in sociology of culture. Indeed, researchers working within particular traditions at times seem deaf and blind to developments in other fields that also deal with media production. But these problems might in themselves partly be a result of the abundance of media industry studies. This isn't just a matter of laziness or a busy schedule; it's getting harder to keep track of everything.

There is an even greater danger for media industries scholarship and teaching: the menace of instrumentalism. Most media industries research takes place outside universities. Much of it is concerned with quantifying the characteristics and behaviors of audiences, and analyzing change. Much of it is futurological, predicting trends and providing perspectives that might inform the strategy of firms.

It is often commissioned or bought by media companies from hundreds of marketing and forecasting firms. And it is usually extremely expensive and closed to public access. University libraries often cannot afford it, let alone ordinary citizens. Some university researchers compete with such organizations to carry out commissioned research.

Most university research on media industries has not been of this instrumentalist kind. Much of it would claim to be *critical*: of concentration and conglomeration, of international inequality, of poor and unequal labor conditions, of organizational dynamics that lead to content that fails adequately to provide public knowledge or rich aesthetic experiences. However, the pressures towards instrumentalism are growing.

What might we mean by *critical*? In one of the earliest and most famous contributions to media studies, Paul Lazarsfeld distinguished between critical and administrative communication research.[2] Lazarsfeld, a major figure in twentieth-century social research, is often cast as villain in a research melodrama, playing the black-hatted positivist against the heroic figures of Theodor Adorno and C. Wright Mills (both of whom he provided with research jobs).[3] Generations of media educators, who have understandably wanted their students to be questioning rather than compliant subjects, used the distinction as a means to explain the value of critique.

Lazarsfeld, his essay, and the critical/administrative distinction, are more complex than the caricatures make out. The core of his essay considered three objections to administrative research. One, from government and businesses, was against the way in which careful empirical work might produce conclusions that were too qualified and complex to be of practical use. Another, from publicly minded sociologists, was that administrative research is too often directed towards rather small issues, and research should instead be oriented to solving major social problems. A third was that the media are much more complex and diffuse in their influence than administrative research, with its focus on specific aims and problems, had been willing to recognize or able to address. This objection, which had been articulated by a group of fellow German émigrés associated with "critical theory," notably Max Horkheimer and Theodor Adorno, was the main focus of Lazarsfeld's attention in his essay. Critical research, explained Lazarsfeld, required that "the general role of our media of communication in the present social system should be studied." Lazarsfeld was by no means hostile to this viewpoint. Much of his essay was about how insights from critical research (those produced by his colleague Adorno) might enrich empirically oriented communication research, and how empirical work might inform critical theory.[4]

We should be suspicious, then, of simplified and Manichean (good versus evil) distinctions between critical and administrative research. Yet some kind of distinction between knowledge that serves more general flourishing and emancipation, and that which does not, seems fundamental to any debate about the value and purpose of research, including media industries research. Arguably, research and education oriented primarily to boosting the dividends of shareholders or the salaries of individuals might be less about such flourishing and emancipation than other types.[5] Such a conception seems to underpin the perspective of Lazarsfeld, pragmatist though he was.

In addressing such issues, and in many other ways, media industries research and education would benefit from a greater engagement with social theory. As Andrew Sayer has explained,[6] philosophical reconstructions of critical social science often emphasize four elements: the identification of problems (false beliefs, suffering, unmet needs, etc.); identification of the causes or sources of those problems, such as forms of domination; negative appraisals of those sources; and approval of actions which reduce or remove those sources. Such a critical social science is most likely to be cogent, coherent, and effective when it addresses normative questions of good and bad, right and wrong, rather than dismissing explicit ethical discourse as Enlightenment will-to-power (as many postmodernists have), or as an unscientific failure to bracket questions of value (as many positivists do). And media industries research informed by a critical social science perspective would involve *explanation* as well as *evaluation*. Often both are missing from research that aspires to be, or merely "feels," critical. Some "critical" researchers seem to think that the first stage of critical social science, the identification of problems, is moot, because, in their view, social media and other features of the digital world will resolve most problems anyway. In the work of some other researchers, it is conceptually far from clear what the problems, sources, and alternatives are meant to be.

In a twenty-first century context where universities are increasingly encouraged to service the requirements of governments and businesses, and to find alternative sources of funding beyond student fees and public research money, the specter of instrumentalism looms larger than ever over *all* research. Few would doubt that recent times have seen an erosion of the Humboldtian vision of the university as a free space centered on the Enlightenment goal that knowledge should ultimately serve social emancipation. That vision and that goal were always compromised by domination and privilege. But their erosion is deeply problematic. A number of factors have contributed to this decline. Attacks on elitism and paternalism have been appropriated and have served to undermine the legitimacy of universities and of (in the broadest sense) scientific knowledge. In an era when private businesses are often dubiously presented as more efficient than public organizations, universities are being pushed in the direction of marketization, promotionalism, and instrumentalism. In an effort to protect research funding in the social sciences and humanities, research councils have increasingly been influenced by the agendas of their political paymasters.[7]

Another push in the direction of instrumentalism is the pressure for academic researchers to accumulate professional capital. Only a saint would have no interest in success; but as Craig Calhoun has pointed out, to the extent that researchers involve themselves in such accumulation they are

> encouraged to accept commonplace understandings of the world. To challenge these too deeply would be to court detachment from those whose "purchase" of their products enables them to accumulate capital…In the spirit of professionalism they betray the calling truly and openly to explore the world.[8]

When many university managers and workers today have an uncertain grasp of the value of the autonomy of their own institutions, it is hardly surprising that others struggle to affirm the legitimacy of those institutions, or appreciate their potential social and cultural contributions.

These problems take a specific form when it comes to media industries research. Many media professionals share a more general distrust of "fusty" academics. Some adopt robust entrepreneurial attitudes and are not shy in saying that academics should be willing to provide directly useful services to them — preferably for free, or subsidized by the public purse. Because the media industries themselves are major producers of knowledge, ideas, and commentary, arguably professionals from these industries are even more inclined to question the value of autonomous research oriented towards emancipation than those working in other sectors. After all, such professionals are in competition with universities. This makes genuine and open collaboration between media workers and academics all the more valuable, and there undoubtedly should be a place for such collaboration alongside independent research. Media professionals who have an understanding of the value of autonomous, independent research can be a joy to work with. But collaborative research still needs to be judged by scientific principles of rigor, originality, and significance, rather than on the basis of whether it contributes to economic prosperity within a particular company, country, or region.

A separate but related problem for media industries research is instrumentalism among students. Many look to media industries education for an entry into what appears to be a desirable form of work.

Given the difficulties for teachers, inside and outside universities, in articulating the value of knowledge and learning, it is hardly surprising that some students seek vocationalist forms of education, and underappreciate open inquiry. Some of these students seem to seek a certain notion of a business school approach to media industries, based on the secrets of media management.

I strongly believe it is possible to give students exposure to media production practices, and an understanding of media management, while emphasizing that media degrees might also have a higher purpose: to provide symbol makers and creative managers with an education that encourages them to live good lives, and to contribute to the flourishing of their fellow citizens. Our main purpose as teachers, and as researchers, should not be to help young people accumulate educational and cultural capital, or to provide training so that the media industries don't have to. It should be to build and share critical understandings of how media industries shape public knowledge and aesthetic experience. To achieve this will mean confronting the menace of instrumentalism.

---

1 See David Hesmondhalgh, "Politics, Theory and Method in Media Industries Research," in *Media Industries: History, Theory, Method*, eds. Jennifer Holt and Alisa Perren (Malden, MA and Oxford: Wiley-Blackwell, 2009), 245-55; David Hesmondhalgh, *The Cultural Industries*, 3rd edition (London and Los Angeles: Sage Publications, 2013), chap. 1.

2 Paul Felix Lazarsfeld, "Remarks on Administrative and Critical Communications Research," *Studies in Philosophy and Social Science* 9 (1941): 2-16.

3 C. Wright Mills' later dismissal of Lazarsfeld's "abstracted empiricism" in *The Sociological Imagination* (New York: Oxford University Press, 1959) cemented Lazarsfeld's role as the bad guy in the critical-versus-administrative soap opera. See Jonathan Sterne's essay "C. Wright Mills, The Bureau for Applied Social Research, and the Meaning of Critical Scholarship," *Cultural Studies/Critical Methodologies* 5(1) (2005): 65-94.

4 Lazarsfeld's essay leaves major problems concerning administrative research untouched: how to fund research, and how funding might affect research.

5 Of course this makes all knowledge "instrumental" in the broadest sense: The term "instrumentalist" is intended here to draw attention to "bad" instrumentality that favours the flourishing of the few over the many, and/or inhibits collective flourishing.

6 Andrew Sayer, *Realism and Social Science* (London: Sage, 2000), 159.

7 See Allison Hearn, "'Through the Looking Glass': The Promotional University 2.0," in *Blowing Up the Brand*, eds. Melissa Aronczyk and Devon Powers (New York: Peter Lang, 2010), 195-218.

[8] Craig Calhoun, *Critical Social Theory* (Oxford: Blackwell, 1995), 2.

Bibliography

Calhoun, Craig. *Critical Social Theory*. Oxford: Blackwell, 1995.

Hearn, Allison. "'Through the Looking Glass': The Promotional University 2.0." In *Blowing Up the Brand*, edited by Melissa Aronczyk and Devon Powers, 195-218. New York: Peter Lang, 2010.

Hesmondhalgh, David. "Politics, Theory and Method in Media Industries Research." In *Media Industries: History, Theory, Method*, edited by Jennifer Holt and Alisa Perren, 245-255. Malden, MA and Oxford: Wiley-Blackwell, 2009.

Hesmondhalgh, David. *The Cultural Industries*, 3rd edition. London and Los Angeles: Sage Publications, 2013.

Lazarsfeld, Paul. "Remarks on Administrative and Critical Communications Research." *Studies in Philosophy and Social Science* 9 (1941): 2-16.

Mills, C. Wright. *The Sociological Imagination*. New York: Oxford University Press, 1959.

Sayer, Andrew. *Realism and Social Science*. London: Sage, 2000.

Sterne, Jonathan. "C. Wright Mills, The Bureau for Applied Social Research, and the Meaning of Critical Scholarship." *Cultural Studies/Critical Methodologies* 5(1) (2005): 65-94.

8.

Transnational TV: What Do We Mean By "Coproduction" Anymore?

MICHELE HILMES

In one sense, coproduction is the natural state of film and television. Every film or television program ever made results from the efforts of more than one person or entity, and when the credits roll, the numerous creative, financial, management, and service companies that contributed to a show's success are acknowledged (or not) in a strict hierarchy. Diffusely shared authorship is the norm. Yet traditionally when the partners come from different national locations rather than occupying the same national space, a whole new set of considerations and terms arise: it becomes an "international coproduction." This is a term used by the film industry since the 1940s, indicating a partnership between two or more different national production entities aimed at taking advantage of locality-specific tax incentives, funding opportunities, locations, and talent. Such international or "treaty" coproduction involves meeting a set of highly specific qualifications and requirements set by national or regional film boards, often rewarded by hefty subsidies. Major production companies long ago developed the practice of setting up subsidiaries in nations around the world to take advantage of international coproduction on an ongoing basis, and many countries have encouraged coproduction as a way to manage and derive greater benefit from "runaway" commercial filmmaking.

In television, the situation has been somewhat more complicated. Given the strong national basis of broadcasting, with most nations supporting their own powerful and well-financed central public broadcasters with mandates for domestic production, international coproduction — particularly with commercial partners — historically met with various forms of resistance and was slower to develop. National broadcasters typically found it preferable simply to import popular foreign television shows, at a relatively low cost, in order to put scarce public funding into preferred types of original, nationally specific programs. However, Britain and the United States began actively coproducing drama and documentary programs in the 1970s, at first primarily for the public-service market but, as cable television opened up new venues in the 1980s, for the commercial market as well. With the expansion of the independent broadcasting sector in Europe in the 1990s, followed by the advent of digital platforms in recent decades, coproduction has exploded to become the "new normal" in high-end drama and documentary, in particular. The United States and the United Kingdom became not only the two largest global exporters of television programs but also each other's biggest customers and most frequent coproduction partners. This relationship has given rise to innovative program forms, newly constituted transnational publics, rich new constellations of cultural engagement, and a host of evolving practices of cooperative production that have been obscured by the attention paid to that other new global phenomenon, the reality format. Here I want to identify issues that arise in studying new forms of transnational television and attempt to pose a few research questions needed to explore them.

From a US vantage point, the world of television suddenly opened up to drama from around the world, focusing not on "reversioned" content to supposedly suit American audiences (and so often failing) but on programs in their original forms, complete with subtitles. The off-piste success of series like *Borgen* (2010-13), *The Fall* (2013), and *Engrenages/Spiral* (2005-)—never carried by US-based cable or broadcast channels but experienced via DVD, Netflix, and other digital means—has awakened a spate of articles directed at US audiences with titles like "Five Great International Shows That Should Be Streaming,"[1] "The International Language of Tube,"[2] and "The Elusive Pleasures of French TV Series."[3] Those titles all share a tone of mild astonishment that such programs exist—where have they been all our lives? This despite the fact that PBS's *Masterpiece* series (1971-) has been coproducing and importing British drama for more than three decades; BBC America brings a steady current of British-produced programs into US cablespace; and of course, a world of Spanish-language television is right there for easy consumption, much of it produced in Mexico and South and Central America (though for the most part only subtitled via closed-captioning and not often noticed or reviewed by English-language outlets).[4] How do certain international programs achieve critical and popular recognition while others are ignored? What role does nontraditional distribution over digital platforms play in opening up the longstanding ethnocentric enclosures of American television? Scholarly attention has mainly focused on the pervasive spread of US-originated forms and narratives, with the influence of other cultures on US television largely neglected.[5] Far more research is needed on the construction of new transnational viewing publics as well as on the largely online spaces where their viewing takes place and where their critical opinions are registered.

From the perspective of other countries, where US-produced programs have long been featured on domestic channels and via satellite, digital globalization has meant wider access to more of the same rather than something completely different. What may prove a more lasting change, however, is the way that domestic drama production around the world is being conceptualized, funded, scripted, and cast with a diverse global market—and, often, global partnerships—foremost in mind. Though *Borgen*, *The Fall*, and *Engrenages* were not coproductions as such, all were produced by a national broadcaster (DR, BBC Two, and Canal+, respectively) with transnational distribution a clear goal; two have since picked up international partners, and all three have attracted considerable transnational audiences and critical attention. Such success has caused industry analysts to note the return of international coproduction to the world of television drama after its decades-long eclipse by reality formats.[6] The staid international, or "treaty," coproductions prominent in television's earlier decades have been transformed into a practice that more and more frequently partners public-sector broadcasters with independents and large commercial companies from two or more nations. The United States still remains the most sought-after partner due to its sizable audience. I call this phenomenon "transnational coproduction" to distinguish it from previous practices, and to indicate the new set of issues it raises.

Transnational coproduction in the current era includes not just cofinancing or presale of distribution rights (i.e., putting money into a series upfront, but contributing very little creatively to the production): it also involves a creative partnership in which national interests must be combined and reconciled, differing audience tastes considered, and, often, the collision of public-service goals with commercial expectations negotiated. Historically, the issue of creative control has been a touchy one since nationally-funded producers like the BBC insist that their coproduction partnerships involve no compromise with public-service goals nor with the best interests of British audiences, sometimes in the face of casting, setting, and plot decisions that clearly bow to their (often American) coproducers. Meanwhile, commercial partners assure their investors that, in fact, the program made with their public service coproducer has broader audiences firmly in mind and will not be held captive to a narrowly national address. Such tensions produce a public discourse that can directly contradict the actual conditions and processes of coproduction. How does creativity work in various forms of coproduced narrative? How do transnational partners negotiate the conflicting demands of national specificity and global appeal? Where can international influences open up a drama productively to broader audiences, creating a text that encourages cross-cultural understanding—and where does it work to destroy or marginalize authentic experience? These questions demand research that looks not just at political-economic conditions but that examines texts, production practices, critical discourses, and audience uses as well.[7]

In the meantime, interesting collisions occur. *Top of the Lake* (2013), the television miniseries written by New Zealand filmmaker Jane Campion, was originally intended as an Australian/UK/US coproduction but lost the participation of the Australian Broadcasting Corporation when American actress Elisabeth Moss was cast in the leading role instead of an Australian or New Zealand lead: an example of global appeal in direct conflict with national or regional specificity. Acclaimed Swedish-Danish coproduction *Bron/Broen* (2011–), a crime drama about a body found on the bridge between the two countries, aired in its original version, subtitled, on the broadcast schedules of many countries, including on BBC Four, and could be widely obtained on DVD. (The online streaming platform Hulu will distribute it in 2014). But two national reversionings have already appeared: the FX channel's *The Bridge* (2013–) sets its action on the border between the United States and Mexico, and a British-French coproduction, *The Tunnel* (2011–), takes the action underwater to the Channel Tunnel on Sky Atlantic and Canal+. In each version, police from two countries must cooperate.

60

The most acclaimed British-American co-production in recent years, *Downton Abbey* (2010–) also highlights the narrative appeal of a program that foregrounds international relationships and provides the opportunity for reflection on cultural similarities and differences. Though set in an aristocratic England of the past, its plot is based on the clash of sensibilities between American and British characters, between upstairs and downstairs, between traditional class hierarchies and a growing resistance to them. As Alessandra Stanley argues, *Downton Abbey* "cleverly filters British social history through the biases and preoccupations of American pop culture . . . what really entrances viewers here isn't Anglophilia or a vestigial yearning for a monarch, but rather the mirror that 'Downton Abbey' holds up to America."[8] It is a mirror that reflects the sensibilities of viewers around the world as well, as its global distribution attests, though its lack of complete realism and many historical improbabilities have attracted considerable criticism. Yet here, perhaps, is one form that the transnational television coproduction might constructively take: interrogating the claims of nation and inflecting them with the intersectionality of identity that is the hallmark of contemporary existence — or, at least, of television viewing. We need to begin to examine the transnational dimensions of the national television "box" precisely by exploring the boundary collisions inherent in transnational coproduction.

---

[1] Margaret Lyons, "5 Great International Shows that Should Be Streaming," *Vulture*, July 10, 2013.

[2] June Thomas, "The International Language of Tube," *Slate*, November 26, 2013.

[3] Alessandra Stanley, "The Elusive Pleasures of French TV Series," *New York Times*, August 29, 2013.

[4] Univision began subtitling its prime-time programs in English in 2012.

[5] With some significant and encouraging exceptions; see Jeffrey S. Miller, *Something Completely Different: British Television and American Culture* (Minneapolis: University of Minnesota Press, 2000); Simone Knox, "*Masterpiece Theatre* and British Drama Imports on US Television: Discourses of Tension," *Critical Studies in Television* 7, no. 1 (2012): 29–48; Elke Weissmann, *Transnational Television Drama: Special*

Relations and Mutual Influence Between the US and the UK (New York: Palgrave Macmillan, 2012).

6 Tim Westcott, "TV Drama Riding High in International Market," *Screen Digest*, April 11, 2013; John Plunkett, "Why British TV Producers Are Going Global," *Guardian*, March 29, 2013.

7 Some excellent new work has made a start at examining these issues: Sheron Neves, "Running a Brothel from Inside a Monastery: Drama Co-Productions at the BBC and the Trade Relationship with America from the 1970s to the 1990s" (PhD diss., University of London-Birkbeck, 2013) and Jonathan Bignell and Simone Knox, *Transatlantic Television: British and American TV Drama* (London: I. B. Tauris, forthcoming).

8 Alessandra Stanley, "A Trans-Atlantic Romance Continues," *New York Times*, January 2, 2014.

Bibliography

Bignell, Jonathan, and Simone Knox. *Transatlantic Television: British and American TV Drama*. London: I. B. Tauris, forthcoming.

Knox, Simone. "*Masterpiece Theatre* and British Drama Imports on US Television: Discourses of Tension." *Critical Studies in Television* 7, no. 1 (2012): 29–48.

Lyons, Margaret. "5 Great International Shows that Should Be Streaming." *Vulture*. Last modified July 10, 2013.

Miller, Jeffrey S. *Something Completely Different: British Television and American Culture*. Minneapolis: University of Minnesota Press, 2000.

Neves, Sheron. "Running a Brothel from Inside a Monastery: Drama Co-Productions at the BBC and the Trade Relationship with America from the 1970s to the 1990s." PhD diss., University of London-Birkbeck, 2013.

Plunkett, John. "Why British TV Produces Are Going Global." *Guardian*, March 29, 2013.

Stanley, Alessandra. "A Trans-Atlantic Romance Continues." *New York Times*, January 2, 2014.

— — —. "The Elusive Pleasures of French TV Series." *New York Times*, August 29, 2013.

Thomas, June. "The International Language of Tube." *Slate*. Last modified November 26, 2013.

Weissmann, Elke. *Transnational Television Drama: Special Relations and Mutual Influence Between the US and the UK*. New York: Palgrave MacMillan, 2012.

Westcott, Tim. "TV Drama Riding High in International Market." *Screen Digest*. Last modified April 11, 2013.

9.

The Film Festival as an Industry Node

DINA IORDANOVA

Today, it has become the norm that film festivals not only show films but also engage with film production and distribution. A variety of models that facilitate this engagement have come about, including talent campuses or filmmaking academies geared toward fostering new talent, preproduction or midproduction pitching sessions meant to create an additional investment stream for the project, and so on. Some festivals have created their own distribution labels, while others have teamed up with TV channels or with specific streaming platforms. These developments have resulted in a situation where the film festival is no longer mainly an exhibition operation (as I argued in my 2009 essay "The Film Festival Circuit"),[1] but becomes a participant in many other aspects of the creative cycle — such as production financing, networking, and distribution — and thus turns into a key player in the film industry, as well as society at large. Indeed, it is increasingly the case that film festivals bridge the film industry with politics and other spheres. In a globalized context, it is the film festivals' inherent transnationalism that counterbalances nationalist tendencies, thus facilitating exchanges in production and circulation. This short essay outlines the changing status of the film festival as a cluster of creativity and commerce and as a node in more general transnational infrastructures.

Traditional classifications of film festivals include a category for the "business" type of festival — or the festival with a "business agenda" (as opposed to an "audience" festival, or a festival that has a "geopolitical agenda," for example).[2] The quintessential "business" festival is Cannes. This festival is so excessively industry oriented — it excludes the audience almost entirely — that many have argued that it should be classified as an industry event rather than a film festival. Indeed, a group of international scholars have proposed that there should be a separate subfield of "Cannes studies."

"Business agenda" festivals also include all those that, over the years, have built up markets and industry networking forums: festivals like Berlinale, Venice International Film Festival (IFF), Toronto IFF, Busan IFF, International Documentary Film Festival, and Amsterdam (IDFA), as well as events in Karlovy Vary, Thessaloniki, Rotterdam, and many more.

This essay focuses particularly on the festival activities that are specifically intended to foster production. However, one must say that, historically, festivals embraced the distribution function first. Indeed, holding parallel markets that facilitated the circulation of new films has been a feature of the Cannes event for many years. In the last decade, however, it is Berlinale and Busan that have garnered the most attention for developing distribution arms. By building its European Film Market in February (and thus early in the calendar year), as of 2001 Berlinale successfully garnered most parts of the film business that had lost access to a single central venue for sales after the collapse of Europe's oldest and best-established autumn film market in Milan (International Market for Cinema and Multimedia; 1960–2005).[3] After emerging as a new kid on the block in 1996, within a decade or so, Busan successfully appropriated most of the Asian film business, rivaling much older and better-known festivals such as those in Hong Kong and Tokyo. One can claim that Busan not only took over existing business from these older festivals and their adjacent market ventures but also developed and expanded the intra-Asian market for visual products to unprecedented proportions.

Recently, a growing number of festival organizations have been capitalizing on the fact that filmmakers, producers, and other professionals congregate for annual festival events and have sought to exploit the presence of these production-oriented stakeholders. Berlinale, for example, pioneered the Talent Campus in 2003. Busan followed in 2005 with its Asian Film Academy (AFA). Many other festivals provide forum space for interpersonal encounters and negotiations between companies and creatives, or hold special events (pitching sessions, development fund awards, sessions for additional financing rounds) that foster production-related activities as part of their festivals. Now so many pitching forums take place across festivals that there are individuals who work the circuit and specialize in hosting such forums; these experts know what films are on offer and who is able and willing to invest in up-and-coming productions. One such individual is Martin Blaney, a journalist at Screen International, who spends significantly more time at pitching engagements across the world than writing stories. Another forum host is the "new world of distribution" consultant Peter Broderick, who also delivers his services mainly through the festival circuit.

"The festival pitch" has become such an established practice that even though many filmmakers have come to recognize the reality of spiraling costs and lessened effectiveness (measured by the smaller stream of incoming investments realized by presenting at festival pitching sessions), the belief that it is essential to pitch still persists. According to a recent survey that scrutinized the cost of attending a pitching forum (based on the official IDFA Forum statistics and list of fees), observers must pay between €200 and €300 and participants between €300 and €400 per person to attend the forum. IDFA earns between €80,000 and €90,000 in revenue from pitching forum fees during each festival.[4] And even though most interviewees expressed reservations about the effectiveness of attending pitching forums and seemed to consider them wasteful, they all acknowledged that online pitching was not a viable alternative, that continued festival attendance is important, and that a representative trailer for their projects should be shown in the context of film festival forums.

New Crowned Hope Festival in Vienna, Austria, was the first festival to engage in direct commissioning of film productions: in 2006, it commissioned films from Asian directors such as Apichatpong Weerasethakul (Thailand) and Garin Nugroho (Indonesia). Long before that, however, festivals distributed production funds to a line of projects that were in the production pipeline and that competed with each other for supplementary funds made available by the respective festivals' schemes. For example, Marco Muller's Montecinemaverita Foundation has operated at Locarno since the 1990s, and Scandinavian festivals have awarded various production funds to filmmakers from across the Third World.

More than a decade ago, the late cultural critic Paul Willemen claimed that although festivals may seem to open up pathways to global exposure and circulation, in fact, they only produce a "bottleneck effect" and ensure that noncommercial films remain outside formal circulation channels. Traditional circulation channels, meanwhile, remain reserved for blockbuster-type mainstream cinema. Festivals, Willemen claimed, do not bring cinema closer to the people. On the contrary, they encapsulate and isolate cinema, shielding it from wider audiences, and thus effectively shrink all chances of proper exposure.[5] Other authors who study the festival galaxy, however, do not feel that festivals play such a restrictive function.[6] In order to balance multiple opinions, one should say that, like most cultural phenomena, film festivals are multifaceted and riddled with inherent contradictions. Festivals enhance the exposure of films, but they also disrupt the traditional distribution process; they may appear networked, but there is also evidence to the contrary. Most importantly, the importance of the film festival as a node in the cinema production and distribution cycle is becoming increasingly recognized by all stakeholders involved in the festival operation, from board members to filmmakers, producers, and critics.

My own research questions gradually crystallized around these dichotomies. They are distilled here in order to reveal several issues explored by my work on festivals, including the importance of film festivals in the context of film culture at large, the reigning logic within the film festival galaxy, and the key features and stakeholders of the film festival. What, if anything, is wrong with the concept of "festival films"? What makes a good film festival *good* or a bad one *bad*?

A mere decade ago, only a handful of publications touched on matters related to film festivals. In recent years, the situation has changed dramatically, with abundant new writing and publications; some even speak of film festival studies as "a field," and a "burgeoning" one at that.[7]

Today, we are witnessing the appearance of a host of studies highlighting important concrete details in the history of cinema and its localization (and globalization) via various festivals — studies that delve deeper into specific aspects of this or that festival, and highlight previously discounted matters of interest.[8] All of these efforts are important in bringing our attention to key phenomena that have been overlooked and denied existence for years; one needs to encourage the compensatory efforts that drive such current scholarship. There is consensus among scholars that media industries research needs to study how the film festival structures and narrates itself, what its components are, what constitutes the play of power between its participants, and how this is reenacted in the time and space of the festival and even beyond. Once such an understanding has been settled, it will lead us to further studies analyzing how the festival inscribes itself into the context of its locality and how it insinuates itself into the global galaxy of other festivals. To employ a technological metaphor in this technological age, such examination focuses on the festival's "hardware" (venues, hub), its "software" (films, programming, sidebars), and the "interface" of its components (the coverage, the party).

---

1 Dina Iordanova, "The Film Festival Circuit," in *Film Festival Yearbook 1: The Festival Circuit*, ed. Dina Iordanova and Ragan Rhyne (St. Andrews: St Andrews Film Studies with College Gate Press, 2009), 23–39.

2 Kenneth Turan, *Sundance to Sarajevo: Film Festivals and the World They Made* (Berkeley: University of California Press, 2002); Mark Peranson, "First You Get the Power, Then You Get the Money: Two Models of Film Festivals," in *Dekalog 3: On Film Festivals*, ed. Richard Porton (London: Wallflower, 2009), 23–37.

3 Dom Serafini, "My 2 Cents: Who Killed MIFED?," *Video Age: The Business Journal of Film, TV, Broadcasting, Broadband, Production, Distribution* (2005).

4 "The Festival Pitch," *DOX: European Documentary Magazine* (2012/2013): 5–10.

5 Dina Iordanova, introduction to *The Film Festival Reader*, ed. Dina Iordanova (St. Andrews: St Andrews Film Studies, 2013), 1.

6 Thomas Elsaesser, "Film Festival Networks: The New Topographies of Cinema in Europe," in *European Cinema: Face to Face with Hollywood* (Amsterdam: Amsterdam University Press, 2005), 82–107; Jean-Michele Frodon, "The Cinema Planet" (lecture, Centre for Film Studies at the University of St Andrews, November 9, 2010).

7 Marijke De Valck and Skadi Loist, "Film Festival Studies: An Overview of a Burgeoning Field," in *Film Festival Yearbook 1: The Festival Circuit*, ed. Dina Iordanova and

Ragan Rhyne (St. Andrews: College Gate Press, 2009), 179–215.

[8] For a listing of published writing related to film festival, please see the FFRN Research Bibliography available at http://www.filmfestivalresearch.org/index.php/ffrn-bibliography/.

Bibliography

De Valck, Marijke, and Skadi Loist. "Film Festival Studies: An Overview of a Burgeoning Field." In *Film Festival Yearbook 1: The Festival Circuit*, edited by Dina Iordanova and Ragan Rhyne, 179–215. St. Andrews: College Gate Press, 2009.

Elsaesser, Thomas. "Film Festival Networks: The New Topographies of Cinema in Europe." In *European Cinema: Face to Face with Hollywood*, 82–107. Amsterdam: Amsterdam University Press, 2005.

Frodon, Jean-Michele. "The Cinema Planet." Lecture, Centre for Film Studies at the University of St Andrews, November 9, 2010.

Iordanova, Dina. "The Film Festival Circuit." In *Film Festival Yearbook 1: The Festival Circuit*, edited by Dina Iordanova and Ragan Rhyne, 23–39. St. Andrews: St Andrews Film Studies with College Gate Press, 2009.

Iordanova, Dina. Introduction to *The Film Festival Reader*, edited by Dina Iordanova, 1–19. St. Andrews: St Andrews Film Studies, 2013.

Peranson, Mark. "First You Get the Power, Then You Get the Money: Two Models of Film Festivals." In *Dekalog 3: On Film Festivals*, edited by Richard Porton, 23–37. London: Wallflower, 2009.

Serafini, Dom. "My 2 Cents: Who Killed MIFED?" *Video Age: The Business Journal of Film, TV, Broadcasting, Broadband, Production, Distribution* (2005).

"The Festival Pitch." *DOX: European Documentary Magazine* (2012/2013): 5–10.

Turan, Kenneth. *Sundance to Sarajevo: Film Festivals and the World They Made*. Berkeley: University of California Press, 2002.

10.

Placing International Media Production

APHRA KERR

Understanding Space and Place

While much of the globalization literature talks of deterritorialization, transnationalism, and global flows, we are seeing at the same time more locational competition and attention being paid to aspects of place and/or space. When I use these terms, it is not in any absolute sense. Rather it is relational and, in terms of cultural production, it means that we need to investigate how and in what ways industries, companies, workers, texts, and users get embedded in particular spaces while simultaneously being involved in global flows. It is to question why a company has located in X or moved its production to Y and if and, in what ways, are the company and their products localized and particular. It is also to note that space and place are experienced both objectively and subjectively – thus companies and workers in the same industry and located in the same city may experience that city quite differently.

This is not a unique perspective. It is, of course, prevalent in more critical and feminist geography but it also appears to varying degrees in media scholarship. In scholarship on the creative industries in the UK, there has been a lot of work that argues for increased sensitivity to spatial and locational factors.[1] In media and communications fields, there is a tradition that explores cross-national geo-cultural and geo-linguistic markets and regional flows.[2] And of course there is the work on a new industrial division of cultural labor.[3] More recently, Vincent Mosco identifies spatialization as a core starting point for any analysis of communication.[4]

Yet the focus on space and place needs some more theoretical development. Mosco draws upon the work of Henri Lefebvre, but still mainly attends to the structure and actions of corporations and states. As I have argued elsewhere, Lefebvre has a richer

73

conceptualization of the social production of space, one that connects the symbolic and representational to practice.[5] Lefebvre stresses the need to attend to the interrelationship between three aspects: spatial practices, representations of space (i.e., formal abstractions like maps), and representational spaces (i.e., lived experiences and actions).[6] For Lefebvre, we must attend to the social, cultural, and everyday lived experiences of people in space.

While Lefebvre's initial work was conducted almost forty years ago in France, it can be productively applied to the study of mobile companies, work, and workers in the context of media capitals and new national and supranational entities (e.g., the EU and Asia-Pacific). However, we need to consider the methodological and theoretical implications of attending to varying spatialities and processes of spatialization. Is it sufficient to compare industries within a country or between two countries? When does a multinational company become a local one? What is the relationship between space, place, and power?

Examples

One can usefully explore space, place, and power through the contemporary digital games industry. To some authors, this is the foremost example of a frictionless post-Fordist informational and promotional capitalism.[7] While clearly it produces informational products and services, the digital games industry has disparate international hardware and software production networks and displays a lot of variance across and within markets.[8] These differences are reinforced by the establishment of technological and organizational regions, like the EMEA region for Europe, the Middle East, and Africa. Within this framework, there are linguistic and other market distinctions. Add increasing competition between states, regions, and cities to attract transnational game companies and you start to see the active social production of spaces.[9] This process is now extending to game content as state support gets tied to national and regional cultural values—a development about which the industry is ambiguous.

It would be inaccurate, therefore, to presume that there is a freely operating global market in digital games and that their development, distribution, and circulation are "footloose." Particular urban locations appear to be important for publishers.

While development and support companies can take advantage of technological changes to locate their operations anywhere, we are still seeing that they prefer to be located in or near major urban markets. Increasingly, these companies locate in cities where other advantages are outweighing the locational costs, or where regional, national, or local subsidies have reduced their costs. Thus, the spatial distribution of the games industry is complex and linked in part to the history of the games industry but more significantly to the regional structure of software production networks interacting with local and regional financial, cultural, and labor markets. As this industry moves towards games as a service rather than simply a product, it is actively negotiating where, when, and for how long it locates in particular places.

One of the first to point to the spatial variations across the value chain of the digital games industry was Jennifer Johns.[10] She noted how finance, uneven power relations between actors in the production network, and cultural embeddedness contribute to the creation of "regional games software production networks." In Ireland, research has found unequal access to state incentives between foreign-owned multinational game companies and locally established start-ups, and between companies involved in production and companies involved in services. In the main, foreign-owned multinational companies engaged in labor-intensive services and community support had better access to state support than local start-ups. Content production is seen as a more risky investment than community support.[11]

Yet, an industrial policy that focuses on attracting mobile multinationals engaged in game services and support is also risky. Surveys of employment in the Irish game industry have found a lot of fluctuation in numbers of employees. In the past three years, Ireland has seen the closure of branches of PopCap and Big Fish games companies as high-tech jobs have been cut due to restructuring in what are, in fact, profitable companies. EA also reduced the number of community support employees in Ireland due to worse-than-expected European player numbers in some of their games. The level of embeddedness of these foreign-owned companies is relatively low but they have all benefitted from state incentives to locate in Ireland.

Finally, we must contend with cultures of production. An important corrective to statistical generalizations are ethnographic studies conducted within game companies or interviews with game company staff, freelancers, and interns. These studies provide important nuance to the image of the digital games production industry as a young, white, mostly-male industry with problematic project management practices and workplace culture. These studies highlight variations between small start-ups, established multinationals, and large indigenous companies. Local start-ups that are acquired by multinational businesses offer another interesting challenge to our assumptions about media ownership as they often, in fact, retain their local managers, linkages, and culture.

An instructive comparison can be made with production processes in broadcast animation companies. In a recent study, we researched a production project from inception to completion and followed the production networks across companies, borders, and continents. In an established cultural industry with a complex set of national and cross-national co-production financing structures as well as variations in local content regulations and regional selling markets, we quickly realized that there were multiple spatialities at work. However, while the production projects sourced their ideas, finance, and labor internationally, they were limited to working with companies in countries where co-production agreements existed, while making use of local specificities to purposefully and productively vary the content. In this case, we are looking at a multi-scalar geography of cultural production shaped by national institutional, cultural, and financial structures. The animation industry developed a range of state, local, and regional supports to offset the risks involved in creative production. These supports were based on the cultural value of animation and were in contrast to the games industry in Ireland, whose funding is mostly based on employment and potential revenue. (Uniquely to date in Europe, France has introduced a tax credit system for games production based on a cultural test.)

While it could be said that we found a high degree of internationalization and distanciated co-operation in these animation projects, this finding was not uniform across the production process. Transnational collaboration in creative conceptualization and financing occurred mainly with the UK,

Canada, and the US and relied on a shared language, cultural heritage, and other forms of proximity.[12] This was in marked contrast to more labor-intensive elements of the production process that were outsourced to the Philippines and which received less creative and managerial input. Again we see that cultural production is spatially distributed, but this distribution is structured by a range of historic, economic, social, and cultural factors.

To empirically understand contemporary international cultural industries, it is necessary to critically examine representations of/by the industry, the structure and boundaries of the industry, and its locational politics. Little independent data exists about the digital games industry; and it is ill-defined. Currently, institutions, including international and national trade associations as well as local and regional governments, are actively trying to legally define and place the digital games industry as they have previously done with the animation, film, and television industries. These institutional struggles should be a key focus of empirical attention. To empirically study production it is also necessary to rethink our methodological approaches. We must look beyond the company and the nation-state and follow the product or service through the various institutional and social networks that shape its spaces of production and consumption. We must examine the spatialization of projects from design through to production and circulation/support; and as the cultural industries increasingly produce services, we must reevaluate the attention paid to "circulation." Production involves a range of practices and creative workers but these concepts are evolving and should not be taken for granted.

1 Andy C. Pratt, Rosalind Gill, and Volker Spelthann, "Work and the City in the e-Society: A Critical Investigation of the Sociospatially Situated Character of Economic Production in the Digital Content Industries in the UK," *Information, Communication and Society* 10, no. 6 (2008): 922-942; Mark Banks, *The Politics of Cultural Work* (New York: Palgrave Macmillan, 2007).

2 David Hesmondhalgh, *The Cultural Industries*, 2nd ed. (London: Sage, 2007); Paschal Preston and Aphra Kerr,

"Digital Media, Nation-States and Local Cultures: The Case of Multimedia 'Content' Production," *Media, Culture and Society* 23, no. 1 (2001): 109-131; Marwan M. Kraidy and Omar Al-Ghazzi, "Neo-Ottoman Cool: Turkish Popular Culture in the Arab Public Sphere," *Popular Communication* 11, no. 1 (2013): 17-29.

3 Toby Miller, "The New International Division of Cultural Labour," in *Global Hollywood*, eds. Toby Miller, Nitin Govil, John McMurria, Ting Wang, and Richard Maxwell (London: BFI, 2005).

4 Vincent Mosco, *The Political Economy of Communication*, 2nd ed. (London: Sage, 2009).

5 Aphra Kerr and Anthony Cawley, "The Spatialisation of the Digital Games Industry: Lessons from Ireland," *International Journal of Cultural Policy* 18, no. 4 (2012): 398-418.

6 Henri Lefebvre, *The Production of Space/Production de L'espace* (Oxford: Blackwell, 1991).

7 Stephen Kline, Nick Dyer-Witheford, and Greig De Peuter, *Digital Play: The Interaction of Technology, Culture and Marketing* (Montreal: McGill-Queen's University Press, 2003).

8 Randy Nichols, "Who Plays, Who Pays? Mapping Video Game Production and Consumption Globally," in *Gaming Globally: Production, Play and Place*, eds. Nina Huntemann and Ben Aslinger (New York Palgrave Macmillan, 2013), 19-39.

9 Aphra Kerr, "Space Wars: The Politics of Games Production in Europe," in *Gaming Globally*, eds. Nina Huntemann and Ben Aslinger (New York: Palgrave, 2013), 215-231.

10 Jennifer Johns, "Video Games Production Networks: Value Capture, Power Relations and Embeddedness," *Journal of Economic Geography* 6, no. 2 (2006): 151-180.

11 Kerr and Cawley, "The Spatialisation of the Digital Games Industry," 398-418.

12 Chris van Egeraat, Sean O'Riain, and Aphra Kerr, "Social and Spatial Structures of Innovation in the Irish Animation Industry," *European Planning Studies* 21, no. 9 (2013): 1-19.

Bibliography

Banks, Mark. *The Politics of Cultural Work*. New York: Palgrave Macmillan, 2007.

Dyer-Witheford, Nick, and Zena Sharman. "The Political Economy of Canada's Video and Computer Game Industry" *Canadian Journal of Communication* 30 (2005): 187-210.

Hesmondhalgh, David. *The Cultural Industries*. 2nd ed. London: Sage, 2007.

Johns, Jennifer. "Video Games Production Networks: Value Capture, Power Relations and Embeddedness." *Journal of Economic Geography* 6, no. 2 (2006): 151-180.

Kerr, Aphra. "Space Wars: The Politics of Games Production in Europe." In *Gaming Globally*, edited by Nina Huntemann and Ben Aslinger, 215-231. New York: Palgrave, 2013.

Kerr, Aphra, and Anthony Cawley. "The Spatialisation of the Digital Games Industry: Lessons from Ireland." *International Journal of Cultural Policy* 18, no. 4 (2012): 398-418.

Kline, Stephen, Nick Dyer-Witheford, and Greig De Peuter. *Digital Play: The Interaction of Technology, Culture and Marketing*. Montreal: McGill-Queen's University Press, 2003.

Kraidy, Marwan M., and Omar Al-Ghazzi. "Neo-Ottoman Cool: Turkish Popular Culture in the Arab Public Sphere." *Popular Communication* 11, no. 1 (2013): 17-29.

Lefebvre, Henri. *The Production of Space/Production de L'espace*. Oxford: Blackwell, 1991.

Miller, Toby. "The New International Division of Cultural Labour." In *Global Hollywood*, edited by Toby Miller, Nitin Govil, John McMurria, Ting Wang, and Richard Maxwell. London: BFI, 2005.

Mosco, Vincent. *The Political Economy of Communication*. 2nd ed. London: Sage, 2009.

Nichols, Randy. "Who Plays, Who Pays? Mapping Video Game Production and Consumption Globally."In *Gaming Globally: Production, Play and Place*, edited by Nina Huntemann and Ben Aslinger, 19-39. New York: Palgrave Macmillan, 2013.

Pratt, Andy C., Rosalind Gill, and Volker Spelthann. "Work and the City in the e-Society. A Critical Investigation of the Sociospatially Situated Character of Economic Production in the Digital Content Industries in the UK." *Information, Communication and Society* 10, no. 6 (2008): 922-942.

Preston, Paschal, and Aphra Kerr. "Digital Media, Nation-States and Local Cultures: The Case of Multimedia 'Content' Production." *Media, Culture and Society* 23, no. 1(2001): 109-131.

van Egeraat, Chris, Sean O'Riain, and Aphra Kerr. "Social and Spatial Structures of Innovation in the Irish Animation Industry."*European Planning Studies* 21, no. 9 (2013): 1-19.

11.

The Industrialization and Globalization of China's Musical Theater

SHIN DONG KIM

The Broadway musical *Chicago* was widely advertised before coming to Shanghai for the first time in February 2014, hitting twelve stages in thirteen days. The price of tickets ranged from 800 RMB to 80 RMB, compared to movie ticket prices averaging 30 to 40 RMB. Many expected tickets to sell out before the show opened. To the great disappointment of musical fans in Shanghai, the show never materialized. The China tour began in the southern city of Fuzhou in December 2013, but the performing team from Broadway hastily left the city for New York after a contentious initial period of production. According to the New York team, the local theater's technology was never properly prepared, and the Chinese partner was unable to resolve the problem in time for the tour to continue. In addition to advance ticket sales, performances at other theaters were already scheduled, which only increased the financial losses associated with the tour.

Although musicals are a relatively new form of entertainment in Shanghai, and in China in general, they have achieved handsome success with Chinese audiences in recent years. In the fall of 2013, *The Phantom of the Opera's* London team toured China and attracted a robust audience in Shanghai, seemingly demonstrating that the local musical market is expanding. Over the last decade, the market has grown with a good number of potential consumers of high-end entertainment, but business practices and technological capabilities in the domestic culture industry have not kept pace with the quickly developing demand.

The Western musical is not a total stranger to young, wealthy audiences in the global city of Shanghai. *The Phantom of Opera* came to the city eight years ago and enjoyed a good response. But foreign musicals have suffered from a fundamental language barrier that has limited their popularity to big cities and a modest number of affluent audiences. The first attempt to adapt this new entertainment model into a fully localized production was *Mamma Mia* in 2011. It was staged 188 times in three major cities: Beijing, Shanghai, and Guangzhou. The successful launch of the show in these big cities paved the way for 97 additional performances in local cities throughout the following year. The show returned to the three big cities again in 2013, with 124 stagings and will likely continue its run for several years. Encouraged by the success of *Mamma Mia*, another classic musical, *Cats*, followed in 2012, with 159 performances in Beijing, Shanghai, and Guangzhou, and 71 in local cities throughout 2013. The original producer in London licensed both productions. A well-organized local producer, the United Asia Live Entertainment (UALE), which represented a joint venture between Korean media company CJ and the Chinese government, were behind the successful introduction of these locally produced musicals into the Chinese market.

Some brief context regarding the development of the music business in China reveals a few fundamental facts. Some Chinese cities are ready for the musical entertainment business. However, although musicals can make a profit in China, they are not always successful. There are more limits placed on foreign musicals than on local productions. The local skills and technological expertise involved in producing musicals do not conform to global business practices. Taking a joint-venture approach, which involves combining foreign musicals with local production practices, seems to work well when the local experience in musicals is limited. In many parts of the world, local productions and foreign tours are the two main types of musical productions. When there is no local capacity to produce musicals, tours by foreign visiting performers are often the only option for this type of entertainment, even if these tours often come up against cultural barriers.

From a slightly different point of view, foreign and local musical productions represent different types of what might be called business globalization. The simplest form of business globalization involves the export of finished goods and services. Foreign tours of musical productions fall into this category. A more developed form of business globalization often establishes the circuit of production, distribution, and consumption through a locally dependent process. UALE entered the musical market by combining musical production technologies and management from Korea with Chinese staffing and marketing. A team of musical production experts arrived in Shanghai and recruited Chinese actors and actresses, who were then trained by Korean producers. All content was translated through collaboration between the Korean team and Chinese crew. After the initial production, the Korean team left, and the Chinese staff and crew managed successive productions. In this way, the collaboration also resulted in technology transfers. UALE, the Korean partner, introduced different types of stories, shows, and levels of production technology into the local industry.

Paralleling the economic development of China, the media and culture industry has experienced remarkable growth in the last decade. In contrast with its success with material goods, China found it difficult to become a global exporter in the area of cultural goods and services. If the growth of the Chinese economy has been dependent on an export-led development strategy, growth in the culture industry has depended mainly on domestic consumption. In a way, this is a natural outcome of the country's rising economic development and prosperity. China's economic development in the last couple of decades following Deng Xiaoping's open and pragmatic policy has produced a thick layer of affluent, middle-class consumers. These were China's new rich, who were able and ready to spend on cultural consumption. The development of a market economy also promoted the expansion of the advertising industry and eventually a competitive commercial media system. Television, film, magazines, books, arts, performances, and all other forms of cultural consumption were initially conceived of as simply the fruits of economic development. However, the notion of "culture as industry" entered the nation's political process in the period surrounding the 2008 Beijing Olympic Games.

In 2007, the Seventeenth National Congress of the Communist Party of China announced that the state would promote "great cultural development and prosperity of socialism," based on Chinese national culture, and hoped to become a leading country in thedomain of global culture. The globalization of Chinese culture became a political goal linked to China's rising soft power. The new policy included structuring the culture industry according to a market-economy system. Led by the Ministry of Culture, this process centered on providing public funding for big state corporations, such as CCTV and the China Arts and Entertainment Group. The state also actively engaged in globalizing Chinese culture through expanding cultural exchanges, establishing overseas posts, and developing foreign cultural partnerships. The rapid expansion of Confucius Institutes to universities around the world and the active proliferation of CCTV to Africa and other parts of the globe were also part of this process.

In 2009, the State Council of the PRC published a "culture industry promotion plan" that aimed at

- developing a new growth engine for restructuring the Chinese industrial structure through the promotion of the culture industry;

- speeding up major projects and strengthening the overall competitiveness, size, and power of culture industry;

- converting state companies involved in the cultural industry into stock companies with diverse types of ownership structures;

- lowering the barriers to entry in order to actively attract foreign capital; and

- expanding the performing arts into a "live entertainment industry," under the Ministry of Culture.

But the expansion of the Chinese culture industry is linked to politically delicate issues. The Chinese government's efforts to open the cultural industry market have been impeded by the old and obstinate ideological systems. On the one hand, the Chinese government aims to promote the development of a globally competitive culture industry. On the other hand, the ruling Communist Party is afraid of exposing the country to "too much" foreign culture. A protective, paternalistic state stands between the task of industrial development and ideological safeguards. However, the development of the culture industry requires increased interactions and transactions with foreign players who could provide advanced content and technology. As is well known, Facebook does not work in China, and Google has experienced many operational challenges. Media are generally under government censorship and the administration tightly controls the supply of foreign cultural content. In these circumstances, industrialization, let alone globalization, of culture is never a simple task. Nevertheless, it is noteworthy that the Chinese government is moving to admit that "culture" is no longer subject to political monopoly. The country is opening its cultural market quickly and widely to the rest of the world and also wants to become a prominent exporter of cultural commodities.

While the Chinese state was busy making plans to develop its culture industry, on the other side of the Yellow Sea social and political discourses about the cultural industries have attracted much Korean media attention. After the successful development and spread of Korean media products such as television dramas, films, and pop music among countries in Asia, major players in the Korean industry have been actively seeking ways to globalize their business practices, from market research to product delivery. Globalization of media businesses, however, provides few models or theories that can be readily recycled. Unlike other business operations, media production and consumption involve cultural-filtering processes that are not easily translated into different social contexts. A global division of labor, for instance, is one of the typical methods of business globalization in many industries ranging from automobile production to beer breweries. In the areas of film production and distribution, a global division of labor has been widely used, but with limited success in most cases. The global film industry's methods of producing and exporting product have changed little after a century of global operation. The global film industry has widely pursued and adopted coproductions, joint investments, and distribution partnerships, but these efforts are minor in comparison to other industry sectors. Musicals, films, and most other genres of the culture industries follow similar patterns.

For the Korean culture businesses, China is a difficult target. It is difficult to deal with the Chinese government, especially for media and cultural businesses. Television programs and films are under the tight control of the Communist Party. Foreign imports are kept to a minimum, as they are viewed as cultural-imperialist products. China is the largest consumer of Korean media culture, from television shows to K-pop. The problem is that most of this consumption is the result of illegal circulation on the internet and via copies of DVDs purchased on the streets. China will only provide returns for Korean media actors if a portion of this illegal flow can be channeled into legal transactions.

Fortunately, the situation seems to be turning a corner, as China seeks industrialization in the media and culture arena. For Korean businesses, this has presented an opportunity to expand their deals with Chinese partners. In the case of the musical, for instance, the Chinese Ministry of Culture initially contacted the world-renowned British theatrical producer Cameron Mackintosh regarding a joint venture. But this attempt never succeeded, as both parties could not agree on the prospective partner's idea of the joint venture. Oftentimes, global business collaborations with Chinese partners, who insist on the Chinese way of controlling shares, create difficulties for foreign firms. Yet this failed collaboration with Mackintosh opened an unexpected opportunity for a Korean firm. Under pressure to develop the culture industry, and responding in part to competition from the Chinese State Administration of Radio, Film, and Television (SARFT), which controls most of media entertainment and thus industrialized mass culture, the Ministry of Culture continued to pursue the expansion of the Chinese musical market. After failed collaboration attempts with the British, and recognizing the significant growth of the Korean musical market over the last decade, the Ministry reached out to Korean partners after the Beijing Olympic Games in 2008.

The growth of the Chinese musical market in many ways parallels what happened in Korea. Common factors are readily observable and include economic growth and rise of disposable personal income; demand for high-level entertainment other than television and film; growing cultural consumption by young single women in their twenties and thirties; the emergence of musical fandom; and the availability of blockbuster franchises such as *The Phantom of Opera*, *Mamma Mia*, and *Cats*. Significantly, China is in the midst of a theater-construction boom. After this infrastructure is complete, China will not be far from Korea in terms of making the musical a successful popular pastime.

There are, however, a few critical differences between the two countries in terms of their ventures into musical theater. Chinese technology of musical production and management lags behind Korea. The political sensitivity of cultural production in China is a second critical difference. Nevertheless, both parties seem to view the case of UALE as a successful international collaboration that

86

promises positive developments within the Chinese musical market. On the Korean side, creating a reliable window through which Korean performing arts businesses can enter the Chinese market was a meaningful gain. To the Chinese, the Korean partner brings accumulated experience and resources to the Chinese industry in the form of new and original content, workforce expertise and training (e.g., creators, designers, and technical staff), and new equipment (e.g., lighting, stage, and sound).

The globalization of the cultural industry comes in many different forms. Wider distribution and consumption of cultural content used to be and still is the most common form of cultural globalization. Joint production is a more complicated form of global collaboration. While China's ambitious plan for the industrialization and globalization of culture is still new, it promises to encourage the country to lower the protective wall surrounding its cultural and political domain to the rest of the world. Musicals are not much different than television, film, or music productions, but they are less politically loaded. Therefore, it might be easier for the Chinese government to start with musicals as a less politically controversial cultural area and then move on to other fields.[1]

---

[1] As this publication goes to press, Chinese television stations are busy reproducing Korean television program formats. Because the government restricts the direct import of Korean programs and the original programs are already widely available on the internet, local stations have quickly picked up a new business strategy of Korean-format purchasing and reproduction, often coupled with importing the production technologies. This is a small but very noticeable development in television production practices, and it promises to bring about significant change to China's central entertainment medium.

12.

Media Industries in Revolutionary Times

MARWAN M. KRAIDY

The popular uprisings that have rocked the Arab world since December 2010 have had a transformational impact on Arab media industries. Old pan-Arab television news networks have changed their editorial orientations and new channels have arisen to challenge incumbents. Musical releases have been slower and fewer, and the music video industry has all but screeched to a halt. In Arab countries that experienced uprisings, national media landscapes have been reshaped. Conservative Islamists like the Muslim Brotherhood in Egypt and the Ennahda movement in Tunisia sought to "cleanse" television through new policies after both groups won elections deemed free and fair, while mobs of their radical brethren, the Salafis, stormed television channels airing content that they judged offensive according to their interpretation of Islam. As established players come under assault, new ones flex their muscles, reflecting newly politically ascendant forces. At the same time, the fortunes of various television genres changed, with talk-show ratings skyrocketing in Egypt to the point that they competed with Ramadan drama in July and August 2013. Shifting relations between states also affect the media industries, most spectacularly in the Egyptian-Turkish row over the military coup that toppled elected Egyptian president Muhammad Morsi, who was supported by Turkey's prime minister Recep Tayyep Erdoğan. The dispute led to a boycott of Turkish drama by Egyptian and other Arab channels starting in August 2013. Since then, the reassertion of military rule in Egypt has spectacularly shown that as enemies of media independence, secular regimes can be worse than Islamists. Media control and censure in revolutionary times are about raw political power more than they are about religious piety.

The most important change in the television news industry brought about by the Arab uprisings has been the editorial realignment of Al Jazeera and the ensuing advent of Al Mayadeen, based in Beirut and led by Al Jazeera's erstwhile bureau chief in the Lebanese capital: the Tunisian journalist Ghassan Bin Jeddu. Throughout the fall of 2011 and spring of 2012, as the Syrian uprising moved into a brutal civil war that increasingly dominated news coverage, Al Jazeera emerged as the chief media cheerleader of the rebels taking arms against Bashar al-Assad. This caused fundamental disagreement within the channel, with several employees resigning from the Beirut bureau, which was in charge of Syria coverage, in protest against "directives from above." I was on research leave in Beirut at the time and did several interviews for Al Jazeera English's program *The Listening Post*, which covers media issues. There, in Al Jazeera's offices in Quntari at the edge of the Hamra district, tension was manifest among the employees. An initial trickle of departures gained momentum as stories emerged of Al Jazeera showing contrived footage of Syrian regime atrocities, and as the contrast between the Qatari channel's histrionic coverage of Syria and its minimal reporting on the popular uprising in Bahrain became flagrant.

Since its launch in 1996, Al Jazeera has been famous for its relentless criticism of the Saudi royal family and its policies. Its talk shows have hosted Saudi dissidents; its newscasts have focused on Saudi domestic problems; and its reports have highlighted negative aspects of Saudi foreign policy. The emir of Qatar launched Al Jazeera after executing a coup against his father, a protégé of the Saudis. The Saudis from the outset led a commercial boycott of the Qatari channel, and in 2003 they launched the Dubai-based Al Arabiya to counter Al Jazeera's onslaught on Saudi interests. In addition to the Saudis not tolerating dissent among the members of the Gulf Cooperation Council (GCC, a club of the region's oil monarchies), some of the seeds of discord came from Qatari support of the Muslim Brotherhood, which the Saudis perceived as a threat to the Wahhabi, or Salafi, doctrine at the heart of the Saudi clerico-political system. The Saudi-Qatari feud animated many a talk show, and Arab analysts and columnists followed its every step.

The Arab Spring upended these political-media dynamics. After an initial period of shock as Tunisia's Ben Ali, Egypt's Mubarak, and Yemen's Saleh—all allies of the Saudis—were unseated, the Gulf monarchies undertook nothing short of a counterrevolution. Qatar emerged as the patron of the Muslim Brotherhood in Egypt and the Brotherhood-affiliated Ennahda in Tunisia, both winners of post-dictatorship elections, while the Saudis sponsored emerging Salafi parties, especially the al-Nour in Egypt. The Saudis fought a losing battle to keep Saleh in power in Yemen, which they consider their backyard. But the Bahraini upheaval, which raised the specter of regime change within the GCC, compelled the Gulf rivals—Qatar and Saudi Arabia—to pull together, though a rift over who is the leading sponsor of the Syrian rebels remains. Under the Peninsula Shield defense clause of the GCC, Saudi armed forces entered Bahrain through the ten-mile causeway (bridge) linking the two kingdoms over Persian Gulf waters to succor the Bahraini monarchy in repressing the rebellion. The Sunni Gulf monarchies have long accused Shiite Iran of meddling in their affairs through Bahrain, which has a Shiite majority. Saudi Arabia and Kuwait also have significant Shiite minorities, and in the former, Shiites predominate the oil- and mineral-rich Eastern Province. In an unfortunate sign of the times, sectarian incitement and mobilization have become both unabashed and systematic, though it is important to recall that the rising intensity and frequency of sectarian agitation stems mainly from geopolitical instrumentalization and much less from fundamental doctrinal disagreements.

As this happened, erstwhile archrivals Al Jazeera and Al Arabiya enacted a stunning editorial convergence—confronting Al Mayadeen, a new channel with a limited following and a smaller audience; Hizbullah's Al Manar; Iran's minor player Al-Alam; and Syrian channels—over the Syrian revolution in what can be characterized as a new Middle Eastern War of the Airwaves. Shifting geopolitical agendas thus shaped a major reshuffling of the pan-Arab television news industry.

At the same time, a renaissance of national broadcasting, terrestrial and satellite, was underway. Egypt is the best illustration of this trend. As Mubarak fell in February 2011 and political life heated up leading to legislative elections, talk-show ratings skyrocketed, driven by newly found freedoms to debate politics in a no-holds-barred fashion. Unexpected ratings boosters happened, such as the resignation of Egypt's first post-Mubarak prime minister on a live television talk show. In moments of upheaval when people are thirsty for information about local politics and security, it is not surprising that local and national news, current affairs, and talk shows take primacy over entertainment fare, which in the Arab world tends to be produced by transnational satellite channels with weak local connections and coverage.

The Arab Spring brought a mixed bag for entertainment. On the one hand, newly enfranchised Islamist parties in Egypt and Tunisia sought to cleanse entertainment of sexual content to bring it in line with their vision of the virtuous society. The security situation in Syria drove Syrian drama production to Beirut, Cairo, and Abu Dhabi. Even in Cairo, deteriorating security conditions delayed or undermined production schedules. Pop stars like Amr Diab and Shereen Abdulwahhab were forced to delay album releases traditionally timed for Eid al-Fitr, the major Muslim holiday that concludes the holy month of Ramadan. In Egypt, Syria, and Tunisia, actors, singers, and other celebrities were dragged into wars of words and ended up on various groups' online walls of fame and walls of shame. Many were threatened, others were kidnapped, some were killed.

The June 30, 2013, military coup in Egypt that unseated elected-president and Muslim Brotherhood figure Muhammad Morsi approximately a year into his tenure reshuffled the media industry chessboard again. Pro-Mubarak celebrities who had been on the defensive during Morsi's rule were newly visible, leading the charge in a vicious media campaign against the Muslim Brotherhood, now labeled terrorists. Many observers were surprised to see that Egyptian and other drama series during Ramadan 2013—Ramadan is the high season of television drama in the Arab world[1]—demonized clerics more than cops and featured the boldest-yet themes and scenes featuring sexuality, addiction, drugs, rape, the marriage of minors, and radicalism. The usual critics aired customary objections, but reactions to increasingly bold treatment of burning social issues by television drama were strangely muffled, as if rendered less problematic by the rough-and-tumble of life in revolutionary times.

The military coup in Egypt also upended Egypt-Turkey relations. Turkey's prime minister, Recep Tayyip Erdoğan, was a strong supporter of Egypt's president, Mohammed Morsi. Erdoğan's party, the Justice and Development Party (Turkish acronym: AKP) and the Muslim Brotherhood are ideological kindred spirits. The Turkish leader was highly critical of the coup that deposed Morsi, and a war of words ensued between Turkish and Egyptian leaders in August 2013, as Ramadan was concluding. As a result, the Egyptian creative class, which chafed under Brotherhood rule and is notoriously prickly when it comes to foreign criticism of Egypt, began promoting the idea of boycotting Turkish television drama, which in the last half decade has competed head-on with Egyptian and Syrian drama for prime-time air time.[2] Erdo an, never known for his rhetorical caution, attacked Al-Azhar, Egypt's venerable religious university, for supporting the coup, saying that history would judge Al-Azhar harshly. Immediately, private Egyptian channels began canceling deals with Turkish production firms, Egyptian op-eds grew more hostile toward Turkey, and several Egyptian celebrities opined that "boycotting Turkish drama is a patriotic duty." In short order, Egyptian-Turkish artistic collaborations were halted, Turkey reconsidered billions in aid it had pledged to Egypt, and the boycott began taking shape. Gulf channels, most visibly Dubai TV and Abu Dhabi TV, announced they were joining the boycott in solidarity with Egypt's media companies, though their real reasons may have been political, since the United Arab Emirates treats the Muslim Brotherhood like a criminal cult and was one of the main backers of the June 30, 2013, military coup that toppled Morsi. In contrast, behind Egyptian media's political posturing lies anxiety about fierce commercial competition of Turkish drama, a boycott of which would create, some believe, breathing room for Egyptian productions (dozens of Egyptian drama series were produced but not broadcast during the last three years, owing to the political situation but also to competition from Syrian and Turkish productions).

Finally, the Arab uprisings spawned a vibrant scene of dissident media and culture. Revolutionary graffiti, dance, theater, puppetry, murals, hip-hop, and poetry exploded from Morocco to Iraq and within months moved from the street to the screen and to art galleries. Remarkable among these is the flourishing of video in all its forms. In Bahrain, Syria, and Tunisia, mobile-phone videos bore witness to atrocities, propagandized for various parties, mocked dictators, and showcased a variety of animation, dance, theater, and song. The rise of more slickly produced satirical videos by groups like Kharabeesh and Masasit Mati is a notable phenomenon because such productions have the potential to find a place in mainstream media industries, infusing them with new, young talent and with the edge of revolutionary aesthetic. Take Masasit Mati's *Top Goon-*

Diary of a Little Dictator, (2011) a satirical finger-puppetry video series on the web that broke through mainstream consciousness in global media coverage. Using a handful of finger puppets to ridicule Assad and the brutality of his regime, the group produced its first season with personal effort, donated labor, and limited personal savings. After Masasit Mati's attempt to crowdfund the second season via a Kickstarter campaign failed, the group's visibility attracted funding from European foundations like the Netherlands' Prince Claus Fund. They now have a slick website, and though there may not be a third season, members of the group are now leveraging their fame for new creative ventures. Because of its low costs and low barriers to entry in the age of YouTube, video has arisen as a key revolutionary medium and a primary path to mainstreaming dissident cultural production.

What do these developments mean for media industries at large? First, they demonstrate that in some parts of the world, media industries are entangled in a political-economic-cultural nexus that is ever shifting and the consequences of which are often unintended. Notably, seemingly unending reserves of petrodollars have enabled the Gulf monarchies to exert enormous influence over the politics and media of revolutionary countries like Egypt, Tunisia, and Syria. Policy differences between Qatar and Saudi Arabia will continue to be a major shaper of transnational and national media industries throughout the Arab world: who would have thought that archrivals Al Jazeera and Al Arabiya would editorially converge to that point?[3] Second, new patterns of creative migration emerge within a region that shares a language and a transnational media industry when various countries experience various levels of violence, insecurity, and persecution of creative workers. Research will need to examine the ultimate impact of the exodus of Syrian directors and producers throughout the Arab world. Already, this is helping reestablish Beirut as a global art and cultural-production city. Third, the work of creative resistance, often created and disseminated under extremely difficult security conditions, gives a new meaning to the notion of precarity in creative labor, broadening its prevailing understanding as economic contingency to include torture-risking and death-defying creative work. Often the work of anonymous collectives, such works will also challenge prevailing notions of authorship and remuneration as they make inroads in the mainstream media industries.

1 Marwan M. Kraidy and Joe F. Khalil, *Arab Television Industries* (London: BFI/Palgrave Macmillan, 2009), particularly chapter 5.

2 Marwan M. Kraidy and Omar Alghazzi, "Neo-Ottoman Cool: Turkish Popular Culture in the Arab Public Sphere," *Popular Communication* 11, no. 1 (2013): 17–29.

3 For a long time, there have been signs of divergent agendas between the two sponsoring countries, and in August 2013 the Saudi-Qatari feud appeared to have returned in full force after the *Wall Street Journal* published statements it attributed to royal prince and head of Saudi intelligence Bandar Bin Sultan, who allegedly said, "Qatar is only 300 people and a TV channel . . . that is not a country," setting the Qatari Twittersphere ablaze with patriotism and condemnation. See Adam Entous, Nour Malas, and Margaret Coker, "A Veteran Saudi Power Player Works to Build Support to Topple Assad," *Wall Street Journal*, August 25, 2013.

Bibliography

Entous, Adam, Nour Malas, and Margaret Coker. "A Veteran Saudi Power Player Works to Build Support to Topple Assad." *Wall Street Journal*, August 25, 2013.

Kraidy, Marwan M., and Joe F. Khalil. *Arab Television Industries*. London: BFI/Palgrave Macmillan, 2009.

Kraidy, Marwan M., and Omar Alghazzi. "Neo-Ottoman Cool: Turkish Popular Culture in the Arab Public Sphere." *Popular Communication* 11, no. 1 (2013): 17–29.

13.

Media Industries in India: An Emerging Regional Framework

SHANTI KUMAR

The digital convergence of hitherto distinct technologies like print, broadcasting, cable, satellite television, film, and online media, along with the privatization of public broadcasting and the telecommunications infrastructure in India, has induced many Indian media companies to radically reshape their organizational structures since the early 2000s. Major players from the telecommunications industry, such as Reliance Industries, have aggressively entered the media production business, and traditional production houses like Network18 (formerly TV18) have expanded operations into online media and created joint ventures with other major national and transnational corporations. By using strategies of conglomeration, many media companies—both traditional production houses in print, radio, television, and film and new players from the telecommunications industry and the information technology sectors—are seeking to expand their audience share across a range of media platforms and across traditionally defined geographical boundaries of national, subnational, and transnational markets. The rapid growth of regional media within and across a range of industry segments, delivery platforms, and programming practices has been a defining characteristic of this new phase of transformation in the Indian media industries.

In the case of Indian cinema, although Mumbai-based Bollywood is still considered the "national" film industry, it is no longer the predominant center for film production, distribution, and consumption. As the record-breaking box office success of the Bollywood blockbuster *Chennai Express* in 2013 reveals, other "regional" film industries, particularly in South India, are becoming not only more integrated with Bollywood but also more integral to the Indian film industry's attempts to reach more diverse and dispersed audiences in the Indian diaspora and within the regional media markets all across India. *Chennai Express* not only smashed box office records in the traditional box office strongholds for Hindi films in North India and in the Indian diaspora; it also doubled the record for the first-week collections of a Hindi film in South India, where Bollywood is not always very popular among moviegoers.[1]

Chennai Express is the love story of a north Indian man, Rahul (Shahrukh Khan), and a South Indian woman, Meenalochani (Deepika Padukone), who meet through a chance encounter in a train journey from Mumbai to Chennai. In many ways, *Chennai Express* is a traditional boy-meets-girl Hindi film with nothing much for a discerning viewer or critic to write home about. But it also varies from the conventional formula of Bollywood romantic comedies in some subtle and significant ways. Unlike other Bollywood films about, or partially set in, South India where the actors speak only in Hindi (or where Hindi subtitles are superimposed on the screen), a very large chunk of the dialogue in *Chennai Express* is in Tamil without any Hindi subtitles, with Meenalochani sometimes translating the Tamil dialogues into Hindi for Rahul and, by extension, for the non-Tamil-speaking Hindi film viewer in the cinema hall. (The DVD version of Chennai Express has subtitles.) Also, unlike many of Shahrukh Khan's films from the 1990s and 2000s where the hero meets the heroine in the diasporic settings of London or New York, *Chennai Express* takes Shahrukh Khan's Rahul deep into the South Indian countryside in a small village near Chennai where Meenalochani's father is a regional mafia don.

In the case of Indian television, reality television genres such as game shows, quiz shows, home improvement shows, and hidden-camera exposés that were first introduced in India and popularized on Hindi television channels like Zee TV and Star TV have fast become the mainstay of programming in other Indian-language networks like Asianet, ETV, and Sun Network. At the same time, popular Hindi reality television shows with national branding such as *Indian Idol* (2004–), *India's Dancing Superstar* (2013–), and *India's Got Talent* (2009–)—which are only marginally popular among non-Hindi speaking audiences—feature contestants increasingly drawn from both Hindi-speaking and non-Hindi speaking regions of India. Recently, these shows have also attracted contestants from the Indian diaspora and non-Indian contestants from Pakistan, the Middle East, Latin America, and North America. By featuring pan-Indian and non-Indian contestants in reality shows, media producers are seeking to invite the participation of viewers across linguistic, cultural, and regional divides. The growing desires of television producers to attract the largest possible share of viewers within and beyond the nation are now fueled by the growing potential of integrating the mass appeal of television shows with the interactive technologies of digital and mobile media to generate new forms of revenue. According to industry analysts, reality television shows in India already derive 30 to 40 percent of their revenues from audience participation in activities such as cell-phone voting, SMS texting, and mobile or online interaction.[2] In the Indian television industry, regionalism is seen as a major avenue for expanding the revenue streams using new programming strategies.

In order to fully recognize the political, economic, and cultural significance of this shift toward regionalization in the narrative conventions, technological transformations, and distribution logics of the Indian media industries, a brief clarification on the definition of regional media in India would be in order. The term *regional media* in many contexts around the world refers to a transnational or supranational constellation of media industries and cultures related to a shared set of geolinguistic traits. For instance, Will Higbee and Song Hwee Lim, in their survey of transnational cinemas, define regional cinemas of the world in terms of geolinguistic categories such as "supranational Chinese" cinema, "regional Nordic" cinema, or "pan-European" cinema.[3]

In India, however, the term *regional media* is traditionally used to describe an intranational or subnational category of media produced in the many regional languages spoken within India. Media produced in Hindi—particularly in cinema and television—are considered "national" since Hindi is the "national" language.

But in other contexts, Hindi media—particularly in print journalism—are considered "regional" in contrast to English media, which circulate predominantly in urban areas and are extremely influential among the political, economic, and cultural elites in the metropolitan centers. Since most states within India are linguistic states, regional media in India are usually defined in relation to the geographic boundaries of the states and the dominant languages within those states.

In his survey of the cinemas of India, Yves Thorval uses the traditional definition of regional cinema to categorize films made in the dominant regional language of each Indian state. For instance, the majority of films in Andhra Pradesh are made in Telugu, which is the dominant regional language in the state. Similarly, Kannada-language films in Karnataka, Malayalam-language films in Kerala, and Tamil-language films in Tamil Nadu constitute the regional cinemas in each of these states. Other regional cinemas in India are similarly indicated in relation to the dominant language of a state. Thus, Bengali cinema is defined as the regional cinema of the state of West Bengal, Gujarati cinema is the regional cinema of the state of Gujarat, Oriya cinema is the regional cinema of the state of Odisha (formerly Orissa), and so on.[4]

In Indian television, regional-language channels were largely absent in the early years of broadcasting in India, following the state-sponsored network Doordarshan's establishment in Delhi in 1959. Although broadcasting services gradually spread across the country in the 1970s and 1980s, regional stations, or *kendras*, were marginal to the imagination of television as a national medium. Regional-language programming was restricted to specific time slots and was generally limited to programming formats like news and film-based shows from regional-language cinemas in India. Occasionally, some of the more established regional television *kendras* such as in Mumbai (then Bombay) and Chennai (then Madras) would produce sitcoms, educational dramas, and religious mythologies in regional languages. The regional broadcasters followed — often grudgingly — Doordarshan's centralized model of "national programming," where the regional was seen as a subnational category. Moreover, successive governments at the national level sought to minimize the growth of regional television as a way to curtail the growth of regional political parties, particularly in states like Tamil Nadu and Andhra Pradesh.[5]

All that began to change in the early 1990s, with the rise of commercial satellite and cable television channels. The growth of the private television channels was fueled by the rise of the first Indian-language television network, Zee TV. Zee TV's Hindi-language programming was wildly successful, and many other regional television channels quickly replicated the Zee model of providing commercial entertainment programs in Indian languages.

Therefore, since the early to mid-1990s, many regional media companies in India — such as the Ramoji Group in Hyderabad, the Sun Group in Chennai, and Zee Entertainment Enterprises in Mumbai, to name a few — have been moving beyond the traditional equation of regional media with regional languages and state boundaries by linking ethnic, linguistic, historical, and geographical elements of identity to material and symbolic mobility of people, products, places, and cultures within India and in the Indian diaspora.[6]

For instance, as Sevanti Ninan insightfully observed in the early 2000s, "When a Ramoji Rao or a Subhash Chandra assesses the market for a Bengali channel, he takes into account both the market in West Bengal as well as in Bangladesh and other parts of the world where Bengalis are."[7] Or more recently, as Aswin Punathambekar writes in his book *From Bombay to Bollywood: The Making of a Global Media Industry*, even traditional production companies in India like Rajshri Productions are nowadays aiming to make films that appeal to audiences from "Bihar to Manhattan."[8] In other words, the holy grail — or, to Indianize the metaphor, the *akshay patra* — of the Indian media industries is content that is sufficiently regionalized to cater to audiences in a heartland state like Bihar and at the same time globally distributed to target the small but lucrative diasporic audiences abroad. Media industry advocates in India now see catering to audiences from Bihar to Manhattan and everyone in between as something that is close at hand because of strategies like regionalization, digitization, and conglomeration.

In March 2013, the Federation of Indian Chambers of Commerce and Industry (FICCI) held its annual convention of media experts and professionals, FICCI-FRAMES, where it boldly proclaimed that the Indian media industry is on a "tryst with destiny" toward "engaging a billion customers."[9] Although India's population crossed the one billion mark several years ago, the FICCI-FRAMES convention resurrected the rhetoric of the "one billion" again in 2013 to announce that the media world's cherished goal of reaching every single one of the one billion-plus Indians as consumers may now be within reach due to the growing power of regional media coupled with the rapid transformations of digitization and media conglomeration.

Established in 1929, FICCI claims to be the largest and oldest nongovernmental, nonprofit business organization in India. FRAMES, the Entertainment Division of FICCI, was established in 2001 as an interface between private media companies and the government of India to work on the process of granting Indian cinema the status of an "industry." Since then, FICCI-FRAMES has been holding a "global convention of the business of entertainment" annually. Coinciding with these annual conventions, FICCI-FRAMES releases its *Annual Report on the Media and Entertainment Industry*. Since 2001, FICCI has commissioned several major consultancy firms to produce its annual reports. KPMG prepared the report first in 2003, and again from 2009 to 2013. PricewaterhouseCoopers produced the annual report for FICCI from 2005-2008, while Ernst & Young was commissioned in 2002 and 2004, and Arthur Andersen in 2001. The FICCI-FRAMES annual reports are among the most comprehensive and exhaustive analyses of the media and entertainment industries in India, and their release is extensively covered and reported upon by various newspapers, magazines, and websites.[10]

Like the FICCI-FRAMES conference, the FICCI–KPMG report for 2013, titled *The Power of a Billion: Realizing the Indian Dream*, also presents regionalization of the media markets along with digitization and media consolidation as three key factors that will enable the media industries in India to reach the magic figure of a billion consumers.[11] Similarly, a report on "India's entertainment economy" released by Ernst & Young in 2011 outlines "new growth opportunities" for global media enterprises in terms of "India's favorable regulatory environment" for media consolidation, digitization as a "new inflection point for consumption," and the diversity of regional markets.[12] Describing regional media as "huge 'markets within a market,'" the Ernst & Young report cautions global media companies of the need to recognize that regional media industries in India work differently due to "diverse content preferences and the low price point and high volumes of content consumption."[13]

In their attempts to reach the magical figure of one billion consumers in the diverse and dispersed Indian markets, the media industries have been actively pursuing strategies of conglomeration, digitization, and regionalization for more than a decade now.

During this period, media critics have pointed out that the largest corporate houses in India, like Reliance Industries Limited and the Aditya Birla Group, have worked to consolidate their media interests to exploit the growing potential of digital media and regional media.[14] For example, a quick look through the FICCI reports and the FICCI-FRAMES conferences since 2001 and other industry reports from the 1990s and 2000s demonstrates how the three strategies of conglomeration, digitization, and regionalization have been aggressively pursued by key players in Indian media industries.

But what is new in the story is that in the past couple of years, the key players in the Indian media industries have started to rethink their global, national, and local strategies for digitization and consolidation almost entirely through a regional framework. In other words, there is a growing consensus that regionalization is the key to the growth of the media industries in India. In industry reports generated by consulting firms like Ernst & Young and KPMG, and in industry conclaves like FICCI-FRAMES, the main reason given for the need to shift toward regionalization in India is that the four metropolitan centers of Delhi, Mumbai, Chennai, Kolkata, as well as other major cities like Bengaluru and Hyderabad, are beginning to show signs of slowdown in consumption patterns or are approaching market saturation.

As a result, the regional market space has emerged as the main target for advertisers who see much higher growth rates of consumption in Tier 2 and Tier 3 cities and towns. The higher consumption pattern in regional markets coupled with lower advertising rates in regional outlets makes the regional spaces more lucrative avenues for advertisers and producers looking to attain their cherished goal of reaching one billion consumers in India. This is particularly evident in print and television, where there have been a spate of regional-market acquisitions and expansion by major players in the Indian media industries. The 2013 FICCI-KPMG report cites examples of consolidation in print, such as Bennet Coleman's launch of the Bengali paper *Ei Shomoy* and the Jagran Group's acquisition of *Nai Duniya*. In the case of the Indian film industry, major film studios Reliance Big Pictures, Disney UTV Motion Pictures, and Eros International are aggressively entering the regional media markets, and Hollywood films are increasingly being dubbed in regional languages such as Tamil and Telugu.

The growth story of regional media in India, as discussed in many industry reports in the 2010s, is indeed impressive. However, a more interesting account that emerges from these industry reports is of the key players in the media industries now imagining the media markets in India almost entirely through a regional framework. Understanding the emergence of regionalization as *the* framework for the business practices of global, national, and local media companies in India is, I argue, a pressing challenge and a critical opportunity for media industry studies.

1 "Chennai Express Collections Smash Box Office Records," *Business Today*, August 13, 2013.
2 Heather Timmons, "In India Reality Television Catches On with Some Qualms," *New York Times*, January 9, 2011.
3 Will Higbee and Song H. Lim, "Concepts of Transnational Cinema: Towards a Transnationalism in Film Studies," *Transnational Cinema* 1, no. 1 (2010): 7–21.
4 Yves Thoraval, *Cinemas of India (1896–2000)* (Delhi: South Asia Books, 2001).
5 Arvind Rajagopal, *Politics after Television: Hindu Nationalism and the Reshaping of the Public in India* (Cambridge: Cambridge University Press, 2001).
6 Shanti Kumar, *Gandhi Meets Primetime: Globalization and Nationalism in Indian Television* (Urbana: University of Illinois Press, 2006).
7 Sevanti Ninan, "Channel after Channel," *The Hindu*, June 18, 2000.
8 Aswin Punathambekar, *From Bombay to Bollywood: The Making of a Global Film Industry* (New York: New York University Press, 2013).
9 Bharati Dubey, "14th Edition of FICCI-FRAMES opens in Mumbai," *Times of India*, March 11, 2013.
10 The FICCI-FRAMES website is online at http://www.ficci-frames.com/.
11 FICCI-KPMG, *The Power of a Billion: Realizing the Indian Dream*, FICCI-KPMG Media and Entertainment Industry Report 2013.

12 "Spotlight on India's Entertainment Economy: Seizing New Growth Opportunities," Ernst & Young, October 2011, 3.

13 Ibid.

14 Paranjoy Guha Thakurta, "Media Ownership Trends in India," *The Hoot*, July 3, 2012.

Bibliography

"Chennai Express Collections Smash Box Office Records." *Business Today*, August 13, 2013.

Dubey, Bharati "14th Edition of FICCI-FRAMES opens in Mumbai," *Times of India*, March 11, 2013.

Ernst & Young. "Spotlight on India's Entertainment Economy: Seizing New Growth Opportunities." October 2011.

FICCI-KPMG. "The Power of a Billion: Realizing the Indian Dream." *FICCI-KPMG Media and Entertainment Industry Report 2013*.

Guha Thakurta, Paranjoy. "Media Ownership Trends in India." *The Hoot*. July 3, 2012.

Higbee, Will, and Song H. Lim. "Concepts of Transnational Cinema: Towards a Transnationalism in Film Studies." *Transnational Cinema* 1, no. 1 (2010): 7–21.

Kumar, Shanti. *Gandhi Meets Primetime: Globalization and Nationalism in Indian Television*. Urbana: University of Illinois Press, 2006.

Ninan, Sevanti. "Channel after Channel." *The Hindu*, June 18, 2000.

Punathambekar, Aswin. *From Bombay to Bollywood: The Making of a Global Film Industry*. New York: New York University Press, 2013.

Rajagopal, Arvind. *Politics after Television: Hindu Nationalism and the Reshaping of the Public in India*. Cambridge: Cambridge University Press, 2001.

Thoraval, Yves. *Cinemas of India (1896–2000)*. Delhi: South Asia Books, 2001.

Timmons, Heather. "In India Reality Television Catches on With Some Qualms." *New York Times*, January 9, 2011.

14.

Assembling a Toolkit

AMANDA D. LOTZ

The study of media industries is developing at a time of constant change in the nature of media and how they are made. Only those who study historical media operations are free to assume that the norms in place at the start of a study will persist to the end. The media industries are being remade and reorganized in profound ways and, though growing more multifaceted, seem only likely to play an increasingly greater role in the lives of individuals and cultures around the globe. These changes are both exciting and challenging for those endeavoring to research them.

Such an environment requires practices of research as dynamic and multifaceted as the industries we study. Fortunately, there is little about media industry studies that is established or entrenched. There were no "media industries" courses available when I studied at the University of Texas at Austin in the late 1990s. Indeed, my collaboration with Tim Havens — with whom I wrote *Understanding Media Industries* — dates to the early 2000s, when we both struggled to inform our developing scholarship with an "industry" perspective and to figure out how to teach these concepts to undergraduate students.[1] I can still remember the sense of being adrift, of searching for a coherent intellectual body within which to place my work, and of clinging to publications that began to offer an approach to media industries that was different than political economy; as that was long the problem, I knew the questions I wanted to ask of media industries weren't those primary among those defining "political economy" at the time, but had no alternative name for it. I assigned a long series of overly demanding books to shell-shocked undergrads in those years (Eric Louw's *The Media and Cultural Production*, David Hesmondhalgh's *The Cultural Industries*) or taught material already outdated (Joseph Turow's *Media Systems in Society*) or just not what I really wanted to teach (Croteau and Hoynes's *The Business of Media*, as well as various media economics texts).[2] But a decade after I had completed my degree, I taught my first graduate media industries class and had a wealth of material to choose from, as Holt and Perren's *Media Industries* and Mayer, Banks, and Caldwell's *Production Studies* were freshly in print and suggested the vibrant conversation increasingly moving from the peripheries into a dynamic subfield.[3]

The point of this detour through a personal aside is to offer some context for my perception that quite substantial change in the study of media industries has developed in a very short period of time. Certainly the creation of a journal such as this one suggests a next stage of development and intellectual institutionalization. Though some might be tempted to seek legitimacy by following paths charted in other fields and disciplines through a survival-of-the-fittest, zero-sum battle to determine *the* canon, approach, and most worthy ideas for studying media industries, here I simply suggest, let's not. Though it might seem that greater cohesion in intellectual endeavors is a mark of a maturing subfield, I would argue: not so. Rather than view the relative youth and variation of the subfield as a deficit, I view our lack of orthodoxy in training, annual meetings, or publication outlet as a strength. Though it might at times seem like the establishment of traditions, standards, and norms provide the next steps toward a more profound presence in the field, there remains great advantage to maintaining dynamic and multifaceted perspectives on this work.

To be sure, the arrival of a journal called *Media Industries* should not become *the* and *only* place where scholarship about media industries is published. Its editors and editorial boards will have tendencies and intellectual proclivities that help shape, but should not alone define, the emerging subfield. Such a journal creates more venues for publication of media industries work and likely allows opportunities for cross-pollination less feasible in the existing journals that publish industry studies, but also a broad range of other media scholarship.

Approaches identified as media industries, production studies, media sociology, and the many others claimed by scholars are valuable for the range of tools their foci provide and should not be considered to be in some competitive death match to become *the* approach to media industry study. Rather, they are made stronger by continued independence and theory building that expands their outlooks and our perspectives on what we can claim to know about media industries and how we arrive at this knowledge. The relative value of these approaches is determined only by the research question at hand. Researchers choose among these tools based on their priorities in the intellectual process. A desire to focus on one area should not be assumed as a categorical disavowal of others. All studies in all approaches are necessarily partial. It is only through conversation across approaches that those bits of knowledge can grow into something larger.

There is much we don't fully understand about how media industries have operated or how they operate today. No one can know how they will operate going forward, though the furious and constant change of the present captures popular and academic fascination alike. As scholars, we have the luxury of taking the long view — of not having the daily deadlines of industry press and bloggers or the weighty pressure of quarterly profit considerations of those working in these industries. This luxury requires that we — regardless of approach — pursue more substantive work than the cataloging of events and developments. We must bring new knowledge by situating events in a historical context, by casting a skeptical eye on the dominant discourses that emerge in superficial trade accounts, and by remembering that the burden of scholarly work is a requirement to articulate a "so what" regarding the matter at hand. The media industry scholar must *consider* the implications of a multiplicity of industrial practices such as new technologies, distribution routes, production practices, and economics for a whole range of groups — audiences, creatives, executives, below-the-line workers, even stockholders — even if we *write* accounts that are more narrowly focused.

Each subtle change in industrial practices brings many unforeseen and unconsidered effects. We must try to see or imagine the "big picture," and doing so requires all levels of inquiry and analysis in our efforts to devise sophisticated understandings of how media industries work and why and how changes in industrial practices affect texts in meaningful ways. Though academic inquiry tends to prioritize analysis, there is much work to be done in first developing more basic descriptive knowledge of actual operations from which to build empirically based analyses. While the youth of media industries studies is an advantage in its lack of entrenched orthodoxies of approach, it also means that there is a great, great deal that we do not truly know. Even many of the things we think we know — such as that advertisers exert influence on the content they advertise in — we don't really know in detail. Many assume a simple process of advertisers objecting to content, when in practice the nature and process by which advertising is sold — in which buyers attend not so much to content but to spreadsheets of demographic data — requires a more nuanced understanding. Of course this is not to say that advertisers don't exert influence: they do so much more by what they don't say or do and through the self-regulation content providers perform in anticipation of advertiser reaction. Simple assumptions of conservative and homogeneous advertisers have prevented interrogation of organizational practices and the acculturation of workers to develop more nuanced understandings. Concepts such as "industry lore" and "discerned savvy" suggest valuable preliminary theory building based in particular sites that might nevertheless prove useful across media contexts.[4]

A robust future for the study of media industries does not require dogmatic adherence to a particular tradition or outlook so much as flexibility that matches research questions and research methods and draws from a vast toolkit of techniques for inquiry. Certainly the naming of a subfield leads toward a tendency of boundary policing: this is what we are or are not; we use these theories or methods, not those. Media industry studies will do well to emphasize its object of study — that of practices and processes of text creation and circulation that precede, although are constitutive of, audience creation. The question should be whether an aspect of these practices and processes is at the core of inquiry, not adherence to a particular approach that determines what is a part of media industry studies. Of course, some of the best work often extends beyond production and industrial operation to unite these practices with analysis of the object created or the response of those engaged by it. Here too, let media industries approach its object broadly.

---

[1] Timothy Havens and Amanda D. Lotz, *Understanding Media Industries* (New York: Oxford University Press, 2011).

2 Eric Louw, *The Media and Cultural Production* (London: Sage, 2001); David Hesmondhalgh, *The Cultural Industries* (London: Sage, 2002); Joseph Turow, *Media Systems in Society: Understanding Industries, Strategies, and Power*, 2nd ed. (White Plains, NY: AB Longman, 1997); David Croteau and William Hoynes, *The Business of Media: Corporate Media and the Public Interest* (Boston: Pine Forge Press, 2001).

3 Jennifer Holt and Alisa Perren, *Media Industries: History, Theory, and Method* (Malden, MA: Wiley-Blackwell, 2009); Vicki Mayer, Miranda J. Banks, and John Thornton Caldwell, *Production Studies: Cultural Studies of Media Industries* (New York: Routledge, 2009).

4 Timothy Havens, "Toward a Structuration Theory of Media Intermediaries," in *Making Media Work: Cultures of Management in the Entertainment Industries*, ed. Derek Johnson, Derek Kompare, and Avi Santo (New York: New York University Press, 2014); Jimmy Draper, "Theorizing Creative Agency through 'Discerned Savvy': A Tool for the Critical Study of Media Industries," *Media, Culture, and Society* 36 no. 8(2014): 1118-1133.

Bibliography

Croteau, David, and William Hoynes. *The Business of Media: Corporate Media and the Public Interest*. Boston: Pine Forge Press, 2001.

Draper, Jimmy. "Theorizing Creative Agency through 'Discerned Savvy': A Tool for the Critical Study of Media Industries." *Media, Culture, and Society* 36 no. 8 (2014): 1118-1133.

Havens, Timothy. "Toward a Structuration Theory of Media Intermediaries." In *Making Media Work: Cultures of Management in the Entertainment Industries*, edited by Derek Johnson, Derek Kompare, and Avi Santo. New York: New York University Press, 2014.

Havens, Timothy, and Amanda D. Lotz. *Understanding Media Industries*. New York: Oxford University Press, 2011.

Hesmondhalgh, David. *The Cultural Industries*. London: Sage, 2002.

Holt, Jennifer, and Alisa Perren. *Media Industries: History, Theory, and Method*. Malden, MA: Wiley-Blackwell, 2009.

Louw, Eric. *The Media and Cultural Production*. London: Sage, 2001.

Mayer, Vicki, Miranda J. Banks, and John Thornton Caldwell. *Production Studies: Cultural Studies of Media Industries*. New York: Routledge: 2009.

Turow, Joseph. *Media Systems in Society: Understanding Industries, Strategies, and Power*. 2nd ed. White Plains, NY: AB Longman, 1997.

15.

Welcome to the Unregulated Wild, Wild, Digital West

DENISE MANN

Google, Microsoft, Apple, and the other internet technology giants desperately want to control Hollywood's premium content, seeing it as the crown jewel in their massive marketing infrastructure via a vast array of smart, mobile technologies and social networking capabilities. However, the internet giants' failure to wrest control over the studios' content business stems from an inherent misunderstanding of the Hollywood system — its inscrutable rules of engagement, rigid hierarchies, and fixed allegiances to strategic partners. Recognizing this impasse between the two sets of corporate behemoths as an opportunity to advance a new culture industry — one less bound by old-fashioned bureaucracies — two types of web-based para-industrial start-ups have emerged with distinct approaches to monetizing the internet. They are the transmedia producers/digital marketing gurus, such as Starlight Runner Entertainment, 42 Entertainment, and Campfire, and the multichannel networks (MCNs), such as Fullscreen, Maker Studios, and Machinima. The MCNs aggregate large numbers of YouTube talent partners as a way to maximize their share of YouTube advertising revenues; in contrast, a number of "independent" web companies (Funny or Die, College Humor, the Collective, Break Media, and Alloy Digital) differentiate themselves from the MCNs by retaining in-house advertising sales teams, production personnel, and their own streaming websites — all strategies designed to make them less dependent on YouTube's revenue-sharing arrangement.[1] However, for the purposes of this article, both types of web-only production companies will be referred to as MCNs, given their joint interest in aggregating web content to attract online advertising dollars in the still-unregulated space of the internet. In exchange for the right to place ads, the MCNs underwrite the production of original, short-form web content, granting creators a degree of creative autonomy rarely seen in Hollywood. Prominent examples of inventive, original web content include Break Media's *Man at Arms* (2013), Maker Studios' *Epic Rap Battles* (2010 - present), and the Collective's *Annoying Orange* (2009–2012).

The transmedia producers, such as Starlight Runner Entertainment and 42 Entertainment, and digital marketers, such as Campfire, are distinct from the MCNs in their approach to reinventing traditional entertainment. Most transmedia producers and digital marketers produce promotional paratexts on behalf of the Hollywood media groups in support of their major media franchises; these indirect, story-driven marketing campaigns are more in line with millennial consumers' tastes than hard-sell approaches are.[2] The transmedia producers have learned to insert themselves in once-immutable studio divisions — licensing, marketing, consumer products — by providing executives with detailed "story bibles" to facilitate oversight of the licensed vendors responsible for designing paratexts. Notably, the transmedia producers are often accused of being marketers rather than creators. However, they have deliberately chosen an alternative path to that of the traditional Hollywood producer, who pitches and packages original projects for presentation to the studios and networks (a process with a high rate of failure and creative micromanagement). Innovative examples of cutting-edge promotional content created by transmedia producers and digital marketers include 42 Entertainment's *Why So Serious?* (2008), an alternate-reality game created to hype Warner Bros.' *The Dark Knight* (2008), and Campfire's "The Five Senses" (2011) campaign, created to tout HBO's drama series *Game of Thrones* (2011 - present).[3] Despite their differences, the transmedia production companies and MCNs are all focused on producing content-promotional hybrids that are designed to be spread by consumers across a variety of social networks (Facebook, Twitter). This consumer-driven distribution helps these hybrid productions rack up maximum "hits," akin to a virtual pinball machine, thereby unleashing a steady stream of Google AdSense earnings for both their creative and brand partners. By enacting this revised media economy — inviting unpaid users to share web promotions and become fans of brands — these transitional production companies have devised a new, advertising-infused culture-industry model that is potentially far more potent than broadcasting's thirty-second ads. As Siva Vaidhyanathan explains in *The Googlization of Everything*, the "product" that is being exploited is the online consumer, who spreads the marketing message among his or her social network of friends and colleagues, producing a vast, exponential reach.[4] Think internet meme *Harlem Shake* (2013); its creator, Filthy Frank, was not paid a dime, while the web-based companies that facilitated its spread across the globe all raked in major profits. Scary business, indeed, as Google's deep infrastructural roots make it the ultimate benefactor of all this sharing and data mining.

Until recently, Google (YouTube's parent company) was largely content agnostic — not caring about the quality of YouTube's user-generated content except as an additional means to generate search-driven "hits." An industrial sea change occurred from 2011 and 2013 when Google-YouTube infused $200 million in production funding into its most successful talent partners as a means of achieving higher advertising rates. The MCNs facilitated this push toward higher production values by forging contractual agreements with YouTube talent partners in exchange for production facilities, social marketing tools, and other resources. In reality, the MCNs only provide production resources for their most successful creators. Paradoxically, it is this same group of web celebrities that tends to accuse the MCNs of exploitative labor practices and to use social media to publicly decry the onerous terms of their agreements, which, in the case of Maker Studios, grants creators 40 percent of shared advertising revenues and 50 percent of the intellectual property rights for their productions in perpetuity.[5] The MCNs counter by arguing that they sink the majority of their profits back into the web productions of their talent partners.

While the transmedia producers and MCNs described above are engaged in the risky business of reinventing content creation for the digital economy, the tech giants — Apple, Microsoft, Google, Intel, and Sony — are pursuing a much bigger prize by seeking to control streaming distribution rights to all content delivered to the home.

Over its hundred-year history, Hollywood has profited by controlling the copyrights on all its premium content, which are leveraged to the tune of $300 billion a year in combined US and European revenues by exploiting a series of windows: DVD/VHS, pay TV, streaming video on demand (SVOD), cable or satellite, broadcast television, the syndicated television markets, and so forth.[6] Despite the marketing fanfare and expense associated with studio theatrical releases, the latter serve primarily as loss leaders that are designed to encourage consumers to rent, buy, or subscribe to watch the content on one or more of the exploitation windows. One of the biggest threats to the traditional Hollywood industry is the potential collapse of these windows as cord-cutting consumers demand that premium content be made accessible online and all at once, also known as "television everywhere." The various tech giants—in particular, Apple, Microsoft, and Google—have made several bold efforts to control the delivery of Hollywood's premium content online via their new smart technologies—Apple TV, Microsoft Xbox, and Google TV—with various degrees of success. Presently, the dominant players in this space are the multichannel video program distributors (MVPDs), in particular, the cable and satellite carriers. As more consumers adapt to smart TVs with built-in Wi-Fi or user-friendly smart-TV interfaces such as Roku and Google's Chromecast, Hollywood licensors may shift from set-top boxes (provided by the MVPDs) to over-the-top, SVOD services such as Netflix, Hulu Plus, and Amazon Prime. The MCNs are eager to position themselves as the primary web content providers of the future, in part by forging deals with the traditional distributors and the new SVOD sites. However, the internet technology companies stand to control the entire Monopoly game board by retaining streaming distribution rights to *all* content via their combined hardware (smart TVs) and software (mobile apps, advertising products) capabilities. By controlling all on-demand entertainment streamed to the home, Google, for instance, could extract an even larger share of its current search-driven, global consumer marketing business.

This brief survey of two para-industries—transmedia producers and MCNs—reveals two sides of the same risky production coin, each group trying to turn web content creation into a viable business. In fact, the ultimate benefactors of this unregulated Wild, Wild, Digital West are Google, Facebook, and other internet technology companies that have turned their surveillance-driven brand-marketing businesses into a multibillion-dollar industry. In *Cultural Industries*, David Hesmondhalgh addresses the game-changing shift that YouTube introduced to the web-based creative industries by launching a new hybrid cultural form—or what legal scholar and intellectual property activist Lawrence Lessig calls a new hybrid economy—based on a community where people interact on terms "which are commerce free, though the motivations for interacting may or may not tie into commerce."[7] Clearly, the days of a commercial-free web zone are gone as companies and creators partner to earn their share of online advertising profits. In the still-unregulated space of the new economy, Google (part of what Jennifer Holt dubbed the "access of evil") has motivated purportedly maker-friendly companies like Maker Studios to bilk their creative partners out of their share of what has become the new-economy equivalent of Monopoly money—AdSense dollars.[8] Some humanities-based scholars focus only on the text-based attributes of prosumer culture celebrate YouTube's "democratic" broadcast system and rejoice in its $200-million-plus investment in its content partners. These scholars risk losing sight of the larger social themes on display—the emergence of a new culture industry dependent on invasive surveillance systems that cast consumers in the role of invisible labor as their consumer preferences are aggregated and sold to advertisers.

As media industry scholars, we need to be mindful of the exploitative practices on display in these new media practices. We should question user-generated-content creators who have been trained by YouTube and its MCN partners to focus on achieving celebrity by any means necessary in order to increase their user count and, hence, their share of AdSense dollars. While the Hollywood media companies are the frequent target of Marxist-themed critiques—from the Frankfurt School, cultural studies, and more recent cultural industries scholarship—the recent collection assembled by Trebor Scholz, *Digital Labor: The Internet as Playground and Factory*, is particularly useful in exposing the dark economy of the internet.[9] Certainly, a fruitful area for future research is the practice of web-based companies hiring semiskilled digital laborers who become *knowing* partners in these exploitative practices.[10]

---

[1] In late 2013, Break Media and Alloy Digital merged to become Defy Media, combining Break's young male audience with Alloy's young female audience.

[2] Michael Serazio, *Your Ad Here: The Cool Sell of Guerilla Marketing* (New York: New York University Press, 2013). Also see Jonathan Gray, *Show Sold Separately: Promos,*

Spoilers, and Other Media Paratexts (New York: New York University Press, 2010).

3 Frank Rose, ". . . And the Final Lesson from 'Game of Thrones' Is, 'Always Support the Bottom," *Deep Media,* January 30, 2012.

4 Siva Vaidhyanathan, *The Googlization of Everything: (And Why We Should Worry)* (Berkeley: University of California Press, 2010).

5 Tessa Stuart, "YouTube Stars Fight Back: Machinima and Maker Studios, Two of YouTube's Most High-Profile Networks, Have Come under Fire from Their Own Talent," *LA Weekly* January 10, 2013.

6 Guy Di Piazza and Martin Olausson, "The Television and Movie Industry Explained: Where Does All the Money Go?" *Digital Media Strategies Service,* June 2007.

7 Hesmondhalgh, *Cultural Industries,* 351.

8 Jennifer Holt, "Access of Evil: Google, Verizon and the Future of Net Neutrality," *In Media Res,* August 25, 2010.

9 Trebor Scholz, ed., *Digital Labor: The Internet as Playground and Factory* (New York: Routledge, 2013).

10 The themes in this essay are drawn from my forthcoming book *Advertaining America: At Work and Play in the Digital Economy.*

Bibliography

Di Piazza, Guy, and Martin Olausson. "The Television and Movie Industry Explained: Where Does All the Money Go?" *Digital Media Strategies Service,* 2007.

Flew, Terry. *The Creative Industries: Culture and Policy.* London: Sage, 2012.

Gray, Jonathan. *Show Sold Separately: Promos, Spoilers, and Other Media Paratexts.* New York: New York University Press, 2010.

Hesmondhalgh, David. *The Cultural Industries.* London: Sage, 2013.

Holt, Jennifer. "Access of Evil: Google, Verizon, and the Future of Net Neutrality." *In Media Res,* August 25, 2010.

Rose, Frank. ". . . And the Final Lesson from 'Game of Thrones' Is, 'Always Support the Bottom.'" *Deep Media*, January 30, 2012.

Scholz, Trebor. *Digital Labor: The Internet as Playground and Factory.* New York: Routledge, 2013.

Serazio, Michael. *Your Ad Here: The Cool Sell of Guerilla Marketing.* New York: New York University Press, 2013.

Stuart, Tessa. "YouTube Stars Fight Back: Machinima and Maker Studios, Two of YouTube's Most High-Profile Networks, Have Come under Fire from Their Own Talent." *LA Weekly*, January 10, 2013.

Vaidhyanathan, Siva. *The Googlization of Everything: (And Why We Should Worry)*. Berkeley: University of California Press, 2010.

16.

Media Industries and the Ecological Crisis

RICHARD MAXWELL

All of today's large media corporations are studying the ecological costs of their operations and have already instituted some kind of greening strategy in response—even News Corp., owner of climate science denier Fox News, has been greening its operations. While the details vary, these companies share a number of laudable green goals: to reduce energy consumption, increase recycling and reuse of inventory, eliminate waste, encourage employees to be good green citizens, and so on.[1] But the scholarship on media industries hasn't paid much attention. My hope is that *Media Industries* journal will change that.

Regardless of naysayers, there is scientific consensus that humans are responsible for harmful climate change caused by the overproduction of carbon dioxide. Ocean acidification is killing off sea habitat, and we've overdosed the planet with nitrogen. Massive levels of conventional pollution are still a problem for the over-developed world and, as we've seen this year in news from Shanghai and elsewhere, in the industrial economies of Asia, too. Many of us of a "certain age" can bear witness to rapidly diminishing biodiversity—this is the Earth's sixth great extinction—and we're responsible for it.

Climate and environmental scientists have different ways of explaining the central point of the eco-crisis: that human activity, *fueled by a growth-obsessed political economic order*, has crossed the line of sustainability. The latter can be defined as the balance between what the Earth can give to support human activity and what the Earth can safely re-absorb from those activities. This balancing function has been called the "scientific prerequisites for ecological sustainability," or more simply, our "planetary boundaries."[2]

But why is this important for media industry studies?

The technologies upon which media industry studies are predicated not only provide the kind of content, institutions, and audiences that form the subject matter of this journal. They also depend on human exploitation of the environment—from the minerals, mechanics, and chemistry used to make them to the energy used to power them.

Media technology is proliferating, with spending on consumer electronics alone reaching $1 trillion in 2012, and rising to nearly $1.1 trillion in 2013, which matched overall annual spending increases of 4 to 5 percent on all information technology for that period. This added up to about $3.7 trillion in spending on consumer electronics by the end of 2013.[3] The major portion of this growth is in sales of mobile devices.

There are many relevant environmental problems associated with our love affair with media technology, but I'll use the issue of energy consumption to illustrate the vital importance of eco-criticism to media industry studies.

I know it's an obvious point, but for some reason we tend to forget that all these gadgets need to be plugged into the electric grid—and remember that batteries, too, have built-in energy costs in production, usage, and disposal. Over ten billion high-tech devices around the world need electricity today. And according to the International Energy Agency (IEA), all this media technology consumes about 15 percent of the total global residential energy in use.

Without any changes to this trend, the residential electricity needed to power this whiz-bang stuff will rise to 30 percent of global consumption by 2022 and 45 percent by 2030, according to the IEA.

Keep in mind that residential use refers to *operational energy* and not to the energy consumed in the manufacturing stage of information and communication technologies. Energy used in the manufacturing of laptops, for example, is 64 percent of the total that's used in a laptop's lifecycle—and this does not account for the energy used to make chemicals and gases that go into the production of semiconductors or the energy used to dispose or recycle the damn things.[4] This problem of measurement applies to all the hardware used in the industry we study.

When we connect the dots between our high-tech lifestyle and the power grid, including the electricity it takes to manufacture and distribute these gadgets, we are talking about aggregate carbon emissions on a scale that matches the footprint of the aerospace industry.

And the story on the so-called *cloud* is similar.

Data centers' energy demand doubled in the first five years of the new century and continues to rise at a steady pace, with business practices that range from serious efforts to reduce reliance on coal-fired energy to widespread examples of waste and thoughtless energy management.

If Google gets its way, small-scale, inefficient data centers will disappear altogether, replaced by the likes of Google, Facebook, IBM, Microsoft, Amazon, and other mega-operators of the cloud. Google backs its play with research showing that the centralization of cloud computing into massive infrastructure systems promises to reduce current energy consumption by 87 percent.[5] That would certainly be a positive change, considering that at their current rate of demand, data centers are such ravenous hogs that, according to Greenpeace, if the cloud were a country it would be the fifth largest energy consumer in the world.

As the media industry moves toward increasing internet delivery of content and audiences via the cloud, the problem of energy provision and consumption becomes an important one for media industry research—a problem complicated by the unsustainable structure of mobile communication business.

A Bell Labs/University of Melbourne study estimates that 90 percent of the total energy consumed by the wireless cloud is attributable to access providers—this is not counting the energy used by the devices themselves.[6] The researchers point to the relatively meager 9 percent share of total energy consumption attributable to data centers.

Behind these projections of rising energy demand is the tremendous growth in sales of electronic equipment that I referred to earlier. This growth is now mostly made up of sales of mobile devices like tablets, notebooks, and smartphones—a quarter of all sales is attributable to the US alone.

Such growth in mobile computing is really astounding, and really bad for the environment. It's the result in part of unrelenting marketing of wireless gadgets promoted as tools to keep us constantly connected to each other and the network. We are told that the convergence around digital technology along with mobility and other supposed innovations of the network society pose big challenges to media industries today.

From an eco-materialist perspective, the intimate relation of media technology and environmental decline poses an important challenge to media industry scholarship. For me, this means reading beyond conventional industry research to study, inter alia, the science on climate change, lifecycle assessment, and the chemistry associated with the production, use, and disposal of media technologies. Most importantly, it means acknowledging the urgent nature of the ecological crisis. Only then can we perform a critical evaluation of the greening strategies currently underway in the media industries.

The environmental problems of media industries should not be understood as a narrow matter relevant only to this sector. The eco-crisis affects every organism on the planet, making this particular problem of general interest—and this means the sub-discipline of media industry studies must venture out into the critique of the wider political economy and ask what kind of society we want to live in. The answer will determine whether our media and cultural industries are rooted in values of sustainability or constrained by a political economic order based on unending and unsustainable growth.

---

[1] For examples, see the site Producers Guild of America's Green.

[2] Johan Rockstrom et al., "Planetary Boundaries: Exploring the Safe Operating Space for Humanity," *Ecology and Society* 14, no. 2 (2009); Thomas Schauer, *The Sustainable Information Society: Vision and Risks* (Vienna: European Support Centre of the Club of Rome, 2003).

[3] Kyle Brown, "Consumer Electronics Show 2013: Global Gadget Spending to Top $1 Trillion this Year," *globalEDGE*, January 8, 2013,; Valli Meenakshi Ramanathan, "Global IT Spending Pegged at $3.7 Trillion;

Gadget Spending Forecast at $1.1 trillion in 2013," *International Business Times*, January 7, 2013.

4 Eric Williams, "Environmental Effects of Information and Communications Technologies," *Nature* 479 (2011): 354-358.

5 Ucilia Wang, "A Google-Funded Study Quantifies Cloud Computing's Environmental Benefits," *Forbes*, June 11, 2013.

6 Centre for Energy-Efficient Telecommunications, "The Power of Wireless Cloud: An Analysis of the Energy Consumption of Wireless Cloud," (Melbourne: Bell Labs and University of Melbourne, April 2013).

Bibliography

Brown, Kyle. "Consumer Electronics Show 2013: Global Gadget Spending to Top $1 Trillion this Year." *globalEDGE*, January 8, 2013. .

Centre for Energy-Efficient Telecommunications. "The Power of Wireless Cloud: An Analysis of the Energy Consumption of Wireless Cloud." Melbourne: Bell Labs and University of Melbourne, April 2013.

Maxwell, Richard and Toby Miller. *Greening the Media*. Oxford: Oxford University Press, 2012.

Ramanathan, Valli Meenakshi. "Global IT Spending Pegged at $3.7 Trillion; Gadget Spending Forecast at $1.1 trillion in 2013." *International Business Times*, last modified January 7, 2013.

Rockstrom, Johan, Will Steffen, Kevin Noone, Åsa Persson, F. Stuart III Chapin, Eric Lambin, Timothy M. Lenton, Martin Scheffer, Carl Folke, Hans Joachim Schellnhuber, et al. "Planetary Boundaries: Exploring the Safe Operating Space for Humanity." *Ecology and Society* 14, no. 2 (2009).

Schauer, Thomas. *The Sustainable Information Society: Vision and Risks*. Vienna: European Support Centre of the Club of Rome, 2003.

Wang, Ucilia. "A Google-Funded Study Quantifies Cloud Computing's Environmental Benefits." *Forbes*, June 11, 2013.

Williams, Eric. "Environmental Effects of Information and Communications Technologies." *Nature* 479 (2011): 354-358.

17.

Media Work, Management, and Greed: A New Agenda?

VICKI MAYER

> *There is romance and magic in the story of the moving*
> *picture industry. The magic of the Midas touch, of*
> *Aladdin's lamp. The romance of poverty turned to wealth,*
> *of millions made from hundreds.* – Diamond Film
> Company (1917) [1]

In a public relations piece that could have been written yesterday, the budding entrepreneurs behind the Diamond Film Company used economic hyperbole and place-based marketing to tout the founding of a new film economy in New Orleans. The company claimed to have everything, from an eager and expert workforce to a state-of-the-art studio in a picturesque location. They reprinted the exuberant newspaper reports of stars that preferred films produced in New Orleans and the six-figure salaries that film executives made after getting their start in the city. Within months of publishing this pamphlet, the company sold its stock and a few reels before going bankrupt.

This would be the end of the story, except that in researching the company's board of directors, I realized that Diamond never actually planned to make films. At least, the films themselves were a small part of the business model. The directors took the money and set up another shell company for bayou oil exploration, selling stock this time to naïve oil, not film, investors. Many of them were eventually caught, ensnared by the energy investors who sued for fraud. And yet the mythology of their magical film industry lives on. With it, I would like to put greed on the agenda for the study of media industries.

In the early twenty-first century, we have entered an era of runaway film romance. Cities and regions compete for major studio and independent house investments. No longer needing a penny stock market for their wares, film production companies may now draw directly from public tills, which offer generous incentives, from direct paybacks, to tradable tax write-offs, to in-kind gifts of infrastructure and labor. In the process, both policy makers and producers proclaim the sure benefits of public financing: a new jobs market for the middle class, shiny new and ecologically clean infrastructure, increased tourism, and other ancillary investments in the overall economy. There have been plenty of debates, mostly among urban geographers and planners, about the veracity of these claims. Like Wall Street, Hollywood is not immune to cycles of boom and bust. Channeling the Diamond profiteers of 1917, however, might raise another set of questions yet to be answered. Namely, to what extent are promotions of film economies laced with avaricious aims? How does greed at the top trickle down, so to speak, through media industries? Or is greed spreadable, like the convergent texts themselves?

Over nearly one hundred years of studies about media industries, two discourses about their workers have dominated, with a third one ascendant today.[2] These discourses organize the kinds of stories we tell about media work and the people who do it. First, in line with studies of organizations and work, media workers' goals could be characterized as the ability to create media within a system of constraining rules and structures. This narrative ran parallel with a second one, which predominated in film and media studies: Media producers have special creative or innovative capacities that can be expressed through their own entrepreneurial activities. Although creative visions were individual in both of these discourses, the pursuit of the visions was universal. The final discourse, which has roots extending at least back to Frankfurt, was that workers may still pursue creative autonomy or even a creative community but only after they secure stable employment. The new economy for media production has succeeded in replacing the narrative of creativity within constraints with one of getting a gig, if not three gigs, each with their various constraints. The studies of media work today pivot on themes of worker flexibility, networking, emotion work, and brand management. I am to be held accountable for at least perpetuating this discourse in my own attempts to humanize the workers that I see on the margins of media industries. The glamour surrounding media jobs has been dulled by the precarity of work and a workload that never seems to end, at least in academic accounts.

Meanwhile, we are surrounded by journalistic accounts of the sheer wealth of media moguls and the continued profitability of media and entertainment industries in an otherwise miserable marketplace. Journalist Ken Auletta was among the first to profile the luxurious lifestyles and naked ambitions of the Hollywood highwaymen, publishing regular stories in *The New Yorker*.[3] Where else does greediness concentrate in media industries? From celebrity hair stylists, to pompous staffers, to legendary assistants willing to do anything for fame, there would seem to be no shortage of ambition driven by envy, anxiety, and greed. Read between the lines of the coverage of new media entrepreneurs and we see how the same qualities that characterize precarious media work can be directed to greed over need. For example, ad agency art director James Ames stays up nights, working long after he put his kids to bed, to make six-second videos on Vine. It's a second job, which he does in a "makeshift studio" on his home couch. Working for major corporations, he was composing a stop-motion video that would take him all night to complete, according to an NPR story.[4] Before we bemoan the needs to make ends meet in the new economy, the reporter tells us Ames is using the money to take his family to Hawaii. This is hardly the kind of goal that scholars typically promote as the ends of media work.

It should be the task of media industry scholars to reconcile the good goals and virtues of media work with those that seem to be neither inherently good nor virtuous. According to the economist David Levine, greed is a natural outgrowth of capitalism, expanding from the basic desire to stockpile capital for the future, and as a way of staving off future losses.[5] Greed is also a capable substitute for community. Those with enough capital can survive hardship solo, while others have to rely on the kindness of others. Yet beyond this means for autonomous survival, capital provides a fantasy of its own limitless reproduction. Unlike income, which comes in exchange for work, capital is generated simply from its present investment and future value. Capital can be wasted in consumption or invested in getting others to work for you. Either way, the owner of the capital pursues the dream of a day when work is unnecessary and when the possibilities of what one does are infinite, since capital can seemingly go towards any goal or direction.

One problem with this common fantasy is when the dream of capital is separated from actual production; that is, somebody has to actually work to generate the things that become the object of the capitalist's desire. Our pursuit of not working must be on the backs of those who do; our pursuit of the limitless life implies more limits for those working under us. Greed also implies competition with others in the same position since, unlike goods, capital has to be regenerated to maintain value. Through competition, capital becomes both the object of desire and the subject of our misery, since we must work harder to get more of it. Levine quotes Durkheim, who called this competition the "disease of the infinite," which manifests as a tendency to devalue what we have in pursuit of what we lack.[6] Greed is the driving force behind the disease. It becomes the agent and individuals are its victims — or its "fetishes," in Marxian terms. Greed, in Levine's exposition, is a system, one that we hope to opt out of one day, whether through meaningful work or freedom from it.

Put in this framework, media industry scholars might take a closer look at the competitive nature of different kinds of media work and media workers. The corrupting fantasy of the infinite life must have various guises. A socio-analysis of greed in media industries would help us better understand the human aspects of labor exploitation, the motivations that pair worthy and less worthy goals in making media. It would also connect media industry studies to those other "greedy bastards," the ones we vilify in media portrayals of banks and hedge fund firms, car dealerships and law offices. After all, imitation still is the sincerest form of flattery.

---

[1] Diamond Film Company, *Filmland: the Kingdom of Fabulous Fortunes* (New Orleans: Schumert-Warfield-Watson, 1917).

[2] Vicki Mayer, *Below the Line: Producers and Production Studies in the New Television Economy* (Durham: Duke University Press, 2011).

[3] Ken Auletta, *The Highwaymen: Warriors of the Information Superhighway* (New York: Harcourt, Brace and Company, 1998).

[4] Daniel Hajek, "On Vine, Brands Look to Deliver their Message in Six Seconds," NPR.org All Tech Considered, August 9, 2013.

[6] David Levine, *Pathology of the Capitalist Spirit: An Essay on Greed, Loss and Hope* (New York: Palgrave Pivot, 2013).

[6] Levine, *Pathology of the Capitalist Spirit*, 20.

Bibliography

Auletta, Ken. *The Highwaymen: Warriors of the Information Superhighway*. New York: Harcourt, Brace and Company, 1998.

Diamond Film Company. *Filmland: the Kingdom of Fabulous Fortunes*. New Orleans: Schumert-Warfield-Watson, 1917. Louisiana Special Collections Archives.

Hajek, Daniel. "On Vine, Brands Look to Deliver their Message in Six Seconds." NPR.org All Tech Considered, August 9, 2013.

Levine, David. *Pathology of the Capitalist Spirit: An Essay on Greed, Loss and Hope*. New York: Palgrave Pivot, 2013.

Mayer, Vicki. *Below the Line: Producers and Production Studies in the New Television Economy*. Durham: Duke University Press, 2011.

18.

"Invisible Work" in the Indian Media Industries

RANJANI MAZUMDAR

The research on media industries in recent years has expanded its scope to include many different kinds of sites and areas. If at one end of this scholarship we have seen work on financial flows, technological transformations, cultural policy, and high-profile production practices, the other end has witnessed a growing interest in the functioning of informal media economies, pirate cultures, and lower-end technological infrastructures. The approaches at both ends remain important and scholarship on media industries will need to continue in this direction. But there is another critical dimension that has not yet received adequate attention: the social, economic, and cultural context of the lowest rung of the workforce in the world's biggest media industries. In contexts such as South Asia, this lower-end workforce of the entertainment industries is sizeable, and its members constitute a major part of the informal sector of the economy. It is this terrain of "informal work" that needs deeper investigation that goes beyond numbers.

Given the scale of invisibility as well as the complex social and cultural structures through which these working lives are mediated, ethnographic approaches seem to hold new attractions. Ethnographies of media industries are not new; in South Asia this turn to field investigations of the entertainment sector has generated an interesting body of work on production contexts,[1] advertising practices,[2] organized and visible fan associations,[3] and television and its audiences.[4] Perhaps it is time now to turn this ethnographic lens to the direction of the lowest rung of industry personnel also. Given the large numbers of people, both skilled and unskilled, involved in film production, the paucity of information and material on them is surprising. Scholarly work on media industries in South Asia needs to take serious note of this amorphous world that many have referred to as "invisible work." These are people whose working practices are central to, but remain on the margins of, big-budget production discourses.

This world of invisible work would include stunt artists, body doubles, dancers, junior artists, makeup artists, lower-end technicians, and spot boys. These are the people who form the backbone of our media industries. Yet the lives of these workers remain largely peripheral to the hype and spectacle generated by media industries. In deeply hierarchical societies like India, production practices tend to reinforce the existing social and class hierarchies, but on a much larger scale given the ubiquitous presence of film production practices in the film cities of India. When industry practices are thought of analytically, these people often appear as statistical information sets. While there are a few documentaries and some journalistic articles available on these film workers, to date, little academic writing exists on this vast body of industry personnel: their lives, social context, and working conditions. We require an approach to production as a form of culture – to recognize that in the making of media output, various kinds of personnel produce themselves as workers in a modern mediatized society. These workers negotiate formal and informal networks, institutionalized hierarchies, and structures. In doing this, shared languages, communities, and identities, come to the fore.[5]

If the popular media in India hypes the expansion of media industries, the critical writings talk of corporate culture, designer dreams, and a downward swing in content. No matter how much we focus on the financial, technological, and cultural movement of media industries, unless the emphasis takes into account production practices beyond the "visible spectacle," forms of media work will continue to remain hidden, reinforced systematically even by academic scholarship. It is here that the turn to ethnography could play a major role in excavating and foregrounding this vast world of industry personnel, their struggle to retain a dignified existence, the associations through which they fight for leverage, and the social and cultural contexts that shape their working practices. A cursory map of the terrain of issues involving this sector of media work shows how new research agendas can be framed to expand the scope of media industry scholarship in South Asia.

Music and dance have played a major role in Indian cinema ever since the arrival of sound. Dance on screen is rarely an individual act done by stars: it is always also a spectacle choreographed with several dancers around the stars. The Cine Dancers Association provides the dancers for all the major choreographed dances in cinema. The Dancers Association is especially active in Chennai and Mumbai. Dancers from diverse backgrounds become members of the association, which remains the contact point for choreographers. In Chennai, several choreographers are also members of the association. The dancers' association functions with a set of norms to which the hiring side must adhere. Thus the eight-hour shift, overtime (if they are made to work beyond eight hours), and a regular, fixed wage per day are issues that the association handles. In return for this, the dancers provide the association with a fee. It is the same story for associations of character artists, junior artists once known as "extras," and stunt artists' associations.

Stunt artists take great risks for action sequences when the star is unable to deliver. The stunt artist's association president in Mumbai insists that almost every star has had to use body doubles at some point.[6] Yet the remuneration received by the stunt artists is usually Rs.2,500–3,500 (approximately US$40–$60) for an eight-hour shift. Suriya Bano Bodiaji works in the film industry as a body double for female stars. She has been admitted to the hospital on several occasions because of the injuries caused by accidents during her stunts.[7] People are drawn to this risky profession because it provides them the "opportunity" to make a little money even if it's nominal. A well-known stunt director, Bhiku Verma, believes that while the quality of stunts in India can be spectacular, the equipment used is not good enough to ensure the safety of the artists.[8] This is largely due to the heavy taxes and duties required for the purchase of these items. While stuntmen and women are insured in other parts of the world, in India they have to rely on the generosity of the producer or the actors for whom they work.[9] The Stunt Artists Association generally fixes the wages for stunts. In general, the fee does not exceed Rs. 10,000 (approximately US$165) for a sequence. But there are a few who have made it big and can therefore charge up to Rs. 50,000 (a little over US$800).[10] Producers pay the association, which then disburses the money. But erratic or no payment is also a regular problem faced by stunt artists. Reportedly 75 percent of the stuntmen registered with the Stunt Artists Association live below the poverty line. Only 20 percent seem to secure regular jobs, and a tiny 5 percent of stunt doubles make it big. Most retire to face bleak and uncertain futures.[11]

There are many female body doubles who perform intimate scenes for the female stars. These doubles work on the condition that their names and faces will not be revealed. To this effect, the double and the producer sign a contract and affidavit. These underpaid doubles remain unknown to the world but are critical to films requiring them to play roles to which the stars would not agree. Doubles are sourced from informal networks to present on screen what the star will refuse to do. There are occasions when these issues turn sour, such as when a star is unhappy about how a double has been used. For example, Manisha Koirala, a well-known actress, had a body double (Jessica Choksi) who performed some of the intimate sequences that were required by the film *Ek Choti Si Luv Story* (2002).[12] The director, Shashilal Nair, promised Jessica that her name and face would not be revealed. She was paid only Rs. 12,500 (approximately US$200) for performing nine scenes and Rs. 9,000 (approximately US$150) for the affidavit guaranteeing her privacy.[13] Jessica's name, however, was dragged into a public spectacle when Manisha quarreled with the director over what she thought was obscene in the film. She revealed Jessica's name and then the press went to town over the issue.[14] A report in the *Times of India* narrated the matter thus: "Manisha alleged that producer Shashilal Nair had used a duplicate in obscene scenes which portrayed her in bad light. Nair said he had used Koirala's duplicate with her permission because she has become obese. Koirala had denied Nair's allegation that she gained weight."[15] Such incidents foreground the lines that separate stardom from this other kind of creative work.

Junior artists were once known as extras. They usually appear as part of the crowd in action scenes, in dance sequences, or any other situation, dramatic or otherwise, that requires their presence. The Junior Artists Association in Mumbai has more than ten thousand registered members.[16] They are now often required by television since so many of the shows require junior artists, who often complain that television pays them lower wages than what they earn in the film industry. The average payment for these artists working for television is approximately Rs. 750 (approximately US$13) per shoot, while in the film industry they are paid between Rs. 900 and 1,000 (approximately US$15–$17).[17] These artists are generally classified into three categories based on experience and acting talent — A, B, and C — and the payment is made according to the classification. An A-level, experienced artist can sometimes get up to Rs. 5,000 (approximately US$80) a day.[18] However, the average remuneration rarely crosses Rs 2,500 (approximately US$40) a day. Junior artists have to operate through coordinators and must be registered with a body under the Cinema India Television Artists Association (CINTAA), an organization that first started in 1959.[19]

In the contemporary transformation of the film industry, junior artists have been the worst hit. One of the arguments for this has been that the urbane quality of the major A-list films requires a certain "look" that is fulfilled by models and foreigners.[20] In 2008, almost one hundred thousand junior artists registered with the Federation of Western India Cine Employees went on strike, demanding regular payment and work for extras. Finally, some of the producers agreed to these demands but also managed to secure a clause that allows the producers to hire outside the association if required.[21] The new scenario has adversely affected the traditional base of junior artists who generally belonged to a particular kind of social background in which they worked as informal labor for a low daily wage. Many migrated into the city in search of work. These traditional junior artists are unable to compete with the glossy, fashionable, and cosmopolitan appearance of many contemporary junior artists who play upper-class roles on screen. The shift in screen culture in the last two decades has resulted in an overwhelming focus on upper-class families; and the traditional junior artist does not easily find a place in many of these new films.

How do we classify this world of work in the larger context of media industry scholarship? Perhaps a methodological concern with excavation, documentation, oral narratives, and memories would invigorate and challenge certain assumptions in scholarly approaches. If media is a form of practice, then we need to open out this world of practice to include not just higher-end, visible professionals such as camerapersons, sound recordists, scriptwriters, directors, and their assistants but also those whose work continues to remain invisible. The term *labor*, or even *cultural labor*, has increasingly become rhetorical and abstract and can hardly represent the lives and experiences of the lowest rung of the media industry's workforce. We need an approach that is fresh and interdisciplinary, one that is not just about reiteration of economic difference in abstract terms. The issues in South Asia that I have briefly discussed remain at the surface level of what journalists have been able to access. We now need to move backward and forward in time, tracking this world of invisible work historically through traces in films and memories of surviving workers, ensuring documentation of those working today and detailed observation of negotiations between associations, unions, and the industries. What we need is not a notion of an amorphous hidden mass of workers but a detailed archeology of the identities and lives of the lowest rung of workers who fuel the media industries of the world. Thus, ethnographic approaches and a desire for oral documentation must fuel the excavation of the lives, identities, and shared imaginations of these invisible cultural workers.

1 Tejaswini Ganti, *Producing Bollywood: Inside the Contemporary Hindi Film Industry* (Durham, NC: Duke University Press, 2012); Rosie Thomas, "Indian Cinema: Pleasures and Popularity," *Screen* 26 (May–August 1985): 3-4, 116–31.

2 William Mazzarella, *Shoveling Smoke: Advertising and Globalization in Contemporary India* (Durham, NC: Duke University Press, 2003).

3 S. V. Srinivas, "Devotion and Defiance in Fan Activity," in *Making Meaning in Indian Cinema*, ed. Ravi Vasudevan (New Delhi: Oxford University Press, 2000), 297–312.

4 Poornima Mankekar, *Screening Culture, Viewing Politics: An Ethnography of Television, Womanhood and Nation in Postcolonial India* (Durham, NC: Duke University Press, 1999); Sara Dickey, *Cinema and the Urban Poor in South India* (Cambridge: Cambridge University Press, 2007).

5 Vicki Mayer, Miranda J. Banks, and John T. Caldwell, eds., *Production Studies: Cultural Studies of Media Industries* (New York: Routledge, 2009), 2.

6 Vidyottama Sharma, "Boomtown Gladiators: for a few rupees more," *Tehelka*, January 7, 2004.

7 "Bollywood stunt artists view for more discipline in the industry," *Oneindia News*, June 7, 2004.

8 Vidyottama Sharma, "Boomtown Gladiators: for a few rupees more," *Tehelka*, January 7, 2004.

9 Ibid.

10 Ibid.

11 Ibid.

12 Piali Bannerjee, "Bollywood's Body Doubles: *Ek Choti Si* Sad Story," *Times of India*, December 8, 2003.

13 Ibid.

14 Ibid. See also Bhawana Somaaya, "Crying Wold," *Screen*, February 20, 2004.

15 "HC Stays Release of *Ek Choti Si Luv Story*," *Times of India*, September 5, 2002.

16 "Bollywood's 'Extras': Story of Dream Unfulfilled," *CNN IBN Live*, June 13, 2011.

17 Ibid.

18 Ibid.

19 Opender Chanana, *The Missing 3 in Bollywood: Safety, Security, Shelter* (Nyon, Switzerland: UNI Global Union, 2011).

20 Meenakshi Ganguly, "This Year's Models," *Time*, July 22, 2002.

21 "Bollywood Junior Artists Feel Threatened by Foreigners," *Indian Express*, October 6, 2008.

Bibliography

Chanana, Opender. *The Missing 3 in Bollywood: Safety, Security, Shelter*. Nyon, Switzerland: UNI Global Union, 2011.

Dickey, Sara. *Cinema and the Urban Poor in South India*. Cambridge: Cambridge University Press, 2007.

Ganti, Tejaswini. *Producing Bollywood: Inside the Contemporary Hindi Film Industry*. Durham, NC: Duke University Press, 2012.

Mankekar, Poornima. *Screening Culture, Viewing Politics: An Ethnography of Television, Womanhood and Nation in Postcolonial India*. Durham, NC: Duke University Press, 1999.

Mayer, Vicki, Miranda J. Banks, and John T. Caldwell, ed. *Production Studies: Cultural Studies of Media Industries.* New York: Routledge, 2009.

Mazzarella, William. *Shoveling Smoke: Advertising and Globalization in Contemporary India.* Durham, NC: Duke University Press, 2003.

Srinivas, S. V. "Devotion and Defiance in Fan Activity." In *Making Meaning in Indian Cinema,* edited by Ravi Vasudevan, 297–312. New Delhi: Oxford University Press, 2000.

Thomas, Rosie. "Indian Cinema: Pleasures and Popularity." *Screen* 26 (May–August 1985): 3–4, 116–31.

19.

The Discourse on Media is Dominated by Reactionary Cant

TOBY MILLER

The dominant discourse on the media industries in the United States and across the *angloparlante* world is profoundly conservative. Reactionary rhetoric characterizes much popular discussion, college teaching, bourgeois journalism, public policy, third-sector activism, and research—whether coin-operated or academic (to the extent that the two can be distinguished).

The discourse takes one or several of the following tacks:

- Because of new technologies and practices of consumption, concentration of media ownership and control no longer matters—information is finally free, thanks to multipoint distribution and destabilized hierarchies.
- Consumers are sovereign and can transcend class and other categories.
- Young people are liberated from media control.
- Journalism is dying as everyone and their owl become sources of both news and reporting.
- Creative destruction is an accurate and desirable description of economic innovation.
- When scholars observe media workers and audiences, they discover that ideology critique is inappropriate.
- Marxist political economy denies the power of audiences and users and the irrelevance of boundaries—it is pessimistic and hidebound.
- Cultural imperialism critiques miss the creativity and resilience of national and subnational forms of life against industrial products.
- Media effects studies are inconsequential—audiences outwit corporate plans and psy-function norms.

What is left out of these seemingly dynamic and innovative but in fact tired and venerable lines?

- the ecological impact of the media
- questions of labor and life in the cognitariat
- those who essentially live outside consumption, beyond multinational markets — without an electricity grid and potable water, for example
- citizenship rights and responsibilities
- concentrated ownership and obedient regulation
- the critique of cultural imperialism that resonates with populations and activists
- the fact that the fantasy of media organizations being vulnerable to the power of the young, consumers being rebellious, and new technology laying waste to all is as old as those organizations themselves
- the expansion of newspapers outside the Global North — people still line up in Barranquilla by the dozen each morning to place classified advertisements in the local paper, for instance
- the *real* use of new technologies — for example, people citing one another's sexting or F- and T-word activity in family courts to undermine claims to parental responsibility, leading to judgments that deny people custody of their children

A key to the reactionary nature of media studies is its devotion to its object of study, and especially its ahistorical celebration of technology. George Orwell dissected the antecedents of this cybertarian rhetoric seventy years ago. His critique resonates today:

> Reading recently a batch of rather shallowly optimistic "progressive" books, I was struck by the automatic way in which people go on repeating certain phrases which were fashionable before 1914. Two great favorites are "the abolition of distance" and "the disappearance of frontiers." I do not know how often I have met with the statements that "the aeroplane and the radio have abolished distance" and "all parts of the world are now interdependent."[1]

Sound familiar? Of course it does. Technological determinists' lack of originality and tendency to repeat exploded myths as if they were new and true refuse to lie down and die. No wonder Facebook claims its social media site can "decrease world conflict" through inter-cultural communication, and Twitter modestly announces itself as "a triumph of humanity."[2] This is yet one more cliché dalliance with new technology's supposedly innate capacity to endow users with transcendence, but no less powerful for its banality because of the interests it serves and the cult of newness it subscribes to.[3]

Equally romantically, but with a franker commitment to capital accumulation, bourgeois economists argue that cell phones have streamlined hitherto inefficient markets in remote areas of the Global South, enriching people in zones where banking services and commercial information are scarce due to distance and terrain. Exaggerated claims for the magic of mobile telephony in places that lack electricity, plumbing, fresh water, hospital care, and the like include "the complete elimination of waste" and massive reductions of poverty and corruption through the empowerment of individuals.[4]

Cell phones and the like are said to obliterate geography, sovereignty, and hierarchy, replacing them with truth and beauty. This deregulated, individuated, technologized world makes consumers into producers, frees the disabled from confinement, encourages new subjectivities, rewards intellect and competitiveness, links people across cultures, and allows billions of flowers to bloom in a postpolitical cornucopia. People fish, film, fornicate, and finance from morning to midnight, from Marx to Godard (minus the struggle). Consumption is privileged, and labor and the environment are forgotten. How very jolly.

Time magazine exemplified the utopic silliness of these tendencies in its choice of "You" as 2006 "Person of the Year," declaring, "You control the Information Age. Welcome to your world."[5] The *Guardian* is prey to the same touching magic: someone called "You" heads its current list of the hundred most important folks in the media.[6] Sweet, isn't it?

The discourse incarnates reader, audience, consumer, and player autonomy — the neoliberal intellectual's wet dream of music, movies, television, and everything else converging under the sign of omniscient, omnipotent, omnipresent populism. The dream invests, with unparalleled gusto, in Schumpeterian entrepreneurs, evolutionary economics, and creative industries. Its true believers have never seen an app they didn't like, or a socialist idea they did. Faith in devolved media-making amounts to a secular religion, offering transcendence in the here and now via a "literature of the eighth day, the day after Genesis."[7] Machinery, not political-economic activity, is the guiding light.

Labor

In cybertarian fantasies of this new era, readers become writers, listeners transform into speakers, viewers emerge as stars, fans are academics, and vice versa, while the economy glides into an ever greener postindustrialism. The comparatively cheap and easy access to making and circulating meaning afforded by internet media and genres is thought to have eroded the one-way hold on culture that saw a small segment of the world as producers and the larger segment as consumers, even as it makes for a cleaner economy. New technologies supposedly allow us all to become simultaneously cultural consumers and producers (prosumers) — no more factory conditions, no more factory emissions.

Zine writers are screenwriters. Bloggers are copywriters. Children are columnists. Bus riders are journalists. And think of the job prospects that follow! Coca-Cola hires African Americans to drive through the inner city selling soda and playing hip-hop. AT&T pays San Francisco buskers to mention the company in their songs. Urban performance poets rhyme about Nissan cars for cash, simultaneously hawking, entertaining, and researching. Subway's sandwich commercials are marketed as made by teenagers. Cultural studies majors become designers. Graduate students in New York and Los Angeles read scripts for producers then pronounce on whether they tap into audience interests. Precariously employed part-timers spy on fellow spectators in theaters to see how they respond to coming attractions. Opportunities to vote in the Eurovision Song Contest or a reality program disclose the profiles and practices of viewers, who can be monitored and wooed in the future. Online end-user licensing agreements for corporate video games ensure that players sign over their cultural moves and perspectives to the very companies they are paying in order to participate.[8]

In other words, corporations are using discounted labor. Business leeches want flexibility in the people they employ, the technologies they use, the places where they do business, and the amounts they pay—and inflexibility of ownership and control. The neoclassical doxa preached by neoliberal chorines favors an economy where competition and opportunity cost are in the litany and dissent is unforgiveable, thought to be as crazed as collective industrial organization. In short, "decent and meaningful work opportunities are reducing at a phenomenal pace in the sense that, for a high proportion of low- and middle-skilled workers, full-time, lifelong employment is unlikely."[9] Even the US National Governors Association recognizes the reality: "routine tasks that once characterized middle class work have either been eliminated by technological change or are now conducted by low-wage but highly skilled workers."[10] The way that cultural workers, from jazz musicians to street artists, have long labored without regular compensation and security now models the expectations we are all supposed to have, rather than our parents' or grandparents' assumptions about lifelong, or at least steady, employment.

Hence the success of Mindworks Global Media, a company outside New Delhi that provides Indian-based journalists and copyeditors who work long distance for newspapers whose reporters are supposedly in the United States and Europe. There are 35–40 percent cost savings.[11] Or consider the advertising agency Poptent, which undercuts big competitors in sales to major clients by exploiting prosumers' labor in the name of "empowerment." That empowerment takes the following form: Poptent pays the creators of homemade commercials US$7,500, it receives a management fee of US$40,000, and the buyer saves about US$300,000 off the usual price.[12]

How might we account for this phenomenon? Antonio Negri redeployed the concept of the cognitariat from the Reaganite futurist Alvin Toffler.[13] Negri defines the cognitariat as people undertaking casualized cultural work who have heady educational backgrounds yet live at the uncertain interstices of capital, qualifications, and government in a post-Fordist era of mass unemployment, limited-term work, and occupational insecurity. They are sometimes complicit with these circumstances because their identities are shrouded in autotelic modes of being: work is pleasure and vice versa; labor becomes its own reward.

The reality is that the media largely remain controlled by communications conglomerates, which frequently seek to impose artist-like conditions on their workforces (the cable versus broadcast TV labor process is a notorious instance). In other words, the cognitariat—interns, volunteers, contestants, and so on—may create "cool stuff," but the primary beneficiaries of their innovations are corporations.[14] This aspect is largely missing from media studies.

In film schools, for example, work is addressed as its own reward, with unpaid internships a prize route to a selfless life to come. In other words, labor is self-sacrifice, a quasi-religious commitment to transcendence where money is grubby and volunteering or activism a higher path. Alternatively, film schools can be seen as assembly lines of masculine privilege. Thirty years ago, Michelle Citron and Ellen Seiter explained that women were marginalized in production classes and victimized in production texts.[15] Seiter recently revisited that work.[16] She found nothing had changed in terms of male film students' taste for having aggression toward women be the touchstone of their art. The University Film and Video Association's 2010 conference dedicated special sessions to the tendency for US film school students from across the world to emphasize brutal violence directed at women in their work.[17] When I was at the Tisch School of the Arts, I served on a committee charged with stopping male directors from cutting female actors' bodies in the name of attaining authentic performances from them.

And quite apart from the misogyny, many film school grads are of course in wonderfully satisfying jobs working for YouTube's 100 new channels, the fruit of Google's US$100 million production (and US$200 million marketing) bet that five-minute online shows will kill off TV. Explosions are routinely filmed for these channels near my old loft in downtown Los Angeles. The workers blowing things up are paid US$15 an hour.[18] Other film school graduates find employment with talent agencies, doing useful things like associating B-list celebrities with social causes in order to raise their profiles: find a major issue such as a new environmental problem or geopolitical hot spot, pitch it to your guy, set up a foundation, and await admiring press coverage. Luxury, really. But they've all got smartphones . . .

Environment

The cell phone may be the *ur*-object of the contemporary cognitariat. What are some of its impacts other than providing a means of connecting postindustrial workers to job "opportunities?" When old and obsolete cell phones, like other media technologies, are junked, they become electronic waste (e-waste), the fastest-growing component of municipal cleanups around the Global North. E-waste generates serious threats to worker health and safety wherever plastics and wires are burnt, monitors smashed and dismantled, and circuit boards grilled or leached with acid, while the toxic chemicals and heavy metals that flow from such practices have perilous implications for local and downstream water, soil, and residents. Much electronic salvage and recycling is undertaken in the Global South by preteen girls, who work with discarded television sets and computers as well as cognitariat phone castoffs to find precious metals and dump the remains in landfills. The e-waste ends up there after export and import by "recyclers" who eschew landfills and labor in the Global North in order to avoid the cost and regulation of recycling in countries that prohibit such destruction to environment and workers. Businesses forbidden to dump in local landfills merrily mail it elsewhere.[1]

There are always contradictions within utopias, of course. I visited London's in August 2013. It had a terrific exhibit that used the notion of an ecological backpack to illustrate the minerals and labor that go into our cell phones. I took a wee photo:

But alongside this excellent work drawing attention to the appalling environmental impact of mobile telephony (though nothing was said of millions killed, enslaved, and raped in the struggle over the conflict minerals that enable these gadgets) the Museum was celebrating what it immodestly called "A New Industrial Revolution." This extraordinary marvel was allegedly already "Here." I'll conclude this rant against cant by engaging the new wonder. Cognitarians, stand by for the latest wonder.

The exciting new arrival in question is three-dimensional printing — sometimes known as "additive manufacturing." 3-D offers "mass customization" — in other words, taking generic commercial designs and matching them to customers' needs through computer-aided design and manufacture. This promises to alter factory assembly, alter the global division of labor, and alter the printing industry.

Now customers are able not only to adjust specifications for home appliances, art works, or apparel online but also to actually make them. Hospitals, for instance, are tailoring hip replacements to patients' individual characteristics and dentists cater to particular gums and teeth. The customization relies on 3-D printers, which transform digital files into material objects by printing slices of molten plastic or powder. Their purchase price can be as low as US$650.[20]

But there are negative sides to this development. The US government has already reacted with concern in the face of the ability to "print" weapons using the technology: the notorious "Liberator" or "Wiki Weapon."[21] Read all about it at the website of Defense Distributed, a group that sees itself as the inheritor of free-speech traditions dating from John Milton. Before these heroes of cybertarianism were ordered to take the site down, one hundred thousand people had downloaded its deadly instructions. Of course, the idea is already under fuller development at the Pentagon, which can hardly wait to deliver customized weaponry to soldiers in the field.[22] In addition to American First and Second Amendment questions and the threat of violence, 3-D printers also raise anxieties about counterfeit and contraband products and consumer safety.[23]

But what concerns me most here is a potentially serious environmental issue, with implications for occupational and amateur health and safety. For while some analysts predict that 3-D printers will have positive environmental effects because they will reduce the amount of carbon used to transport goods over large distances, [24] recent research suggests the need for caution.[25]

Many desktop 3-D printers use heated thermoplastic extrusion and deposition. Numerous factory studies have associated such processes with dangerous aerosol emissions, but little research has been done into the new printers—and they generally lack exhaust ventilation or filtration systems. The first such investigation focuses on particle emissions, specifically ultrafine particle (UFP) concentrations, within an office using 3-D printing. The UFP emissions were alarmingly sizable. Why alarming? The trouble is that UFPs are very efficient at depositing themselves in our lungs, airways, and brains, and they may produce high concentrations of other absorbed and condensed compounds. What are the results of such exposure? The epidemiological record associates UFP concentrations with cardiorespiratory mortality, strokes, and asthma.[26]

So what should our attitude be as analysts of the media industries? The precautionary principle places the burden of proof onto proponents of industrial processes to show that they are environmentally safe. The idea is to prevent harm rather than clean up messes after the fact, with potentially fatal consequences for life—so it is about prevention rather than cure.[27] The doctrine is opposed to the more common cost-benefit analysis, which looks at the pluses and minuses of consumer satisfaction versus safety.[28] That should be a motif and guide for all our work.

Back at the Design Museum, it was quite shocking to see workers and visitors interacting directly with 3-D printers in the absence of any obvious warnings. Instead, this was a grand new cornucopia on display, with all the fun of the fair.

Celebratory endorsements as per "The Future Is Here" have become generic advertisements for an industry that may deliver far more than new kinds of efficiency and customization. And that delivery could be very toxic indeed. The partial job done by the museum in covering the horrors of cell phones is inadequate. Its appalling embrace of new toxic technologies compromises that achievement. The exhibit shows the impact of cybertarianism as the latest technological determinism — reinvented with retreads each time it is rolled out; seemingly new, but relying on the built-in obsolescence of gadgets and theories that imbue historical forgetfulness and fealty to capital. The show urges us to bind together labor and the environment in our analyses and use them to deter our seemingly overwhelming desire to find the beautiful in the new (that is actually ugly and old).

Oh, if you're still a true believer, listen to the Hot Toddies' song "HTML."

1 George Orwell, "As I Please," *Tribune*, May 12, 1944.
2 "A Cyber-House Divided," *Economist*, September 4, 2012, 61–62.
3 Christine L. Ogan, Manaf Bashir, Lindita Camaj, Yunjuan Luo, Brian Gaddie, Rosemary Pennington, Sonia Rana, and Mohammed Salih, "Development Communication: The State of Research in an Era of ICTs and Globalization," *Gazette* 71, no. 8(2009): 655–70.
4 Robert Jensen, "The Digital Provide: Information Technology, Market Performance, and Welfare in the South Indian Fisheries Sector," *Quarterly Journal of Economics* 122, no. 3 (2007): 879–924.
5 Lev Grossman, "*Time*'s Person of the Year: You," *Time*, last modified December 13, 2006.
6 "1. You.," Media Guardian 100, *Guardian*, September 1, 2013.
7 James W. Carey, "Historical Pragmatism and the Internet," *New Media & Society* 7, no. 4 (2005): 443–55.
8 Toby Miller, "The Shameful Trinity: Game Studies, Empire, and the Cognitariat," in *Guns, Grenades, and Grunts: First-Person Shooter Games*, ed. Gerald A. Voorhees, Josh Call, and Katie Whitlock (New York: Continuum, 2012), 113–30.
9 Cosma Orsi, "Knowledge-Based Society, Peer Production and the Common Good," *Capital & Class* 33 (2009): 31–51.
10 Erin Sparks and Mary Jo Watts, *Degrees for What Jobs? Raising Expectations for Universities and Colleges in a Global Economy* (Washington, DC: National Governors Association for Best Practices, 2011).

[11] Nandini Lakshman, "Copyediting? Ship the Work Out to India," *Business Week*, July 8, 2008.

[12] Ibid.

[13] Antonio Negri, *Goodbye Mister Socialism* (Paris: Seuil, 2007); Alvin Toffler, *Previews and Premises* (New York: William Morrow, 1983).

[14] Toby Miller, "The Cognitariat," *Cognitariat: Journal of Contingent Labor* 1 (2013).

[15] Michelle Citron and Ellen Seiter, "The Woman with the Movie Camera," *JumpCut: A Review of Contemporary Cinema* 26 (1981): 61–62.

[16] Ellen Seiter, "On Cable, Tech Gods, and the Hidden Costs of DIY Filmmaking: Thoughts on "The Woman with the Movie Camera," *JumpCut: A Review of Contemporary Cinema* 53 (2011).

[17] Jennifer Proctor, River E. Branch, and Kyja Kristjansson-Nelson, "Woman with the Movie Camera Redux: Revisiting the Position of Women in the Production Classroom," *JumpCut: A Review of Contemporary Cinema* 53 (2011).

[18] Sam Thielman, "YouTube Commits $200 Million in Marketing Support to Channels," *AdWeek*, May 3, 2012.

[19] Richard Maxwell and Toby Miller, *Greening the Media* (New York: Oxford University Press, 2012).

[20] Shan Li, "3D Printers Are Beginning to Make an Impression," *Los Angeles Times*, last modified July 27, 2013.

[21] Ibid.

[22] Robert Beckhusen, "In Tomorrow's Wars, Battles Will Be Fought with a 3-D Printer," *Wired,* last modified May 17, 2013.

[23] "Your Future Will Be Manufactured on a 3-D Printer," *Bloomberg.com*, last modified May 12, 2013.

[24] Thomas Campbell, Christopher Williams, Olga Ivanova, and Banning Garrett, Could 3D Printing Change the World? Technologies, Potential, and Implications of Additive Manuacturing, Atlantic Council, 2011.

25 Brent Stephens, Parham Azimi, Zeineb El Orch, and Tiffanie Ramos, "Ultrafine Particle Emissions from Desktop 3D Printers," *Atmospheric Environment* 79 (2013): 334–39.

26 Ibid.

27 Maxwell and Miller, *Greening the Media*.

28 See, for example, "The Wingspread Consensus Statement on the Precautionary Principle," the Science and Environmental Health Network, January 26, 1998.

Bibliography

"1. You." Media Guardian 100, *The Guardian*, September 1, 2013.

"A Cyber-House Divided." *Economist*, September 4, 2012.

Beckhusen, Robert. "In Tomorrow's Wars, Battles Will Be Fought with a 3-D Printer." *Wired.* Last modified May 17, 2013.

Campbell, Thomas, Christopher Williams, Olga Ivanova, and Banning Garrett. *Could 3D Printing Change the World? Technologies, Potential, and Implications of Additive Manuacturing.* Atlantic Council, 2011. Last modified October 17, 2011.

Carey, James W. "Historical Pragmatism and the Internet." *New Media & Society* 7, no. 4 (2005): 443–55.

Chmielewski, Dawn C. "Poptent's Amateurs Sell Cheap Commercials to Big Brands." *Los Angeles Times*, May 8, 2012.

Citron, Michelle, and Ellen Seiter. "The Woman with the Movie Camera." JUMP CUT: A REVIEW OF CONTEMPORARY MEDIA 26 (1981): 61–62.

Grossman, Lev. "*Time*'s Person of the Year: You." *Time.* Last modified December 13, 2006.

Jensen, Robert. "The Digital Provide: Information Technology, Market Performance, and Welfare in the South Indian Fisheries Sector." *Quarterly Journal of Economics* 122, no. 3 (2007): 879–924

Lakshman, Nandini. "Copyediting? Ship the Work Out to India." *Business Week*, July 8, 2008.

Li, Shan. "3D Printers Are Beginning to Make an Impression." *Los Angeles Times*. Last modified July 27, 2013. Maxwell, Richard, and Toby Miller. *Greening the Media*. New York: Oxford University Press, 2012.

Miller, Toby. "The Shameful Trinity: Game Studies, Empire, and the Cognitariat." In *Guns, Grenades, and Grunts: First-Person Shooter Games*, edited by Gerald A. Voorhees, Josh Call, and Katie Whitlock, 113–30. New York: Continuum, 2012.

Miller, Toby. (2013). "The Cognitariat." *Cognitariat: Journal of Contingent Labor* 1. Negri, Antonio. *Goodbye Mister Socialism*. Paris: Seuil, 2007.

Ogan, Christine L., Manaf Bashir, Lindita Camaj, Yunjuan Luo, Brian Gaddie, Rosemary Pennington, Sonia Rana, and Mohammed Salih. "Development Communication: The State of Research in an Era of ICTs and Globalization." *Gazette* 71, no. 8 (2009): 655–70.

Orsi, Cosma. "Knowledge-Based Society, Peer Production and the Common Good." *Capital & Class* 33 (2009): 31–51.

Orwell, George. "As I Please." *Tribune*. Last modified May 12, 1944.

Proctor, Jennifer, River E. Branch, and Kyja Kristjansson-Nelson. "Woman with the Movie Camera Redux: Revisiting the Position of Women in the Production Classroom." *Jump Cut: A Review of Contemporary Cinema* 53 (2011).

Seiter, Ellen. "On Cable, Tech Gods, and the Hidden Costs of DIY Filmmaking: Thoughts on 'The Woman with the Movie Camera.'" *Jump Cut: A Review of Contemporary Cinema* 53 (2011).

Sparks, Erin, and Mary Jo Watts. *Degrees for What Jobs? Raising Expectations for Universities and Colleges in a Global Economy*. Washington, DC: National Governors Association Center for Best Practices, 2011.

Stephens, Brent, Parham Azimi, Zeineb El Orch, and Tiffanie Ramos. "Ultrafine Particle Emissions from Desktop 3D Printers." *Atmospheric Environment* 79 (2013): 334–39.

Thielman, Sam. "YouTube Commits $200 Million in Marketing Support to Channels." *AdWeek*, May 3, 2012.

Toffler, Alvin. *Previews and Premises*. New York: William Morrow, 1983.

"Your Future Will Be Manufactured on a 3-D Printer." *Bloomberg.com*. Last modified May 12, 2013.

20.

On Automation in Media Industries: Integrating Algorithmic
Media Production into Media Industries Scholarship

PHILIP M. NAPOLI

Introduction

As recent efforts to define the contours of media industries
scholarship illustrate, one of the core objectives of the field is to
develop deeper understandings of the processes via which media
content is produced, consumed, and interpreted by media
audiences.[1] Such a focus inevitably requires exploring the decision-
making dynamics that take place at the individual, organizational,
and supra-organizational levels. Decision making in this context
should be understood broadly to encompass aspects such as: the
constructions of the environmental cognitions of decision makers;
the inputs that inform these decisions; and the institutional and
organizational structures that guide and constrain them.

For these lines of inquiry to respond effectively and adapt to the
rapidly changing technological conditions under which
contemporary media industries operate, a key point of focus going
forward should be on the role of algorithmically-driven automation
and how it is affecting the dynamics of media production and
consumption. Due to space constraints, the focus here will be on the
production dimension.[2] In addressing this issue, this essay provides
an overview of the roles and functions that algorithms are serving
in the dynamics of media production, and how these roles and
functions connect with core areas of media industries scholarship.
Drawing from this analysis, this essay then proposes directions for
future research.

The Algorithmic Turn in Media Production

Perhaps one of the most visible and potentially significant
transformations currently affecting media industries is the
increasingly prominent role that algorithms play in the production
of media content.[3] As the media environment grows more complex,

with audiences increasingly fragmented and empowered, and with a growing array of technologies and platforms at their disposal, media organizations are increasingly turning to "big data" and algorithms to help them effectively navigate this complex environment.[4] The two primary functions that algorithms currently perform in the media production realm are: a) serving as a demand predictor; and b) serving as a content creator.

The Algorithm as Demand Predictor

A common point of focus in media industries scholarship has been examining and critiquing the mechanisms via which media organizations navigate the inherently unpredictable marketplace demand for various forms of media content.[5] A key pattern that has been illuminated by this line of research has been a steady although contentious process of "rationalization," in which impressionistic modes of decision-making are replaced by more data-driven, analytical approaches.[6] In this big-data era, media organizations have an ever-expanding supply of data on audiences' media consumption patterns and preferences to draw upon,[7] and algorithms play a central role in extracting actionable insights and producing decision outcomes from these data stores. These are the fundamental elements of the most recent—and perhaps most dramatic—step forward in this long-running process of rationalization.

The motion picture industry, for instance, has begun to rely on predictive software packages such as Epagogix, which employs algorithms to predict the success of prospective film projects based upon the plot elements contained within the individual film scripts, linking these content characteristics with historical data on box office grosses.[8] Similarly, Netflix has been developing its slate of original programming by feeding its enormous trove of audience behavior and ratings data into a predictive algorithm that then identifies the type of original programming most likely to succeed.[9] The inputs in the Netflix case are obviously very different from the inputs being utilized by a system such as Epagogix, but the outcome is essentially the same: algorithmically-derived performance forecasts that are increasingly dictating production decisions.

Perhaps the most controversial application of such algorithmically-driven demand predictors has been in the realm of journalism. In some cases (such as Patch, AOL's hyper-local news venture), algorithms that analyze demographic, social, and political variables related to specific geographic communities and their anticipated demand for local news have been used to determine where local news outlets are established.[10] Thus, the very existence of local news operations is, to some extent, being algorithmically dictated. In other cases (but also including Patch), news organizations are increasingly relying on analyses of various forms of user behavior and feedback data to more precisely calibrate their newsgathering and reporting activities. Many newsrooms now operate with comprehensive and immediate feedback related to various aspects of online news consumption, ranging from page views to time spent on a site/story, to ratings, to volume and valence of comments.[11]

Consider also the case of "content farms." Content farms mine search-engine data to estimate demand for content on various topics, and then produce that content rapidly and cheaply in order to meet that demand.[12] Once again, the process is algorithmically-driven. Leading content farm Demand Media for instance, feeds its algorithm three types of data: a) popular search terms from search engines; b) the ad market for keywords (i.e., which keywords are currently being sought and how much is being paid for them); and c) the competitive environment (in terms of content that's already available online).[13] The output then represents a prediction of the type of content for which there is the highest unmet audience and advertiser demand, and Demand Media produces that content accordingly.[14]

The Algorithm as Content Creator

The algorithmic turn in media production is, in some instances, being enhanced in ways that go beyond demand prediction and extend into the realm of content creation. This is not to say that the human element is being eliminated from content creation. Algorithms are human creations. Rather, the point here is that the human role in content creation is migrating from a direct to an indirect role.

Algorithms already have been developed and employed to perform comparably to human content creators in areas such as poetry and music composition.[15] They are also playing an increasingly prominent role in areas of online content creation such as tweets, where a large number of tweets are automatically generated by algorithmically-driven bots.[16] This model is at the core of Narrative Science, a start-up based around a software package that can generate complete news stories once it is fed the core data on which the stories will be based (e.g., sporting event scores and statistics, company financial reports, housing data, survey data).[17]

Discussion

As should be clear, the production of media content is now, in many instances, being conducted in ways that increasingly delegate important analytical and decision-making authority to sophisticated algorithms. The long traditions of media industries scholarship that have sought to comprehend how media industries seek to understand their audiences, anticipate demand for content, and generate content must now consider how these processes are being reconfigured by this algorithmic turn in decision-making processes. Algorithms may even need to be considered a distinct media institution in their own right within the context of the production of content.[18] Understanding algorithms from this broader institutional perspective means examining not only how algorithms are being used and the outputs that result, but also the inputs — the ways in which algorithms are being constructed, and the assumptions, priorities, and inputs that underlie their construction. As much as media industries research has enhanced our understanding of the ways in which films, television programs, and music are produced, the field must similarly begin to investigate the still-opaque processes of algorithm construction.

Conclusion

Developing a deeper understanding of algorithms, their construction, and the role they play in the dynamics of media production should be a focal point of media industries scholarship. Such a focus is a natural extension of a well-established line of media industries scholarship that has sought to illuminate the decision-making dynamics that surround media industries' efforts to understand their audiences and produce the content that most effectively meets their audiences' interests.

Future research should delve into the organizational dynamics of algorithmic development, deployment, and calibration. For example, we know little at this point about the organizational dynamics surrounding the adoption and usage of algorithmic tools in the media sector. Are there intra-organizational tensions, and if so, how are they being resolved? How are established professional norms, identities, and practices adapting? How are algorithmic tools becoming legitimized in organizational processes? How are the criteria that are utilized in the construction of media industry-specific algorithms developed? How and why are they adjusted and recalibrated over time? And perhaps most importantly, how exactly are algorithms affecting the nature of the content that is produced? Are they having their intended effects in terms of improving the success rates of various forms of media content? Are there any unintended effects (either positive or negative) that have yet to be realized? Exploring questions such as these will help to ensure that media industries scholarship fully reflects the contemporary dynamics surrounding the production of media content.

1   John T. Caldwell, "Para-Industry: Research Hollywood's Blackwaters," *Cinema Journal* 52, no. 3 (2013): 157-165; Nitin Govil, "Recognizing 'Industry'," *Cinema Journal* 52, no. 3 (2013): 172-176.

2   Philip M. Napoli, "The Algorithm as Institution" (paper presented at the Media in Transition Conference, Cambridge, Massachusetts, May 2013).

3   Tarleton Gillespie, "The Relevance of Algorithms," in *Media Technologies*, eds. Tarleton Gillespie, Pablo Boczkowski, and Kirsten Foot (Cambridge: MIT Press, 2014); Napoli, "The Algorithm as Institution."

4   Thomas Davenport and Jean Harris, "What People Want to Know (and How to Predict It)," *MIT Sloan Management Review* 50, no. 2 (2009): 23-31.

5   Todd Gitlin, *Inside Prime Time* (Berkeley: University of California Press, 2000).

6   Jarl A. Ahlkvist, "Programming Philosophies and the Rationalization of Music Radio," *Media, Culture & Society* 23, no. 3 (2001): 339-358; Philip M. Napoli, *Audience Evolution: New Technologies and the Transformation of Media Audiences* (New York: Columbia University Press, 2011).

7   Napoli, *Audience Evolution*.

8   Davenport and Harris, "What People Want to Know," 23-31; Malcolm Gladwell, "The Formula: What If You Built a Machine to Predict Hit Movies?" *The New Yorker*, October 16, 2006.

9   David Carr, "Giving Viewers What They Want," *The New York Times*, February 24, 2013; Andrew Leonard, "How Netflix is Turning Viewers into Puppets," *Salon*, February 1, 2013.

10 Joseph Tartakoff, "AOL's Patch Aims to Quintuple Size by Year-End," *paidContent*, August 17, 2010.

11 C.W. Anderson, "Between Creative and Quantified Audiences: Web Metrics and Changing Patterns of Newswork in Local U.S. Newsrooms," *Journalism: Theory, Practice, Criticism* 12, no. 5 (2011b): 550-566.

12 Piet Bakker, "Aggregation, Content Farms, and Huffinization: The Rise of Low-Pay and No-Pay Journalism," *Journalism Practice* 6, no. 5-6 (2012): 627-637.

13 Daniel Roth, "The Answer Factory: Demand Media and the Fast, Disposable, and Profitable as Hell Media Model," *Wired*, November 2009.

14 Christopher W. Anderson, "Deliberative, Agonistic, and Algorithmic Audiences: Journalism's Vision of its Public in an Age of Audience Transparency," *International Journal of Communication* 5 (2011a): 529-547.

15 Christopher Steiner, *Automate This: How Algorithms Came to Rule Our World* (New York: Portfolio, 2012).

16 Zi Chu, Steven Gianvecchio, Haining Wang, and Sushil Jajodia, "Who Is Tweeting on Twitter: Human, Bot, or Cyborg?" (paper presented at the ACSAC Conference, Austin, Texas, December 6-10, 2010).

17 Steve Lohr, "In Case You Wondered, A Real Human Wrote This," *The New York Times*, September 10, 2011.

18 Napoli, "The Algorithm as Institution."

Bibliography

Ahlkvist, Jarl A. "Programming Philosophies and the Rationalization of Music Radio." *Media, Culture & Society* 23, no. 3 (2001): 339-358.

Anderson, C.W. "Deliberative, Agonistic, and Algorithmic Audiences: Journalism's Vision of Its Public in an Age of Audience Transparency." *International Journal of Communication* 5 (2011a): 529-547.

Anderson, C.W. "Between Creative and Quantified Audiences: Web Metrics and Changing Patterns of Newswork in Local U.S. Newsrooms." *Journalism: Theory, Practice, Criticism* 12, no. 5 (2011b): 550-566.

Bakker, Piet. "Aggregation, Content Farms, and Huffinization: The Rise of Low-Pay and No-Pay Journalism." *Journalism Practice* 6, no. 5-6 (2012): 627-637.

Caldwell, John T. "Para-Industry: Research Hollywood's Blackwaters." *Cinema Journal* 52, no. 3   (2013): 157-165.

Carr, David. "Giving Viewers What They Want." *The New York Times*, February 24, 2013.

Chu, Zi, Steven Gianvecchio, Haining Wang, and Sushil Jajodia. "Who is Tweeting on Twitter: Human, Bot, or Cyborg?" Paper presented at the ACSAC Conference, Austin, Texas, December 6-10, 2010.

Davenport, Thomas and Jean Harris. "What People Want to Know (and How to Predict It)." *MIT Sloan Management Review* 50, no. 2 (2009): 23-31.

Gillespie, Tarleton. "The Relevance of Algorithms." In *Media Technologies*, Tarleton Gillespie, Pablo Boczkowski, and Kristen Foot, eds. Cambridge: MIT Press, 2014.

Gitlin, Todd. *Inside Prime Time*. Berkeley: University of California Press, 2000.

Gladwell, Malcolm. "The Formula: What If You Built a Machine to Predict Hit Movies?" *The New Yorker*, October 16, 2006.

Govil, Nitin. "Recognizing 'Industry'." *Cinema Journal*, 52, no. 3 (2013): 172-176.

Leonard, Andrew. "How Netflix is Turning Viewers into Puppets." *Salon*, February 1, 2013. Lohr, Steve. "In Case You Wondered, A Real Human Wrote This." *The New York Times*, September 10, 2011.

Napoli, Philip M. *Audience Evolution: New Technologies and the Transformation of Media Audiences.* New York: Columbia University Press, 2011.

Napoli, Philip M. "The Algorithm as Institution." Paper presented at the Media in Transition Conference, Cambridge, Massachusetts, May 2013.

Roth, Daniel. "The Answer Factory: Demand Media and the Fast, Disposable, and Profitable as Hell Media Model." *Wired*, November 2009.

Steiner, Christopher. *Automate This: How Algorithms Came to Rule Our World.* New York: Portfolio, 2012.

Tartakoff, Joseph. "AOL's Patch Aims to Quintuple Size by Year-End." *paidContent*, August 17, 2010.

21.

"It's TV's Fault I Am This Way": Learning From Love
Hating the Media Industries

PHIL OPPENHEIM

This essay, which suggests potential directions for students and critics of media industry studies to consider, began not as a critical analysis but as a tirade.[1] Neil Genzlinger, the television critic for the *New York Times*, aimed for a bit of whimsy during the height of the 2013 summer cable original series season. Recognizing that we were experiencing many good television programs at once — *too* many, really, enough to create a "surplus" — Genzlinger suggested that the federal government might need to intervene.[2] What we "need," he argued, is something comparable to the Agricultural Adjustment Act of 1933, a way to control the creative spigot so that our troughs don't overflow with stuff we're unable to consume. TV has never produced more great series, "but we can't choke them down as fast as they're being produced. We need a Television Adjustment Act of 2013."[3] I got the joke, of course. Still, I bristled at the snarky, but ultimately industry-cheerleading, message. Gentzlinger's piece stirred pent-up suspicions that I had similarly felt after attending presentations at academic media conferences heralding our current "golden age" of television and the triumph of recent "quality television." Had academics as well as journalists unwittingly joined the PR departments of the networks?

More recently, Michael Wolff, professional gadfly and columnist for *USA Today*, restored my faith in skeptical journalism with a hilariously mean-spirited, probably unfair troll targeting a handful of network executives. He attacked them as "empty suits" whose skill sets consisted not of creating or shepherding golden-age content but instead of "managing up, hogging credit, grabbing power, terrifying staff and relentlessly managing . . . [their] own press."[4] The executives Wolff named all wore "the emperor's empty suits," but Wolff's article suggests that the aesthetic, intellectual, and business vacuum at their core was endemic to the industry as a whole. "That's network television!" his screed concludes, "as it has always been, and as it remains, even with just about everyone saying how passionately they are focused on reinventing the business."[5] My amusement at whiffing Wolff's stink-bomb editorial was short lived, however, for within five hours I happened upon *TV Week* managing director Chuck Ross's apologist rejoinder.[6] According to Ross, not only was Wolff (who is himself, in the words of an anonymously cited friend, "well, an 'empty suit,' and . . . a rather unpleasant person") wrong in his assessment of executives ("I have rarely interviewed a top executive who I actually thought was an empty suit"): he was also wrong about the entire industry. "The jobs are real," Ross opines, "and these executives—like most everyone involved in network TV, from those at the studios to those at the stations to those at the networks themselves—are working their asses off trying to figure out how to put on programming that most of us want to watch and will tune in to."[7]

Ross's rebuff of Wolff might have made me, by proxy, feel pretty good about myself, my career, and my industry. To confessionally out myself, *I* am a TV executive. In reality, it made me once again worry about the state of industrial criticism. Believe me, I love when all kinds of critics, journalists, and academics champion and praise our programming. I am both proud of and humbly grateful for the networks' accolades, awards, and—most gratifyingly—the viewers. But, perhaps perversely, I also revel in bare-knuckled takedowns, aggressive criticisms, and scorchingly passionate attacks on the industry. I think it makes for a healthier cultural ecosystem. And, like the best TV, it's also fun to watch.

My fondness for diatribes aimed at my cherished vocation isn't a function of mere pathological perversity. Coming of age in the late 1970s and early '80s, flirting with academia in the mid-eighties, and landing in cable TV in 1989, waves of antimedia discourses shaped my sense of the media industries.

As a teenager, I may have been blissfully ignorant of Jerry Mander (and his *Four Arguments for the Elimination of Television*, 1978), but I was painfully, repeatedly made aware of Ronny Zamora.[8] Zamora was the fifteen-year-old Floridian who killed his eighty-three-year-old neighbor after watching too many hours of TV and one too many episodes of *Kojak* (1973–1978)—or so went his defense. As my high school teachers lectured, it was TV's fault that Ronny was this way. (The court, of course, found otherwise, and Zamora — not the defense's witness Telly Savalas — was found guilty.) "If you and I can be influenced to buy products by a 30-second commercial, an hour commercial for murder is going to get through to his [and your] head thousands of times," argued the defense.[9] As one might expect, anti-television hectoring by adult authority figures had the opposite of the intended effect: television's dangerousness made it more attractive, not less.

At the same time, I was lucky enough to be the right age (sixteen), in the right place (New York), at the right time (1977); the explosion of punk played a constitutional role in my identity formation. My sense of media culture was fundamentally rooted in punk. While there was never an agreed-upon consensus of what punk aesthetics were — being oppositional, reifying its sensibilities would serve to only to kill it — one could (safety) pin together a loosely formed punk critique of mass media.

On the one hand, punks argued that television and radio were stultifying cultural industry manufacturers that churned out a homogenized culture and slathered it onto a passive, narcotized, captive audience, defusing any of its potential to provoke thought or feeling. Radio "is in the hands of such a lot of fools trying to anesthetize the way that you feel," Elvis Costello famously spat; the medium is littered with generic acts that "all sound . . . the same to me."[10] Television was as bad, if not worse, peopled with gun-toting Starskys and Kojaks who were "always on the TV / 'cause killers in America / work seven days a week."[11] All in all, radio and TV were banal and boring, prompting punks to become their own creative producers, bashing out three-chord (or fewer) anthems and DIY distribution and marketing strategies. As the Desperate Bicycles proclaimed in the title of their 1977 self-produced classic 45, "The Medium Was Tedium": if you didn't make your own culture, you were doomed to consume somebody else's mass-produced junk, the last stop in an assembly line of "just another commercial venture."[12]

On the other hand, punk's position toward mass culture wasn't simply total rejection. Punks hated television and radio in many ways because of what it had become. Punky retrofuturism helped them embrace what they thought media once was and to imagine its future promise. Punk godfathers the Velvet Underground understood that "despite all the amputations / you could just dance to a radio station," and radio-blasted rock 'n' roll could still save your life.[13] AM radio still had a mystical power, and "help[ed] me from being lonely late at night," especially when it was infused with "the spirit of 1956."[14] The Ramones articulated the sensibility well: they fervently felt that radio was important and reclaimable, which is why "we want the airwaves, baby / if rock is gonna stay alive."[15]

Similarly, when punks didn't hate television, they loved it.[16] Again, they directed most of their love toward retro series — whether it was by "watchin' *Get Smart* on TV," covering theme songs from sixties cartoons, or mix-mastering old sci-fi and dance-party TV shows (e.g., anything from the B-52s' first album, in 1979).[17] Even contemporary shows were lovable, given enough beer. While Black Flag's embrace of pop TV was ironic in its 1981 single "TV Party", a function of boredom and stupidity more than connoisseurship ("I don't bother to use my brain anymore / There's nothing left in it"), they still managed to reveal a funny fan's view of favorite shows: "*That's Incredible! / Hill Street Blues! / Dallas!...Saturday Night Live! Monday Night Football! Dynasty! Fridays!*" Punk's oppositional aesthetics valorized trash and embraced no-budget "junk," like the *Joe Franklin Show* (1950–1983) in one famous example. Meanwhile, punk viewed middlebrow culture with suspicion, loathed "quality," and spurned well-packaged products that critics, teachers, and parents acknowledged as high art. My punk-inspired hatred for media culture was concomitant with my punky love for it.

By the time I actually began my career in the industry — I joined TNT during its first year, in September 1989 — punk had been dead for nearly a decade,[18] but a new antimedia critique had entered my landscape. The students and faculty I'd left behind in graduate school (Emory PhD dropout, 1989) started affixing a strange new sticker to their bumpers: we, the loyal listeners of NPR and readers of the *New Yorker*, were all now commanded to "kill your television." TV was still mind-rotting garbage, but now we could do something more dramatic than "eliminate" it. We could *destroy* this home invader, make like Elvis and blast it to smithereens.[19] Bruce Springsteen's unavoidable 1992 hit "57 Channels (and Nothin' On)" provided the movement with an anthem. He borrowed from Ant Farm's famous 1975 stunt *Media Burn* for his music video, which crashed a Cadillac into a flaming wall of TVs as part of a vague, impressionistic critique. Giggling pyromaniacs Beavis and Butt-head added fuel to the fire—literally—a year later. In the Plasmatics' punk video that also appropriated *Media Burn*, they expressed their love for burning stuff, thus throwing their show into the middle of debates about imitative behavior and ultimately getting the episode "banned" from the air.[20] In 1994—the same year in which my colleagues and I launched Turner Classic Movies—TV-Free America launched as a nonprofit dedicated to consciousness-raising about our national dependence on TV. They instituted TV Turnoff Week as a way to make us aware of how addicted we really were. In part, I understood and sympathized with the middlebrow assault on television; a lot of what was on the air was junk. Yet I still *loved* a lot of that junk. The 1990s and 2000s TNT institutions like *MonsterVision* (1993-2000), *100% Weird!* (1993-2000), *Lunchbox TV* (1995-1999), and *Bad Movies We Love* (1993-1994) were all testimonies (along with TBS reruns of Minow-baiting[21] sitcom *Gilligan's Island*, 1964-1967, among many others) that proved I was not alone. And, of course, we at the network were proud of running great shows, movies, cable original movies, and (soon) original series. Indeed, we reached the point of bragging that we were the home of "The Good Stuff" (one of TNT's earliest slogans).

I'm belaboring this decades-old, perhaps solipsistic industrial autobiography not to gloat over the failed efforts to euthanize my industry or to try to bring back punk (as unrevivable as my seventies-era hair or waistline, alas) but to suggest some ways for media industry students and scholars to think about their work. I hope my example proves a simple truth: it's okay and healthy to be conflicted about the media. I've met many students in media programs who seem all too willing to embrace roles as sort of adjuncts to the industry, squelching criticisms of the media as a pre-professional defense strategy so as not to jeopardize their first steps on their media career ladders. As my own experiences demonstrate, self-critical reflection is not an impediment to a TV gig or career. Other students seem to ascribe semi-supernatural abilities to media executives, believing their focus to be laser-like and their strategic executions flawless as they draw eyeballs to their products and money from everyone's wallets. While I'd admit to thinking that we're a pretty smart bunch of folks who have extraordinary batting averages, I'd also strongly suggest that students would learn much from investigating our failed product rollouts, botched mergers, dead-end technologies, missed opportunities, and outright flops. I have been glad to see that so many scholars at so many conference panels want to talk about a newly canonical set of TV series—I love those shows too. I would, however, also love to see more conversations about series entrepreneurs, phenomena, oddball performers, atypical viewers, weird trends, industrial misreadings of shifting market dynamics, and technological and corporate initiatives that never bore fruit, as well as analyses of artifacts of *unpopular* popular culture. With apologies to legendary DJ (and punk icon) John Peel, I want to hear something I haven't heard before. Who knows: perhaps we in the culture industries can learn something about ourselves from the kind of fractured reflection such critiques will reveal to us? Might we thereby achieve an oft-imagined and rarely realized reciprocity—at arm's length—between academe and industry?

Finally, like Chuck Ross, I've never met an empty suit, and all of my industrial colleagues are proud of what they do and *do* work their asses off—but it's fine with me if you think otherwise, and say so in print and conferences. Have fun at our expense. I look forward to reading and hearing what you've got to say.

---

1 The quote in the title of this article is taken from the song: Ramones, "Carbona, Not Glue," Sire, 1977, LP.

2 Neil Genzlinger, "A Television Adjustment Act for Viewers Who Can't Keep Up," *New York Times*, August 19, 2013.

3 Ibid.

4 Michael Wolff, "How Empty Are Television's Suits?," *USA Today*, October 7, 2013.

5 Ibid.

6 Chuck Ross, "You Know That Executive the Network Just Hired? What an A-Hole!" *TVWeek* (blog), October 7, 2013.

7 Ibid.

8 Jerry Mander, *Four Arguments for the Elimination of Television* (New York: Quill, 1978).

9 B. Drummond Ayres Jr., "Influence of TV Fails as Defense Plea," *New York Times*, October 7, 1977.

10 Ramones, "Do You Remember Rock and Roll Radio?" *End of the Century*, Sire, 1980, 33 ⅓ rpm.

11 Clash, The. "I'm So Bored with the USA," *The Clash*, CBS, 1979, 33⅓ rpm (single originally released in 1977).

12 Desperate Bicycles, "The Medium Was Tedium," *The Medium Was Tedium / Don't Back the Front*, Refill Records, 1977, 45 rpm.

13 The Velvet Underground, "Rock and Roll," *Loaded*, Warner, 1990, compact disc (originally recorded 1970).

14 Modern Lovers, "Roadrunner," *Modern Lovers*, Rhino/Berserkley, 1989, compact disc.

15 Their love also contained a threat: "Keep rock 'n' roll music alive / Mr. Programmer / I got my hammer / And I'm gonna / Smash my / Smash my / Radio." Ramones, "We Want the Airwaves," *Pleasant Dreams*, Sire, 1981, 33⅓ rpm.

16 When mass media struck back and responded to punk, its reaction was less equivocal. Phil Donahue, for instance, staged a shouting match between "punkers" and their unfairly treated moms ("Parents of Punkers," *Phil Donahue Show*, 1984). The eponymous forensics pathologist *Quincy, M. E.* infamously offered punk music as a murder weapon in the infamous episode "Next Stop, Nowhere" (1982). Tom Snyder mocked punk with condescending fogeyism on *The Tomorrow Show* (1973–1981, see particularly his Johnny Rotten/John Lydon interview from 1980). Officer Poncherello upstaged a gang of punkers when he broke out a rendition of "Celebration" in the finale to the 1982 *CHiPs* episode "Battle of the Bands," and Vicki Lawrence's geriatric alter ego taught a trio of female punk rockers to dress like housewives and warble like the Andrews Sisters in 1989's *Mama's Family* episode "Bubba's House Band" — both of which ran ad nauseam on (unsurprisingly, perhaps) TNT and TBS, respectively.

17 Ramones, "Danny Says," *End of the Century*, Sire, 1980, 33□ rpm; The Dickies, "Gigantor," *The Incredible Shrinking Dickies*, A&M, 1979, 33⅓ rpm.

18 Punk's echo boom — fueled largely by MTV — began in the late 1980s with the rise of "grunge" and crested in 1991, *The Year Punk Broke* (the name of an influential 1993

documentary). I'll leave the debate over the importance of this movement to bar arguments and Twitter fights.

[19] The Elvis-shot-at-TV myth was itself a distortion, of course. As real fans know, Elvis shot at Robert Goulet while in his Vegas hotel room; he hated the singer, not the medium. Visitors to Graceland know that TV held a special place in Elvis's heart: three side-by-side sets line one wall of his "TV Room."

[20] Kristofor Brown and Mike Judge, "Scared Straight," *Beavis and Butt-head*, MTV, September 27, 1993.

[21] Newton Minow was US Federal Communications Chairman from 1961 to 1963. Fueled by his ire over the "dictatorial power" that Minow bequeathed to the networks in the wake of his "vast wasteland" jeremiad, *Gilligan*'s creator, Sherwood Schwartz famously christened the ill-fated tiny ship the *S.S. Minnow*. For more details, see Robert M. Jarvis, "Legal Tales from *Gilligan's Island*." *Santa Clara Law Review* 39.1 (1998): 185-205. Quotation from page 202.

Bibliography

Ayres, B. Drummond, Jr. "Influence of TV Fails as Defense Plea." *New York Times*, October 7, 1977.

Genzlinger, Neil. "A Surplus of Good TV? Try Depression Economics." *New York Times*, August 19, 2013.

Jarvis, Robert M. "Legal Tales from *Gilligan's Island*." *Santa Clara Law Review* 39.1 (1998): 185-205.

Ross, Chuck. "You Know That Executive the Network Just Hired? What an A-Hole!" *TV Week*, October 7, 2013.

Wolff, Michael. "How Empty Are Television's Suits?" *USA Today*, October 7, 2013

22.

Politically Charged Media Sites: The "Right," the "Left," and the Self in Research

YEIDY RIVERO

German novelist Thomas Mann famously quipped that "everything is politics." Even if as researchers we recognize the truth of that statement, we are often not prepared to confront the complicated politics of our own ideologically charged sites of study in media. With right-wing dictatorships, scholars generally analyze the media within the broader context of that totalitarian system. More challenging, however, are the locations in which political rule is aligned with the left but those in power have appropriated some dictatorial practices similar to those in right-wing regimes. Because intellectuals have regularly constructed these places associated with the left as somewhat utopian (for example, less racist, less elitist, less capitalist driven), they have regularly failed to critique the idealized regimes' undemocratic practices. This sightlessness, of course, has an impact on those who conduct media research on these "utopian" sites.

I was unaware of this scholarly shortcoming until I gave a presentation seven years ago at a Society for Film and Media Studies Conference. At the time, I was beginning my research on Cuban commercial television (1950–1960), and I wanted to share some of my early "discoveries." My talk focused specifically on media practices from 1950 to 1953, well before the triumph of the Cuban Revolution, which was thus not mentioned in the presentation. My remarks included the terms *dictator* and *dictatorship* in reference to President Fulgencio Batista and his regime during that period. I had mentioned Batista's name at the beginning of the talk and, for the sake of variety and avoiding repetition, I subsequently sprinkled in the other terms. Given that the audience comprised highly educated people, I assumed they all knew the basic political history involving Cuba and Batista. In other words, I assumed that at the very least, they had seen *The Godfather: Part II* (1974). Then the question-and-answer period began, and the first comment for me came from a man who said, "I do not know why you are referring to Castro as a dictator when there are much worse leaders who deserve that title and are not called as such." Confused—in part because I had never even uttered the "C" word—I replied, "I am sorry, I do not understand." The man repeated his question. With a smile on my face I channeled all the poise and etiquette lessons I was forced to learn as an adolescent and answered, "There seems to be a misunderstanding. I was talking about Fulgencio Batista not Fidel Castro," and I moved on to the next question.

Perhaps the guy had been dozing during the presentation or was daydreaming about revolutions in general, or maybe he showed up late. Regardless, his comment and the assumptions behind it did more than produce an awkward conference moment for me. The experience revealed to me that revolutionary Cuba and Fidel Castro were untouchable subjects for many US scholars. As a recent article observes regarding the lack of criticism of Cuban policies by left-wing North American and Latin American intellectuals, no one has "recognize[d] it [Cuba] as a dictatorship."[1] A similar process also occurs with the topic of Venezuela. As a left-wing and highly educated Venezuelan colleague recently told me, "left-wing intellectuals in the US defend the concept of the [Venezuelan] revolution, the idea. Most of the time they lack concrete data or even partial data." But the problem with these idealized research sites is not only that many intellectuals avoid critical assessment; the problem for the researcher is that regardless of one's political position, what is said about the media in the "utopian" sites or about media artifacts produced by people against the "utopian" regimes tends to put the scholar on one side of the ideological spectrum. As a result, scholars find it necessary to provide extra information to justify why the research is relevant. Let me provide an example.

In her seminal essay, "Greater Cuba," film scholar Ana López takes up the task of charting the creative trajectory and artistic production of Cuban exiles and Cuban American filmmakers from the 1970s to the 1990s. [2] Early in the piece she raises an intriguing quandary: why is it that when cinema scholars analyze exile cinema, the studies unavoidably focus on the production of exiles escaping conservative and murderous regimes, leaving aside the creators

172

who have left socialist states such as Cuba? As López writes regarding the marginalization of Cuban exile filmmakers, "Although buttressed by official U.S. policies and actions against Cuba since 1961, Cuban exile film- and video-makers have paradoxically had a difficult time articulating their arguments and being heard. Within artistic circles, their exile has, in general, not been a privileged position from which to speak."[3] While López convincingly explains the relevance and ideological diversity of the Cuban exiles' cinematic productions, the fact that she needs to justify her analysis or clarify that not all Cuban exiles are reactionary rich people who want to see the system collapse reveals some of the issues facing those researching politically charged media sites. Certainly, in López's case, the fact that she is a Cuban American scholar probably added another layer of meaning to her writing on Cuban exiles' films. As a Cuban American woman (and accordingly a daughter of Cuban exiles), she is already grouped with the ideological right wing regardless of her own political views. But despite a researcher's ethnicity, dealing with politically charged sites invariably comes with left-wing or right-wing baggage that might impact the reception of one's research. Believe me, no one will question your political views if your research topic is *Breaking Bad* (2008–2013), *The Golden Girls* (1985–1992), or the rise and decline of *Buffy the Vampire Slayer* (1997–2003). How then should one deal with the complexities of politically charged media sites? How do you prepare for the guy who might have been dozing and who thinks you called Castro a dictator?

I asked colleagues who conduct research in Cuba and Venezuela to provide some advice to graduate students and young scholars who are researching politically charged media sites. The following tips would in fact apply to most research sites. However, given the complexities of "utopian" sites where the political terrain can be slippery, the tips below from my colleagues and me are important to stress.

1. Do not reject or embrace a particular ideological position before conducting the research.

2. Have a strong historical understanding of the location, its political shifts, and its media industries before conducting the research.

3. Be fluent in the language of your research site and engage with the literature produced in the site as well as the one produced outside the site (beyond the United States).

4. Treat institutional responses, pamphlets, and information as sources to be questioned and analyzed, not as "the truth."

5. If possible, talk to people from a diverse range of political positions.

6. Always remember to be respectful of other people's opinions even if you disagree with what is being said.

7. Recognize your own assumptions and remember that those assumptions may not translate to other places. For example, saying that market competition among networks and cable has improved the quality of US programs might be offensive to people who are critical of capitalism.

8. Support your claims with solid data rather than with romanticized generalizations.

9. If you are being questioned or attacked at a conference, be calm and always go back to your sources.

While paying heed to this advice, one should also enjoy the research process. I found it very rewarding to spend time with people who, while sharing the same language and many cultural traits, had a drastically different upbringing and worldview form my own. And yes, I need to admit that even though I was cautious about the comments I made at the center where I conducted my research in a socialist country, some members of the Communist Party were nonetheless shocked by some of my "cautious" remarks. Live and learn. However, despite a few awkward moments and the risk of being called a Castro hater or a Castro lover, I do not regret the selection of the topic and research site. What I do regret is that, because of the politics of academia and the left-wing and right-wing baggage associated with Cuba, in the introduction of my forthcoming book I felt the need to disclose my ethnic background and discuss the fact that I have no personal investment in the past, present, or future of Cuba. I would never have needed to make that sort of qualification if I were simply analyzing sexuality in *The Golden Girls*.

1 Duanel Díaz Infante,"Revolución Cubana, Crítica Latinoamericana, y Academia Norteamericana," *Diario de Cuba,* accessed April 29, 2013, http://www.diariodecuba.com/de-leer/1367137602_2990.html.

2 Ana López, "Greater Cuba," in *The Ethnic Eye: Latino Media Arts,* ed. Chon Noriega and Ana López (Minneapolis: University of Minnesota Press, 1996), 38–58.

3 Ibid., 40.

Bibliography

Infante, Duanel Díaz. "Revolución Cubana, Crítica Latinoamericana, y Academia Norteamericana." *Diario de Cuba.* Accessed April 29, 2013.

López, Ana. "Greater Cuba." In *The Ethnic Eye: Latino Media Arts,* edited by Chon Noriega and Ana López, 38–58. Minneapolis: University of Minnesota Press, 1996.

23.

Film Studies, Cultural Studies, and Media Industries
Studies

THOMAS SCHATZ

I'll begin with an anecdote. A few years back, I contributed an essay on Hollywood history to the collection *Media Industries: History, Theory, and Method*.[1] When I submitted the piece, co-editor Jennifer Holt mentioned that she was delighted to have something that dealt with authorship and film style. I thought that a bit odd at the time, but when the book was published I understood what she meant. While I was pleased to be included in that excellent collection, the volume as a whole had little to say — remarkably little, it seemed to me — about individual agency in the creation of media content, about the formal style and expressive qualities of individual works, and about the analysis and assessment of media texts. I immediately flashed back to that moment of realization when I was invited to write this brief reflection on media industries research. I find myself asking whether the issues that were so crucial to the emergence of film studies back in the 1960s and '70s are of central importance, or of any real importance at all, to the burgeoning field of media industries studies.

The centrality of these questions to film studies a half century ago was the result of conditions in both the film industry and the academy. American cinema and indeed world cinema were then in the throes of profound change, with the rise of national movements like the French New Wave and New German Cinema; the prominence of international auteurs like Bergman, Fellini, and Kurosawa; and the surprising emergence of the Hollywood renaissance. Cinema suddenly was being taken seriously as an art form as well as a social and cultural phenomenon, particularly by a new generation of critics — Andrew Sarris, Pauline Kael, et al. — and by a new generation of scholars in the arts and humanities programs where film studies first took hold. For these critics and scholars, individual artists and great works were the coin of the realm, and thus their preoccupation with auteurism and canon

177

formation. Meanwhile, on another academic front, the truly explosive impact of structuralism and semiotics had scholars and intellectuals radically rethinking the very notion of culture and reassessing the once reviled "culture industries." This laid the groundwork for cultural studies, which coalesced during the 1970s in close confluence with film studies in the US and UK.

Both the industrial and academic landscapes have changed considerably since then. The prospect of a "directors' cinema" in the US or anywhere else has become increasingly remote since the 1970s, as have the modernist and art-cinema impulses that fueled that unique, exceptional era. The critical and theoretical agendas evolved as well, due largely to industry changes but also to more complex approaches by film scholars (if not critics and journalists) to questions of authorship, aesthetics, and the production of culture. These issues still fuel film studies, obviously enough. But whether (and how) they pertain to media industries studies remains to be seen—and remains, for me, a crucial issue. It seems to me imperative that we keep in mind the fact that the media industries are *cultural* industries involving the systematic production and consumption of expressive, meaningful works that manifest our shared sense of ourselves, our lives, our values. We who study the media are obliged to examine the industrial process, with its necessary compulsion for standardization and commodification. But we are also obliged to identify and account for instances of disruption and innovation, the differences that truly *make a difference* in the industrial production of culture.

As the study of media industries develops, I cannot help but notice a decided slant toward a political economy approach—analyses that focus on ownership and control, on technology and policy, on marketing and consumption, with only incidental concern for the creative and cultural dynamics involved. I do not wish to rehash the political economy versus cultural studies debate. On the contrary, media industries studies demands that we integrate these two vital and complementary (if seemingly contrary) ways of seeing and assessing the media. It demands that we consider not only media ownership but also the means and modes of production as well as the products themselves. It demands that we examine the mainstream and the margins of media production and consumption, trying to understand and assess a broad range of expressive, meaningful work. It demands that we ask what constitutes authorship in the context of cultural production, and what creative and administrative work roles really matter in the production process. We must ask whether the industrial machinery functions to facilitate, enable, or even allow for individual human agency, let alone personal expression. Under what circumstance, and to what ends, do the media industries promote (pun intended) the individual author? Has the very notion of authorship in contemporary media-making become little more than a discursive construction, a necessary journalistic fiction, and a marketing ploy?

These questions of creativity, commerce, and cultural production are cogently addressed in a recent essay in *Critical Studies in Media Communication*, "Culture Industries in a Postindustrial Age: Entertainment, Leisure, Creativity, Design," by Raúl Rodríguez-Ferrándiz.[2] As his title suggests, Rodríguez-Ferrándiz advocates a return to the Frankfurt School's original term *culture industries*. The label dates back to the 1940s, of course, to Adorno and Horkheimer's devastating critique of mass media and mass culture. [3] But as Rodríguez-Ferrándiz points out, our view of culture and its systematic (re)production has been recast and rehabilitated by Umberto Eco, Stuart Hall, John Fiske, Pierre Bourdieu, and other scholars. From their more nuanced perspective, "Consumption in general and its most eminent form, the consumption of culture, constituted an arena for a genuine construction of meaning, or at the very least, for a reappropriation for purposes that could not be anticipated, rather than a mere displaying of the meanings which had been craftily placed there by the producers of culture." [4]

Rodríguez-Ferrándiz prefers the term *culture industries* to other current labels — *entertainment industries, leisure industries*, and particularly, *creative industries*. The latter is widely used in Europe and Australia, he notes, and tends to dominate the discussions (and policy legislation) related to cultural production. In the process, the very concept of "creative work" has been diluted of all nuance and precision: "We have passed from the anguish and disappointment

Adorno felt on seeing the creative act of the artist swallowed up by the logic of industry, to qualifying the entire industry as 'creative,' to place creativity itself at the very heart of this industry." [5] Rodríguez-Ferrándiz does not include *media industries* in his inventory of labels, although he acknowledges "the communicative explosion of all industrial production in a media environment."[6] This is scarcely an oversight, since he is considering industries like fashion design and the performing arts that do not involve media in their delivery and consumption. But clearly the study of media industries falls within his general purview and is subject to the same essential questions about the "genuine construction of meaning" and the tendency simply to take for granted—and thus, ultimately, to overlook—the creative practices and protocols involved.

With the media industries expanding and cross-pollinating at a furious pace, these questions of innovation and authorship have never been more acute, and in fact a good many film and television scholars are addressing them. Consider the work being done in television studies on cable series programming and the role of the showrunner, for instance, and the ongoing wrangle in film studies over the indie movement and the role of the indie auteur. But significantly enough, particularly for my purposes here, it's worth noting that this work is being done in very separate scholarly quarters, and for the most part outside the media industries studies arena as well.[7] This seems shortsighted and rather ironic for several reasons. One is that the emerging media industries studies field itself owes such an obvious debt to breakthrough authorship studies in the 1980s—Tino Balio's two-volume history of United Artists, for instance, and the work by Jane Feuer, et al., on MTM Enterprises and "quality television."[8] A second is that the scholarly work both on showrunners and on indie auteurs is so clearly attuned to the industrial milieu in which these content creators are operating. And yet a third reason is that industry conditions in the convergent, conglomerate era are actively compelling the migration of top talent between the film and television sectors—in both directions, in fact, and at a dizzying rate.

Media Industries provides a venue in which these developments can and should be assessed, along with the larger theoretical issues involving the entrenched and very different conceptions of individual agency and authorship in film and television studies. Film scholars continue to focus authorship studies on the director, a work role that is rarely even mentioned, let alone seriously considered, in discussions of TV series authorship. Television scholars, meanwhile, tend to gauge authorship in terms of the producer or the writer — or both in the case of the showrunner, who invariably rose through the writers' ranks to a management role, and who oversees the series as an executive producer while directly supervising the writing staff. These very different views of authorship are a function of the distinct modes of production involved, although these distinctions are rapidly blurring under current industry conditions. What are we to make, for example, of Lena Dunham, who reworked a modest indie film-festival hit into an auteur-driven HBO series (*Girls*, 2012 –), and who did so as a multi-hyphenate, twenty-something female — an unthinkable achievement in the retrograde movie industry? Or *True Detective* (2014 –), perhaps the single best example to date of cable television's — and particularly HBO's — appropriation of the indie film ethos on both sides of the camera? Or J.J. Abrams and the billion-dollar reboot of Paramount's primordial Star Trek franchise?

The list goes on and on, and spans a widening array of media industries, each with its own regimes of production and expression. As the forces of convergence and conglomeration bring these industries — and these regimes — into closer accord, issues of production and expression become ever more important and more complex. Indeed, the challenges posed when dealing with adjacent industries like film and television seem rather modest once we begin to factor, say, the gaming and software industries into the equation. But as the established culture industries evolve and as new industries coalesce, the same core questions pertain. How do these industries systematically create both capital and culture? How do they value standardization and innovation in the production and consumption of media content? What work is required to produce that content, and which work roles — and which workers — are privileged in that process? Questions of ownership and control pertain as well, of course, but these should be considered alongside — and in dynamic interaction with — those that address the expressive power and appeal of culture industry products.

---

1 Jennifer Holt and Alisa Perren, eds., *Media Industries: History, Theory, and Method* (Malden, MA: Wiley-Blackwell, 2009).

2 Raúl Rodríguez-Ferrándiz, "Culture Industries in a Postindustrial Age: Entertainment, Leisure, Creativity,

Design," *Critical Studies in Media Communication* (2013): 1-15, accessed October 20, 2013, doi:org/10.1080/15295036.2013.840388

3 Horkheimer, Max, and Theodor W. Adorno. Dialectic of Enlightenment: Philosophical Fragments. (Stanford, CA: Stanford University Press, 2002).

4 Rodríguez-Ferrándiz, " "Culture Industries in a Postindustrial Age," 2.

5 Ibid., 11.

6 Ibid., 1.

7 There are as few exceptions here, particularly among recent books on the indie film movement that focus on individual and corporate authorship within an industrial context. These include Geoff King, *Indiewood USA: Where Hollywood Meets Independent Cinema* (London: Tauris, 2009); Yannis Tzioumakis, *Hollywood's Indies: Classics Division, Specialty Labels, and American Independent Cinema* (Edinburgh: Edinburgh University Press, 2012); and Alisa Perren, *Indie, Inc.: Miramax and the Transformation of Hollywood in the 1990s* (Austin: University of Texas Press, 2013).

8 Tino Balio, *United Artists, Volume 1, 1919-1950: The Company Built by the Stars* (Madison: University of Wisconsin Press, 2009); Tino Balio, *United Artists, Volume 2, 1951-1978: The Company That Changed the Film Industry* (Madison: University of Wisconsin Press, 2009); Jane Feuer, Paul Kerr, and Tise Vahimagi, eds., *MTM 'Quality Television'* (London: British Film Institute, 1985).

Bibliography

Balio, Tino. *United Artists, Volume 1, 1919-1950: The Company Built by the Stars*. Madison: University of Wisconsin Press, 2009.

Balio, Tino. *United Artists, Volume 2, 1951-1978: The Company That Changed the Film Industry*. Madison: University of Wisconsin Press, 2009.

Feuer, Jane, Paul Kerr, and Tise Vahimagi, eds. *MTM 'Quality Television.'* London: British Film Institute, 1985.

Holt, Jennifer, and Alisa Perren, eds. *Media Industries: History, Theory, and Method.* Malden, MA: Wiley-Blackwell, 2009.

Horkheimer, Max, and Theodor W. Adorno. *Dialectic of Enlightenment: Philosophical Fragments.* Stanford, CA: Stanford University Press, 2002.

King, Geoff. *Indiewood USA: Where Hollywood Meets Independent Cinema.* London: Tauris, 2009.

Perren, Alisa. *Indie, Inc.: Miramax and the Transformation of Hollywood in the 1990s.* Austin: University of Texas Press, 2013.

Rodríguez-Ferrándiz, Raúl. "Culture Industries in a Postindustrial Age: Entertainment, Leisure, Creativity, Design." *Critical Studies in Media Communication* (2013): 1-15.

Tzioumakis, Yannis. *Hollywood's Indies: Classics Division, Specialty Labels, and American Independent Cinema.* Edinburgh: Edinburgh University Press, 2012.

24.

Navigating the Two Worlds of Research

JAMES SCWOCH

When I posit that there are Two Worlds of research, I imagine at least three general reactions. One reaction for many might well be "what a silly thing to say" or similar (with wits and wags adding "well look at who said it, what else would you expect?"). A second reaction for many others might be to say "Yes, and the Two Worlds are . . ." and state the two worlds they happen to see. And a few might say I am simply preparing my riff mannered on the philosophy of Andy Warhol, getting ready to go from A to B and back again.[1] Those with the first reaction may well choose to read no further. Those with the second reaction may find what follows something to ponder. And to those with the third reaction: thank you for associating me, even fleetingly, with someone who understood media industries far more brilliantly than I do.

Many problems pop up with the claim of Two Worlds of research, not the least of which is: why two? Why not one; why not many; why not several? In part, I choose two in resigned recognition of what seems to be the habit, choice, insistence, realpolitik, or dream of so many: simply put, you (or me, or whoever) either do "this" or "that" form of research. Qualitative or quantitative. Institutional or critical. Humanities or social sciences. Well, these are some of the Two Worlds out there, and readers can doubtless identify even more sets of Two Worlds. Mind you, I myself do not particularly like the lived experience of the Two Worlds, whatever Two Worlds happen to be on the table at the moment. I much prefer a world without Two Worlds (and I prefer the possibilities of a multiverse of research worlds). Often when the Two Worlds concept crops up (whichever set of Two Worlds has emerged at the moment) and the advocates of either one or the other of the Two Worlds launch their discursive gyrations in favor of their one world of preference, the momentum surges into claiming the one-world identity for those present who are not adherents to either of the Two Worlds. Yet despite your personal silence or voiced objections, claims are made by others on your behalf as to whether you are, or are not, an authentic member of their world (and truth be told, the real problems emerge when these same claims by others about you are made in your absence, because that increases the probability that those claims might stick). When this happens to me, sometimes I remember an essay written a while back by Linda Alcoff, who wrote eloquently about the problems and misunderstandings that can arise when one speaks for another. In this regard, making claims by, for, and about others — especially when those others are not present or are otherwise unable to speak for themselves — risks misrepresentation and divisiveness in research communities. An alternative is to navigate through research communities in ways that seek inclusiveness while also respecting the value of differences.[2]

By now you likely gather I personally find the whole Two Worlds thing a bit painful. But I assure you, dear reader, this missive is not my oblique way of turning you into my therapist. It's not my emotional discomfort that leads me to write about navigating the Two Worlds of research but rather my deep pragmatism. Much as I may prefer things otherwise, the pragmatist in me recognizes that Two Worlds is a concept that courses through much of the lived experience of participating in research communities. Two Worlds in some variant or another will regularly rear its head: in the faculty meeting, the research seminar, the grant proposal, the interview, the book prospectus, the journal review — well, the possibilities are endless. Two Worlds is a construct that needs to be navigated — again and again — in order to have a productive research experience.

I have two suggestions for researchers navigating the Two Worlds (or, to shuffle the title of this essay, Two Worlds of research navigation). Again, my pragmatism surfaces with offering two suggestions: simply put, having more than one route among your options is more often than not an advantage. In that vein, multiple routes of navigation probably increase the range of advantages (at least up to a point where confusion might begin to surface through a welter of options, but remember, this essay is about the Two Worlds — no more, no less). Hopefully, offering two suggestions for navigation also helps me to diminish any perceptions that my goal for this essay is to be prescriptive. I'm skeptical about the value of prescriptiveness, because I believe it (intentionally or not) undermines the value of difference, and I value difference. Therefore, I suggest.

My first suggestion may ring a note of familiarity: maximizing, when feasible, the use-value of transforming Two Worlds separated by the word *or* into Two Worlds separated by the word *and*. Qualitative *and* quantitative. Critical *and* institutional. Humanities *and* social sciences. This transformation increases the possibilities of difference, it increases the possibilities of inclusiveness, and it is resonant with multidisciplinarity.

My second suggestion is to expand the multiverse of Two Worlds by offering a wider range of conceptual possibilities for Two Worlds. This may seem counterintuitive in that expanding the sets of Two Worlds might raise the risk of additional navigation challenges, and this is true. However, this expansion might also present new navigational challenges that are in fact easier to navigate than a smaller, more traditional collection of Two Worlds. Put another way, if navigating the Two Worlds is a familiar challenge of research — and it is for many — having a bigger set of Two Worlds to choose from might increase your ability to find, at any given moment, one particular set of Two Worlds that can be successfully navigated. In other words, look for opportunities to see the world — indeed, see two worlds — in new ways, and in ways that foster inclusiveness. Some sets beyond the traditional concepts mentioned earlier that I — and likely many of you — have from time to time found useful include:

- global and/or local
- old media and/or new media
- creating data to analyze and/or analyzing preexisting data

More sets of Two Worlds can be generated, and I welcome the emergence of additional sets for *Media Industries*. Having a multiverse of Two Worlds at hand will better enable *Media Industries* to navigate the vexing problems of excluding work on the basis that it does not represent the one world preferred over the other. Preference of one or the other world is not to be avoided, but rather might be done in ways that minimize the risks from diminishing the values of difference. Having many sets of Two Worlds to choose from and navigate will also allow *Media Industries* to better navigate in ways that sail toward the values of research evident in work that is compelling, controversial, rigorous, finely crafted, and carefully detailed, and work that opens new avenues for future research opportunities, because *Media Industries* will have more options for navigating toward those research values.

Navigating a multiverse of Two Worlds of research sets the stage for *Media Industries* to be prodigious in its quantity, and also creates the conditions for the journal to achieve distinction in its quality. Congratulations to *Media Industries* on its launch, and best wishes as the voyage to navigate many worlds of research now gets underway.

---

[1] Andy Warhol, *The Philosophy of Andy Warhol (From A to B and Back Again)* (New York: Harcourt Brace Jovanovich, 1975).

[2] Linda Alcoff, "The Problem of Speaking for Others," *Cultural Critique* 20 (Winter 1991–92): 5-32.

Bibliography

Alcoff, Linda. "The Problem of Speaking for Others." *Cultural Critique* 20 (Winter 1991–92): 5-32.

Warhol, Andy. *The Philosophy of Andy Warhol (From A to B and Back Again)*. New York: Harcourt Brace Jovanovich, 1975.

25.

Advertising, the Media, and Globalization

JOHN SINCLAIR

The media industries are different from other industries because of
their privileged place in social communication and the perception
that they wield extensive influence on public opinion, cultural
norms and values, and the popular imaginary. This truism applies
particularly to the advertising industry, for not only does
advertising have a high visibility in the cultural environment: it is
also the most vital source of the revenue that supports and
motivates the vast majority of commercial media. It could even be
said that advertising is the media industry that stands behind all
the other media industries. However, research approaches of past
decades have tended to concentrate upon the products of the
advertising industry — that is, advertisements and their cultural
significance — rather than penetrating beyond to the industry as
such, including its political and cultural economy; the relations
between advertisers, advertising agencies, and the media; and
actual advertising practices. More contemporary research has
focused directly on these fundamentals, particularly in the context
of globalization and the complex transition from "old" to "new"
media.[1]

The very meaning of "advertising" is in flux, for the advent of the
internet has transformed the character of advertising media as we
have known it. The comfortable relationship between advertisers,
agencies, and media that existed throughout the golden age of mass
media in decades past — in which the media would offer content
that could attract audiences so as to sell access to those audiences to
advertisers via the agencies — is a business model that is now under
severe pressure. The interactive properties of the internet, with the
affordances of social networking and direct commercial
transactions, have precipitated a shift in the balance of power
between advertisers and consumers. These properties have also
caused advertising revenue for television, still the dominant
medium for advertising in most national markets, to grow more

slowly as advertisers increasingly favor the internet. Meanwhile, on the internet itself, emergent business models compete for hegemony.

With the growth of the internet, it becomes more evident that advertising is just the most visible and public dimension of a much broader, but still quite familiar, set of practices intent upon harnessing our ways of life for commercial purposes. These practices include sponsorship, notably of sport and the arts; in-store displays, sales promotions, competitions and giveaways; and direct marketing, such as telemarketing. In the past, media advertising was referred to in the industry as "above the line," while the various forms of nonmedia marketing, such as those just mentioned, were deemed "below the line." However, the line has been crisscrossed so much now that it is obliterated. Not only is media advertising ever more incorporated into sales promotions — for instance, television commercials promoting giveaway toys in McDonald's — but advertising campaigns are now devised on a "cross-platform" basis, meaning that such campaigns are mounted across traditional media, the internet, and perhaps other, more direct "touchpoints" where they can reach prospective consumers. Marketing practitioners and textbooks now tend to conceive of advertising in the context of what they like to call "integrated marketing communications." This may sound like empty industry hype, but the phrase does express how advertising is now linked strategically to the other dimensions of marketing, and to other forms of promotion.[2]

Given the triumph of neoliberal ideology in recent decades, it may be difficult to appreciate that there was a time when Marxism — or at least, a "cultural" version of it — was extremely influential in setting the agenda for media and communication research. In conjunction with feminist perspectives, this neo-Marxism generated a great deal of research and theoretical critique in the 1980s, when advertising was considered to be a prime instrument for the reproduction of consumer capitalism and patriarchy, as revealed by semiological-structuralist analysis. The classic example is Judith Williamson's *Decoding Advertisements*.[3] This type of scholarship put emphasis on advertisements rather than advertising as such, a focus of inquiry that was interesting and useful for a time but that ultimately exhausted itself. A version of Marxism more attuned to political economy instead paid attention to advertising's role in "commodification," that is, how advertisements endow goods with an "exchange value" beyond their actual usefulness. This concept is still part of the critical lexicon, but is not so much a heuristic and analytic concept as a rhetorical trope used to denounce all cultural forms in which commerce encroaches upon spheres of life where it ought not belong.

In the 1990s, the study of advertising came to be seen within a larger, more inclusive context, framed within a broad critique of "consumer culture" and the society that supported it. The same decade saw attention shift to the dynamics of the advertising agency. Several researchers, such as William Mazzarella,[4] drew upon anthropology, employing that discipline's characteristic methodology of ethnography, usually by working in advertising agencies as participant-observers. This work represented something of a focal shift, centered less on advertising and the media as such and more on advertising practice.

A prominent theoretical contribution came from Scott Lash and John Urry, who argued that the economy and culture were becoming ever more integrated.[5] They particularly saw a "culturalization" of economic production, meaning that goods and services were designed to attract certain kinds of consumers and to fit with their lifestyles. This work typified the "cultural turn" of the 1990s, a broad movement away from political economy in favor of more emphasis on systems of symbolic meaning and the reflexivity of subjects within culture, a trend that attracted attention to the study of advertising as the complex fusion of economy and culture. Prior to the cultural turn, it was sufficient to "get a life," but both the discourse of marketing and its critique promoted the idea that what we each needed was a lifestyle as a way of defining our individuality by knowingly constructing a distinctive pattern of consumption for ourselves.

However, a recurrent criticism of Lash and Urry's thesis about the "aestheticization" of goods and services in "consumer society" is that it is too "epochal" to posit as a new and decisive phase in the history of capitalist modernity.[6] If it makes any sense at all to talk about a consumer society, critics say, its genesis is better thought of, and studied empirically, as the result of incremental shifts rather than a qualitative, epoch-defining leap. There is also the issue of the complex moral baggage carried not so much by the consumer culture–society couplet in itself as by *consumerism*, the total ethos of social values on which it is said to rest. This is a term familiar from both academic and popular critiques of how we live now, and used by both conservative and progressive sides of the spectrum. Yet it is a normative term, almost devoid of analytic meaning. Everybody is opposed to consumerism, from the Pope to Occupy Wall Street.

The 2000s have seen a shift of attention toward a quite specific marketing and advertising practice, namely that of branding, particularly in its relation to popular culture and new media. Some of the best contemporary academic work is on branding, rather than on advertising as such.[7] Particularly since the era of large-scale corporate takeovers of brands in the 1980s, advertising has become consciously harnessed to the process of branding. More than uniquely identifying a product or its manufacturer, advertising enables brands to acquire cultural meanings, such as status distinctions (Harrod's versus Marks & Spencer), associations with certain kinds of people (the Marlboro man), and even something like their own personalities. Just as mediated popular culture sustains a world of celebrities, so it does also for the world of goods. However, if brands are the celebrities, then commodities are the masses — and, as Marx could not have anticipated, it is actually brands, not commodities, that are fetishized. Modern-day Marxists can agree that branding contributes to a mystique that conceals the value of the labor that made the product: branding is a process through which commodification takes place.

Indeed, one influential theorist of branding, Adam Arvidsson, invokes "autonomous" Marxism to make the argument that — although it is people (whether a nation or a subculture) who create "trust, affect and shared meanings" — what brand marketers do is to pick up on these meanings and exploit them by associating these meanings with particular products and services.[8] This is a capitalism that is more reflexive in the sense that it recognizes the rise of an independent popular culture but seeks to bring it under the control of commercial interests. Consumers, in this view, are more reflexive in understanding their own responses in relation to advertised goods. Yet Arvidsson also acknowledges that consumer perceptions are "beyond the direct control of capital."[9] Far from imposing brand images upon unwitting targets, brand managers have to protect their brands from falling victim to ridicule or disrepute. Young consumers in particular are inclined to participate in ruthless parodies and spoofs of branded advertising that they discern to be manipulative and inauthentic, and new social media such as YouTube, Facebook, and Twitter allow the diffusion of such material on a global scale. At the same time, advertisers and their agencies are fascinated by the internet's ability not only to target young consumers but also to exploit their social networking behavior, so they play the dangerous game of strategically planting advertising or other marketing material on the internet that they hope will go viral, that is, be picked up and passed on by users, thus creating buzz around the brand.

Many, perhaps most, of the brand names that we know via advertising and other modes of marketing in our national markets are in fact owned by global corporations. Some of these corporations are companies that grew from local to national scale, mainly in the United States and Western European countries, becoming in the 1960s and 1970s what were called the multinational, or transnational, corporations. Others, the colossi of the internet age, have become global only in recent decades, notably Google, Microsoft, and Apple. Among all these, the main clients of the advertising agencies and big spenders on media are the manufacturers of "FMCG" (fast-moving consumer goods), or everyday packaged food, household, and personal products. Corporations like Procter & Gamble and Unilever, both with hundreds of brands under their corporate umbrellas, can be found on the lists of biggest advertisers in most countries of the world.

In step with the globalization of such clients and the media carrying their advertising, the advertising agency business itself has become highly globalized in its organization. The real crucible of the present era was the 1980s, when the UK-, France-, and Japan-based agencies rose to challenge US industry domination at a global level. Certain British agencies, buoyed by stock market "financialization," bought out several Madison Avenue agencies. This was the beginning of globalization proper. The putative national origin of agencies became less important than the combined interpenetration of capital from different national origins; and more importantly, a completely new stratospheric level of ownership and management was created in the form of the global advertising group, or "mega-group." The world advertising industry has since evolved into a small number of complexly integrated holding groups that, to use the trade discourse, incorporate "creative" advertising agency networks along with "media-buying" specialist agencies, and businesses in a series of related marketing "disciplines," which include internet or digital advertising, as well as public relations, market research, direct mail, and similar "marketing services." These structures are a manifestation of how "integrated marketing communications" have eclipsed the mediacentric advertising of the past.

Indeed, with the remarkable growth of social media and other internet use, digital advertising is attracting ever more advertising revenue. Apart from the crisis this trend has presented for "legacy" media, particularly print, it has given rise to more commercio-technical areas of advertising practice, such as in the exploitation of "big data," and in "programmatic advertising," the computer-programmed placement of advertisements. The avid attention that advertising agencies are now giving to digital media is an index of the degree to which the once-comfortable relations between agencies, media, and advertisers now have been destabilized as the era of mass media morphs into the age of the algorithm.

---

[1] John Sinclair, *Advertising, the Media and Globalisation: A World in Motion* (New York: Routledge, 2012).

[2] George E. Belch, Michael Belch, Gayle Kerr, and Irene Powell, *Advertising and Promotion: An Integrated Marketing Communication Perspective* (Sydney: McGraw Hill Australia, 2014, 3e).

[3] Judith Williamson, *Decoding Advertisements* (London: Marion Boyars, 1978).

[4] William Mazzarella, *Shovelling Smoke: Advertising and Globalization in Contemporary India* (Durham, NC: Duke University Press, 2003).

[5] Scott Lash and John Urry, *Economies of Signs and Space* (London: Sage, 1994).

[6] Liz McFall, *Advertising: A Cultural Economy* (London: Sage, 2004), 99.

---

7 Melissa Aronczyk and Devon Powers, eds., *Blowing Up the Brand* (New York: Peter Lang, 2010).

8 Adam Arvidsson, "Brands: A Critical Perspective," *Journal of Consumer Culture* 5 (2005): 236–37.

9 Ibid., 242.

Bibliography

Aronczyk, Melissa and Devon Powers, eds. *Blowing Up the Brand.* New York: Peter Lang, 2010.

Arvidsson, Adam. "Brands: A Critical Perspective." *Journal of Consumer Culture* 5 (2005): 235–58.

Belch, George E., Michael Belch, Gayle Kerr, and Irene Powell. *Advertising and Promotion: An Integrated Marketing Communication Perspective.* Sydney: McGraw Hill Australia, 2014 3e.

Lash, Scott, and John Urry. *Economies of Signs and Space.* London: Sage, 1994.

Mazzarella, William. *Shovelling Smoke: Advertising and Globalization in Contemporary India.* Durham, NC: Duke University Press, 2003.

McFall, Liz. *Advertising: A Cultural Economy.* London: Sage, 2004.

Sinclair, John. *Advertising, the Media and Globalisation: A World in Motion.* New York: Routledge, 2012.

Williamson, Judith. *Decoding Advertisements.* London: Marion Boyars, 1978.

26.

Selling Television: Addressing Transformations in the
International Distribution of Television Content

JEANETTE STEEMERS

> *Over the coming decades and across the
> world, internet TV will replace Linear TV.
> Apps will replace channels, remote controls
> will disappear and screens will proliferate.
> As internet TV grows from millions to
> billions, Netflix, HBO, and ESPN are
> leading the way"*[1] - Netflix (2013)

The demise of television, and broadcasting in particular, has long
been forecast and debated. Current discussion suggests that linear
television either faces imminent oblivion or a future that looks only
mildly promising. Instead of the top-down model practiced by
broadcasters in the past, there are now opportunities for a
multitude of organizations and individuals to post, distribute, and
react to content on many different platforms — and this of course
includes the international distribution of television-type content. If
it all goes according to plan there will be a further shift from the
idea of scheduled, appointment–based viewing towards an
audiovisual environment that is more on-demand and engagement-
based.

What is interesting about US internet television provider Netflix's
assertion above, however, is the total belief in the demise of linear
television and confidence in the ability of commercial US-based
players to adapt to the new realities "across the world." Non-US
players do not feature in Netflix's vision of the future at all. What is
also interesting is the implicit emphasis on distribution, what Alisa
Perren has usefully pinpointed as the "space in between"
production and consumption.[2]

What is interesting about US internet television provider Netflix's
assertion above, however, is the total belief in the demise of linear
television and confidence in the ability of commercial US-based

players to adapt to the new realities "across the world." Non-US players do not feature in Netflix's vision of the future at all. What is also interesting is the implicit emphasis on distribution, what Alisa Perren has usefully pinpointed as the "space in between" production and consumption.[3]

The emphasis on distribution is also significant because it stresses the technicalities of distribution (the internet, channels, remote controls, screens, etc.) rather than content itself and the wider political, economic, and social context, which are part and parcel of distribution. A lot of industrial and academic attention has been paid to current trends associated with digitization and the emergence of alternative distribution platforms, but technology is only one factor in the transformation of the screen industries that also encompasses longstanding trends such as commercialization and deregulation,[4] which influence the circumstances under which content is produced, circulated, and received.

What can't be denied is that while television, or perhaps more accurately, audiovisual media, are unlikely to die any time soon, the way they are delivered is set to radically change.[5] At this point, some distinctions have to be made. For the purpose of this piece, the focus is on the international trade in television programming as distinct from film distribution, the practice of transporting content using physical infrastructure, or individuals uploading content online. International television distribution has traditionally taken place between companies (distributors) that have content to license (either their own or their clients') and buyers (broadcasters, but also cable and satellite networks, DVD companies, product licensees, and more recently online players such as iTunes and Netflix) who require licensed content to satisfy their schedules, on-demand offerings, and product lines. International television distributors, who are often producers as well, are now also heavily involved in other aspects of the business, including co-production financing, the management of format production in different markets, intellectual property, licensing merchandise, and brand marketing across different platforms and markets (which are still largely determined by geography). In regard to international distribution, however, scholarly focus still tends to be on the circulation of film (and mainly US films at that), rather than the distribution of television content, let alone television content that is not produced in the US.[6]

From this perspective, it is useful to review how the international television distribution market has changed in recent years in order to establish possible avenues for future research. The last big transformation in distribution occurred in the 1980s and 1990s, when a combination of deregulation and satellite television led to a massive expansion in the number of TV channels worldwide, increasing opportunities for trade in television programs and formats. US media conglomerates vigorously pursued these opportunities for international expansion by establishing "localized" versions of their globally branded channels.[7] At the same time, some non-US players also sought to take advantage of what appeared to be a growing marketplace.[8]

British players were especially active in looking overseas to expand their business. This was the focus of my 2004 monograph, *Selling Television: British Television in the Global Marketplace*, in which I discussed Britain as the world's second largest exporter of television programming after the US. At the time, British exporters were experiencing one of their periodic highs with big-budget factual programming (*Walking with Dinosaurs*, 1999), game show formats (*Who Wants to be a Millionaire?*, 1998 - present) and children's content (*Teletubbies*, 1997 - 2001) selling well globally due to demand in that most lucrative yet typically difficult-to-penetrate of international markets, the US, which rarely acquired overseas material at all. This situation reflected the larger television environment at the time. There were some countries (primarily the US) that made internationally attractive television content (mainly drama) that sold well worldwide. For those with the right content, it was a lucrative business. But in the case of completed ready-to-air programs (as opposed to formats), it was a market dominated in 2007 by US companies who accounted for an estimated 76 percent of all finished programs exported, compared to 7 percent from the UK, which followed in second place.[9]

Some UK policymakers and industry executives felt that Britain was seriously underperforming as an exporter, especially in the contemporary drama genre which was deemed "too dark; too slow; unattractive; too gritty or socio-political"[10] with "distasteful characters," "storylines," and downmarket lifestyles that reinforced a negative image of Britain.[11] UK government policies became focused on consolidating the television industry, which in turn allowed for the emergence of larger "super-indies" — independent producers. Those super-indies were better equipped at raising funding for and producing glossy, internationally attractive content,[12] including formats, for which the UK was estimated to account for half of all exported hours in 2007.[13] Nevertheless, for all of globalization's assumed impact and the expansion in television channels and formats at this time, complex national markets with their cultural, legal, and regulatory barriers; the preference for local production if it was available; and the role of national buyers as gatekeepers who regulated the flow of imports still really mattered. Unless you were a US company with lots of movies and TV series, it was difficult to sell content to overseas buyers because they usually had limited slots and/or limited budgets.[14]

Moving forward to 2013, a great deal has changed. The creation of new digital channels and on-demand services on the internet is dramatically altering the market, which in turn demands new ways of examining complex and evolving trends in the cross-border distribution and flow of content. Yet some things haven't changed much at all. In 1990, Richard Collins wrote about British television presenting to the world "a costumed image of Britain as a rigidly but harmoniously hierarchized class society" through the likes of *Brideshead Revisited* (1981) and *Upstairs Downstairs* (1971 – 1975).[15] British costume dramas still pull in viewers in the US but don't typically attract audiences in non-English speaking markets. In 2012, Britain's biggest international drama success was *Downton Abbey* (2010 – present), the upstairs-downstairs saga of an English aristocratic family, which attracted good audiences for PBS in the US and appreciative press. What was different, however, was that US company NBCUniversal has owned Carnivals Films, the company behind *Downton Abbey*, since 2008. In this respect,

Downton Abbey represents a good example of the challenges around the production of expensive dramas. With the fragmentation of audiences and revenues in recent years, we have seen more company consolidation and international co-production to support the high costs of origination. We have also seen a rise in sales of reality entertainment and factual formats by UK content owners.

Now the international market for television appears to be changing yet again. The latest developments in more mature markets focus on over-the-top video delivery directly to television sets via the internet through major US players Apple, Netflix, Google, and Amazon. This has been accompanied by suggestions that linear TV will disappear in the face of multiple multimedia platforms and that on-demand content might eventually replace scheduled programming. Looking beyond the US, what do these changes mean for the funding and delivery of televisual content? Is there a conceptualization of the processes and theories associated with the international circulation of content that will help explain its implications for production industries?

Media industry studies, as formulated by this journal, offers a good way of tackling these shifts and recognizing the interrelated nature of production, distribution, and consumption rather than pursuing the more narrowly defined paths adopted by the fields of political economy and cultural studies. It also offers a means for us to explore what is meant by distribution and how it functions internationally:

- In what ways, for example, do content aggregators like YouTube change old distribution patterns by providing access to new content from new players, as well as circulating content from traditional players?
- To what extent will the YouTube model or models offered by Amazon and Netflix stimulate and fund productions that individuals can locate easily and are willing to purchase?
- Who are the new players in international television distribution? In what ways are they different from existing players and how are existing players responding?
- How will the business of international distribution, which has traditionally been based on personal relationships between sellers and buyers (also gatekeepers) in different countries, adapt to more direct channels of distribution over the internet?
- What is the role of governments in stimulating the export and restricting the import of cultural products, including audiovisual content? How effective are government policies that seek to provide tax breaks for what is seen as particularly exportable content such as drama, animation, and video games—a policy recently adopted by the UK treasury to assist UK content producers?

- Is it possible to pinpoint longer-term patterns that connect with the past rather than pursuing a raft of contemporary developments that might not have long-term explanatory value?

For scholars looking at the increasingly complex ways in which television content is circulated internationally, it is important to track how industry practices are changing in regard to development, fundraising, and marketing to international markets. If the distinction between production and consumption is blurring, how does this blurring impact the international marketplace? Above all, it is important that scholars no longer focus primarily on North America and those developed markets that have been the traditional target markets of American product. With emerging media economies in Asia, Latin America, the Arab world, and Africa it is important that we expand the scope of our analysis to include more comparison across cultures and across media to reflect both the growing diversity of distribution and the extent to which television might share distribution characteristics with other media. Finally, it is crucial that we access and dialogue with industry respondents from different parts of the distribution business (sales, acquisitions, licensing, legal affairs, format production, intellectual property, marketing) in order to illuminate the complexities of a business that is about much more than just selling television shows internationally.

---

[1] Netflix Corporation, "Netflix Long Term View," last modified October 21, 2013.

[2] Alisa Perren, "Rethinking Distribution for the Future of Media Industry Studies," *Cinema Journal* 52(3) (2013): 166.

[3] Alisa Perren, "Rethinking Distribution for the Future of Media Industry Studies," *Cinema Journal* 52(3) (2013): 166.

[4] Maria Michalis, "Thirty Years of Private Television in Europe – Trends and Key Moments," in *Private Television in Western Europe*, eds. Karen Donders, Caroline Pauwels, and Jan Loisen (Basingstoke: Palgrave, 2013), 38.

[5] Timothy Havens and Amanda Lotz, *Understanding Media Industries* (Oxford: Oxford University Press, 2012), 206.

6 Exceptions include: Stuart Cunningham and Elizabeth Jacka, *Australian Television and International Mediascapes* (Cambridge: Cambridge University Press, 1996); Timothy Havens, *Global Television Marketplace* (London: British Film Institute, 2006); and Jeanette Steemers, *Selling Television: British Television in the Global Marketplace* (London: British Film Institute, 2004).

7 Jean K. Chalaby, "Television for a New Global Order: Transnational Television Networks and the Formation of Global Systems." *Gazette: The International Journal for Communication Studies* 65(6) (2003): 457–472.

8 John Sinclair, Elizabeth Jacka, Stuart Cunningham, eds., *New Patterns in Global Television: Peripheral Vision* (Oxford: Oxford University Press, 1996).

9 Television Research Partnership, *Rights of Passage* (London: PACT, 2008), 20.

10 David Graham and Associates, *Building a Global Audience: British Television in Overseas Markets* (London: Department for Culture, Media and Sport, Broadcasting Policy Division, 1999), 24.

11 Ibid.

12 See Jean K. Chalaby, "The Rise of Britain's Super-Indies: Policy-Making in the Age of the Global Media Market, " *International Communication Gazette* 72(8) (2010): 675.

13 Television Research Partnership, *Rights of Passage,* 28.

14 Steemers, *Selling Television.*

15 Richard Collins, *Television, Policy and Culture* (London: Unwin Hyman, 1990), 158.

Bibliography

Chalaby, Jean K. "The Rise of Britain's Super-indies: Policy-making in the Age of the Global Media Market." *International Communication Gazette* 72(8) (2010): 675–693.

Chalaby, Jean K. "Television for a New Global Order Transnational Television Networks and the Formation of Global Systems." *Gazette: The International Journal for Communication Studies* 65(6) (2003): 457–472.

Collins, Richard. *Television: Policy and Culture.* London: Unwin, 1990.

Cunningham, Stuart, and Elizabeth Jacka. *Australian Television and International Mediascapes.* Cambridge: Cambridge University Press, 1996.

Graham, David and Associates. *Building a Global Audience: British Television in Overseas Markets.* London: Department for Culture, Media and Sport, Broadcasting Policy Division, 1999.

Havens, Timothy. *Global Television Marketplace.* London: BFI, 2006.

Havens, Timothy, and Amanda D. Lotz. *Understanding Media Industries.* Oxford: Oxford University Press, 2011.

Michalis, Maria. "Thirty Years of Private Television in Europe – Trends and Key Moments." In *Private Television in Western Europe: Content, Markets, Policies,* edited by Karen Donders, Caroline Pauwels, and Jan Loisen, 37–55. Basingstoke: Palgrave Macmillan, 2013.

Netflix Corporation, "Netflix Long Term View." Last modified October 21, 2013.

Perren, Alisa. "Rethinking Distribution for the Future of Media Industry Studies." *Cinema Journal* 52(3) (2013): 165–171.

Sinclair, John, Elizabeth Jacka, and Stuart Cunningham, eds. *New Patterns in Global Television: Peripheral Vision.* Oxford: Oxford University Press, 1996.

Steemers, Jeanette. *Selling Television: British Television in the Global Marketplace.* London: BFI, 2004.

Television Research Partnership. *Rights of Passage.* London: PACT, 2008.

27.

Global, Regional, Transnational, Translocal

JOE STRAUBHAAR

In the excitement and hubris of youth and doctoral study fieldwork in the late 1970s, I argued that cultural dependency and cultural imperialism, at least in the Brazilian television industry, were being transformed, or Brazilianized. Given what I had read in graduate school by Herbert Schiller and others in terms of cultural imperialism and dependency,[1] I had expected a penetration of Brazil's media by US-style capitalism, by institutions such as advertising agencies,[2] by multinational advertisers,[3] by direct investment from US companies,[4] and by the co-optation of national elites.[5] Further, Schiller argued that both US industry and government had a desire to control media in other countries in order to create ideological support for a capitalist transformation. Looking at Latin America in the 1970s, Luis Ramiro Beltrán, a contemporary of Schiller and one of the main critics of development in Latin American communications study, thought he saw evidence of such ideological dominance.[6] Both theory and initial empirical studies predicted an overwhelming one-way flow of film,[7] news,[8] and television from the US to other countries.[9] Some went so far as to predict "Wall-to-Wall Dallas,"[10] in part because US culture, genres, and production values were assumed to be overwhelmingly attractive to audiences elsewhere. The outcome most feared by political economy scholars was cultural homogenization,[11] or synchronization and loss of autonomy on the part of individual nations.[12]

Yet what I had found already by the late 1970s in Brazil did not fit the holistic pattern of imperialism argued for by Schiller. Instead, I discovered a Brazilian television prime time full of local telenovelas, whose ratings showed that they were much more popular than any imported US programs. This observation led me eventually to articulate a counter-theory of the attraction of cultural proximity: that the cultural products most relevant to a local culture — either its own or from nearby or similar cultures — would be most popular.[13]

Foreign capital, at least in the television industry, had been chased out in the early 1970s, particularly since it violated the Brazilian constitution, which anticipated and prohibited such outside interference. Brazilian entrepreneurs clearly used US network models, but they also adapted them heavily.

The then proponents of cultural dependency and cultural imperialism theories were committing a mistake much like the one being made by some globalization theorists and researchers today. They overgeneralized from rapid changes in economics, economic paradigms, technology, and infrastructure to presume equivalent changes in production, content, and reception. However, my approach risked underestimating the accurate core of what political economists perceived because of the overreach of cultural imperialism theory.

In the 1970s, I did see evidence for a real trend toward the active agency of owners, administrators, producers, writers, and so forth. These Brazilian industry professionals were blending US and Brazilian economic models, administrative models, and programming ideas, thereby creating distinctive genres, like the telenovela, from a variety of sources, including US genres like the soap opera. In the 1980s, when I had a chance to do more reception-oriented research, I found a distinct preference for Brazilian programming, which was linked to a notable national impact of television in creating an imagined national community and identity.[14] However, I severely underestimated the underlying power of increasingly global capitalism, of the implantation of a mass consumer model, and of the increasing incorporation of Brazil into an integrated global economy. A key question, then, is how to resolve these tensions between what political economy tends to perceive accurately and what cultural studies tends to perceive accurately — hopefully seeing more clearly the impacts of both structure and agency in the process.

Problematizing the Global, Transnational, and National

The (over)use of the word global often tends to lead people to expect that most of the things we look at, above and below the level of the nation-state itself, are global. While macro political-economic structures and technological infrastructures may have truly global impacts, many other aspects of media industry are more often constrained or structured within domains of language and culture.

The capitalist system has been steadily penetrating more and more of the world, slowly pulling even those countries that resisted it most, such as Albania, China, and the USSR, into its orbit.[15] Advertisers, ad agencies, international program sellers, US commercial networks, media equipment manufacturers, and so forth have all tended to pull media institutions around the world into a more commercial mode of operation that articulated better with global capitalism.

In Brazil, older institutions—those not so attuned to advertising as the prime base of support, less well structured as commercial networks, and less well positioned to produce commercial programming that pleased both advertisers and audiences—declined in ratings in the 1960s and '70s. The new institutions that arose, like TV Globo, were far more adept at creating a national network,[16] refining genres like telenovelas for commercial production,[17] selling advertising,[18] and, in a broad sense, helping to pull the population into a commercial economy and to cast them as consumers. Some of this transformation and adaptation took place earlier at the regional level, where both commercial broadcasting and genre ideas from the United States were already being adapted and transformed in Cuba since the 1950s.

The case of telenovelas is a key example, carrying national, regional, and transnational cultural-linguistic, and global resonance, since TV Globo has been one of the few developing-country networks to export globally since the 1970s.[19] At one level, the expansion of global capitalism succeeded dramatically in terms of advertising global products and pulling millions of people into an upcoming economy (what are called the BRICs—Brazil, Russia, India, and China) as consumers. Observing this success, one economist pondered whether, if programming in Brazil still helped to sell soap, it mattered that the programming was Brazilian.[20] This inquiry shows both the strengths and weaknesses of political economy as an approach: it is quite right at the level of economics and the sociology of consumer society but misses the importance of culture itself. A wave of nationally oriented cultural studies in Latin America in the 1980s and 1990s showed that the cultural content of television programming mattered a great deal to individuals' understanding of cultural identity—national identity plus racial, gender, class, subcultural, and religious identities and subjectivities, as well.[21]

Another wave of studies since the 1990s, heralded most prominently by Sinclair, Jacka, and Cunningham, has attended to the regional level of analysis of media industry.[22] This includes examining national networks as primary actors but also involves fleshing out levels of analysis between the local, national, and global. Similarly, others are looking at cultural-linguistic spaces such as the Anglophone, Francophone, or Lusophone, which have built on older empires that reached beyond geographic regions like Latin America.[23]

To conclude, let us return to Brazil as an example. To understand the media industry there, one must examine it on multiple levels: the country's internal media regionalism,[24] the strong national media such as TV Globo, and its global media cities, Rio de Janeiro and São Paulo.[25] Transnationally, one must look at Brazil's role as exporter of programs, genres, formats, and models in the region of Latin America and its similar, even more dominant role in the Lusophone cultural-linguistic space that includes Angola, Mozambique, and Portugal.[26] An understanding of Brazil's political economic place in the global capitalist system—where it has been elevated into the ranks of up-and-coming global BRICs—is essential.[27] But so is an understanding of the cultural complexity of its racial, religious, and other mixtures in the context of the African diaspora,[28] as well as its diverse internal cultural geography of cities, distinctive state, and regions.[29]

---

[1] Herbert I. Schiller, *Mass Communication and American Empire* (Boston: Beacon, 1969).

[2] Fred Fejes, "The Growth of Multinational Advertising Agencies in Latin America," *Journal of Communication* 30, no. 4 (1980): 36–49.

[3] Elizabeth de Cardona, "Multinational Television," *Journal of Communication* 25, no. 2 (1975): 122–27; Luis Ramiro Beltran and Elizabeth Fox de Cordona, *Comunicacion Dominada: Estados Unidos en Los Medios de America Latina* (Mexico City: Instituto Latinoamericano de Estudios Transnacionales, Editorial Nueva Imagen, 1980).

4 Luis Ramiro Beltran and Elizabeth Fox de Cordona, *Comunicacion Dominada*

5 Theotonio dos Santos, "The Crisis of Development Theory and Problems of Departure in Latin America," in *Underdevelopment and Development: The Third World Today*, ed. Henry Bernstein (Baltimore: Penguin, 1973): 64-76.

6 Luis Ramiro Beltran, "TV Etchings in the Minds of Latin Americans: Conservatism, Materialism, and Conformism," *Gazette* 24, no. 1 (1978): 61–65.

7 Schiller, *Mass Communication and American Empire*; Kaarle Nordenstreng and Tapio Varis, *Television Traffic: A One-Way Street* (Paris: UNESCO, 1974); Thomas Guback, "International Circulation of US Theatrical Films and Television Programming," in *World Communications*, ed. George Gerber and Marsha Siefert (New York: Longman Incorporated, 1984), 153–63.

8 Oliver Boyd-Barrett, *The International News Agencies* (Beverly Hills: Sage, 1980).

9 Nordenstreng and Varis, *Television Traffic*.

10 Richard Collins, "Wall-to-Wall Dallas? The US-UK Trade in Television," *Screen* (May–August): 66–77.

11 Chin-Chaun Lee, *Media Imperialism Reconsidered* (Beverly Hills: Sage, 1980).

12 Cees J. Hamelink, "Cultural Autonomy Threatened," in *Cultural Autonomy in Global Communications*, ed. Cees J. Hamelink (London: Langman Group, 1983), 1–25.

13 Joseph Straubhaar, "Beyond Media Imperialism: Asymmetrical Interdependence and Cultural Proximity," *Critical Studies in Mass Communication* 8 (1991): 39–59.

14 Benedict Anderson, *Imagined Communities: Reflections on the Origin and Spread of Nationalism* (New York: Verso, 1983); Mauro Pereira Porto, "Telenovelas and Representations of National Identity in Brazil," *Media, Culture & Society* 33, no. 1 (2011): 53–69.

15 Immanuel Wallerstein, *The Capitalist World Economy* (Cambridge: Cambridge University Press, 1979).

16 J. Wallach, *Meu Capítulo na TV Globo* (Rio de Janiero: Editora Topbooks, 2011).

[17] Jose Bonifácio de Oliveira Sobrinho, *O Livro Do Boni* (Rio: A Casa de Palavra, 2011).

[18] Wallach, *Meu Capítulo na TV Globo.*

[19] Jose Marques de Melo, *As Telenovelas de Globo* (Sao Paulo: Summus, 1988).

[20] Omar Souki Oliveira, "Brazilian Soaps Outshine Hollywood: Is Cultural Imperialism Fading Out?," in *Beyond National Sovereignty: International Communication in the 1990s,* ed. Kaarle Nordenstreng and Herbert Schiller (Norwood: Ablex, 1993), pp. 116-31.

[21] O. F. Leal, *A Leitura Social da Novela das Oito* (Petropolis, Brazil: Vozes, 1986).

[22] John Sinclair, Elizabeth Jacka, and Stuart Cunningham, eds., *New Patterns in Global Television* (New York: Oxford University Press, 1996).

[23] Joseph D. Straubhaar, *World Television: From Global to Local.* Thousand Oaks, CA: Sage, 2007).

[24] Cicilia M. Krohling Peruzzo, "Mídia Regional e Local: Aspectos Conceituais e Tendências," *Comunicação & Sociedade* 1, no. 38 (2005): 67-84.

[25] Michael Curtin, "Media Capital: Towards the Study of Spatial Flows," *International Journal of Cultural Studies* 6, no. 6 (2003): 202–28.

[26] John Sinclair and Joseph Straubhaar, *Latin American Television Industries* (London: British Film Institute, 2013).

[27] Jim O'Neill, "Building Better Global Economic BRICs," Goldman-Sachs, GS Global Economics, last modified 2001.

[28] Michael L. Conniff, and T. J. Davis, *Africans in the Americas: A History of the Black Diaspora* (New York: St. Martin's, 1994).

[29] Arturo Escobar, "Culture Sits in Places: Reflections on Globalism and Subaltern Strategies of localization," *Political Geography* 20, no. 2 (2001): 139–74; Charles A. Perrone and Christopher Dunn, eds., *Brazilian Popular Music & Globalization* (London: Routledge, 2012).

Bibliography

Anderson, Benedict. *Imagined Communities: Reflections on the Origin and Spread of Nationalism.* New York: Verso, 1983.

Beltran, Luis Ramiro. "TV Etchings in the Minds of Latin Americans: Conservatism, Materialism and Conformism." *Gazette* 24, no. 1 (1978): 61–65.

Beltran, Luis Ramiro, and Elizabeth Fox de Cardona. *Comunicacion dominada: Estados Unidos en los medios de America Latina.* Mexico City: Instituto Latinoamericano de Estudios Transnacionales, Editorial Nueva Imagen, 1980.

Bonifácio de Oliveira Sobrinho, Jose. *O Livro Do Boni.* Rio: A Casa de Palavra, 2011.

Boyd-Barrett, Oliver. *The International News Agencies.* Beverly Hills: Sage, 1980.

Cardona. Elizabeth de. "Multinational Television." *Journal of Communication* 25, no. 2 (1975): 122–27.

Collins, Richard. "Wall-to-Wall Dallas? The US-UK Trade in Television." *Screen* (May–August): 66–77.

Conniff, Michael L., and T. J. Davis. *Africans in the Americas: A History of the Black Diaspora.* New York: St. Martin's, 1994.

Cunningham, Stuart, Elizabeth Jacka, and John Sinclair, eds. *New Patterns in Global Television.* New York: Oxford University Press, 1996.

Curtin, Michael. "Media Capital: Towards the Study of Spatial Flows." *International Journal of Cultural Studies* 6, no. 6 (2003): 202–28.

Dos Santos, Theotonio. "The Crisis of Development Theory and Problems of Departure in Latin America." In *Underdevelopment and Development: The Third World Today,* edited by Henry Bernstein. Baltimore: Penguin, 1973: 64-76

Escobar, Arturo. "Culture Sits in Places: Reflections on Globalism and Subaltern Strategies of Localization." *Political Geography* 20, no. 2 (2001): 139–74.

Fejes, Fred. "The Growth of Multinational Advertising Agencies in Latin America." *Journal of Communication* 30, no. 4 (1980): 36–49.

Guback, Thomas. "International Circulation of US Theatrical Films and Television Programming." In *World Communications*, edited by G. Gerber and M. Siefert, 153–63. New York: Longman, 1984.

Hamelink, Cees J. "Cultual Autonomy Threatened." In *Cultural Autonomy in Global Communications*, edited by Cees J. Hamelink, 1–25. New York: Longman, 1983.

Lee, Chin-Chuan. *Media Imperialism Reconsidered*. Beverly Hills: Sage, 1980.

Marques de Melo, José. *As Telenovelas da Globo*. Sao Paulo: Summus, 1988.

Nordenstreng, Kaarle, and Tapio Varis. *Television Traffic: A One-Way Street*. Paris: UNESCO, 1974.

O'Neill, Jim. "Building Better Global Economic BRICs." Goldman-Sachs. GS Global Economics. Last modified 2001.

Oliveira, Omar Souki. "Brazilian Soaps Outshine Hollywood: Is Cultural Imperialism Fading Out?" In *Beyond National Sovereignty: International Communication in the 1990s*, edited by Kaarle Nordenstreng and Herbert Schiller, 116–47. Norwood: Ablex, 1993.

Peruzzo, Cicilia M. Krohling. "Mídia Regional e Local: Aspectos Conceituais e Tendências." *Comunicação & Sociedade* 1, no. 38 (2005): 67-84.

Porto, Mauro Pereira. "Telenovelas and Representations of National Identity in Brazil." *Media, Culture & Society* 33, no. 1 (2011): 53-69.

Schiller, Herbert I. *Mass Communication and American Empire*. Boston: Beacon, 1969.

Sinclair, John, and Joseph Straubhaar. *Television Industries in Latin America*. London: British Film Institute, Palgrave Macmillan, 2013.

Straubhaar, Joseph. "Beyond Media Imperialism: Asymmetrical Interdependence and Cultural Proximity," *Critical Studies in Mass Communication* 8 (1991): 39–59

Straubhaar, Joseph. *World Television: From Global to Local.* Beverly Hills: Sage, 2007.

Straubhaar, Joseph. "Telenovelas in Brazil: From Traveling Scripts to a Genre and Proto-Format Both National and Transnational." In *Global Television Formats: Understanding Television across Borders,* edited by Tasha Oren and Sharon Shahaf, 148–77. New York: Routledge, 2011.

Wallach, Joe. *Meu Capítulo na TV Globo.* Rio de Janiero: Editora Topbooks, 2011.

Wallerstein, Immanuel. *The Capitalist World Economy.* Cambridge: Cambridge University Press, 1979.

28.

There Is No Music Industry

JONATHAN STERNE

The term "music industry" remains in wide circulation among academics, as well as in common journalistic discourse. We can find it in research on political economy, scholarship on file sharing, studies of musicians, and aesthetic analyses of recording practices. The term generally refers to the sale and purchase of recordings, the bundles of rights that go with them, and the livelihoods of people involved in that economy, ranging from musicians and fans to accountants, artists and repertoire (A&R) people, street teams, engineers, producers, lawyers, and record company executives, among others. In this conceptualization, "the music industry" is broadly concerned with the monetization of music recordings. When people write about a music industry "in crisis" or "the future of the music industry," they are generally referring to the monetization-of-recordings construct.

As I will argue, this is an incredibly limited way to understand how media industries and music interact. But first, we should understand why this nomenclature persists in media industries scholarship. There are at least two key reasons. First, to reduce the music industries to those involved with the monetization of recordings in fact adopts a public relations tactic used by groups such as the Recording Industry Association of America, in which companies that sell recordings claim to speak for musicians and by extension, music itself as a part of our cultural life. It's not that scholars are on the PR payrolls of companies but rather that we have been insufficiently attentive to the construction of our objects of research. We have accepted the "pregiven" in Pierre Bourdieu's words, rather than beginning with constructing our own objects.[1]

The "music industry" locution crystallizes a particular historical formation of music production, circulation, and consumption as ideal-typical. Some components of this formulation are worth considering as they have come under significant criticism by scholars in a number of fields:

1. An idea of "music industry" generally assumes that recordings are made up of "works," whether songs, movements, or pieces. These works have an author, are original, can be copyrighted, and can be protected by (theoretically) limited-term monopolies on circulation afforded by copyright and international trade agreements.

2. In the above model, successful musicianship is tied to successful commercialization of recordings; that is, making a living off the rights to one's original works. Of course, this immediately begs the question of what counts as originality, a matter settled in copyright law but not settled in aesthetics. We can copyright melodies, lyrics, and some timbres, but not rhythms. Therefore, only some kinds of originality count. Regardless of the genre to which this model is applied, it requires the notion of an "artist" who produces the original work, and can either hold copyright for that "work" or sell it to a holding company (i.e., a label) that will collect rent. Implied in this economic relationship is a notion of originality as the highest aesthetic ideal. Presumably that originality is a product of creativity, which is a quality that resides in the artist. Moreover, it privileges "the work" as the most important aspect of musical activity, as the work is the thing that is given monetary value and is the basis of exchange.

For several decades now, these ideas have been under criticism in a number of fields. Media industries scholars may be most familiar with the scholarship on the complexity of copyright, from Siva Vaidhyanathan's critique of "property talk" to Kembrew McLeod's critiques of the ideas of ownership of culture.[2] But an equally vital tradition exists in interdisciplinary music studies. Ethnomusicologists have attacked the work-based notion of music since at least Alan P. Merriam's 1964 *Anthropology of Music*. Writers like LeRoi Jones and Charles Keil, based on their analysis of African-American blues and jazz traditions, argue that musical meaning is inhered in collective activity and participation, not in a static text. Christopher Small's work is particularly important here.

His 1977 text *Music-Society-Education* built on Ivan Illich's philosophy of technology to argue for a diffusion of musical education and against the idea that musical talent inheres in only some people and not others. [3]

But it is Small's later book, *Musicking* (1998), which provides a particularly useful jumping-off point for media industries scholars interested in music. Small builds his argument around a simple turn: "Music" should be understood as a verb instead of a noun. As he defines it:

> To music is to take part, in any capacity, in a musical performance, whether by performing, by listening, by rehearsing or practicing, by providing material for performance (what is called composing), or by dancing. We might at times even extend its meaning to what the person is doing who takes the tickets at the door or the hefty men who shift the piano and the drums or the roadies who set up the instruments and carry out the sound checks or the cleaners who clean up after everyone else has gone. They, too, are all contributing to the nature of the event that is a musical performance.[4]

Small's point is essential: We miss a lot by focusing everything around the musicians-audiences-recordings nexus and we miss even more when we limit our understanding of music as a social practice to the objects sold as "music" in its wake. Louise Meintjes's classic ethnography of a South African recording studio also illustrates this way of thinking: behind the "making of a record" lie many varied social relations that crisscross race, gender, nation, and economy.[5]

Today we can extend Small's argument in dozens of directions. To begin with, defining "music" as a commodity is extremely limited considering the range of commodities sold through, with, or around music, ranging from musical instruments, to hardware and software, to smartphones, to speakers and room architectures.

To understand music as an industrial phenomenon goes far beyond those industries directly involved with the sale of recordings. For instance, we need to consider the music instrument industries (manufacturing, sales, marketing, development, retail, etc.), which have consistently grown during the same years that sales in the so-called "music industry" have been in decline. We need to consider rights-based work, such as soundtracks and music supervision, so central to the sound of modern television, film, and video games. We need to consider sound design in high-end automobiles, as well as sound insulation in trendy condo developments in gentrifying mixed-use urban districts. We need to consider the vast consumer electronics, computing, and bandwidth industries, not to mention companies like YouTube, which have used recorded music to market their products. Even though they don't sell music, they sell musical experiences. People pay their monthly internet bills, buy their smartphones, and visit internet sites to play music and have musical experiences.

Thus, as with its cultural life, music's economic life extends far beyond remediations of live performance. It touches upon various manufacturing industries; computer hardware and software; media conglomerates' synergy proposals and other media holdings; materials extraction, mining, refinement, and recycling; containerized shipping industries; higher education and vernacular forms of music education; real estate; the postal system; fashion; and countless other industries.

In his classic study of musical instrument industries, Paul Théberge adopted "multisectorial innovation," a term from agricultural economics, to describe what happened to electronic musicians in the 1980s and 1990s.[6] As they used devices with microchips, memory, and software, musicians and the music industry became more dependent on economic cycles in other industrial sectors—in this case, computers. The cycle toward obsolescence of musical instruments accelerated greatly during this time. These same factors also spawned a number of interesting retro and vintage markets due to the association of certain instruments with certain genres, as well as platforms for international second-hand trade, like *craigslist* or *eBay* (though to be clear, the vintage market in musical instruments has a considerably longer history than the internet).[7]

While Théberge's point is specific to instruments, it is generalizable to pretty much all industries involved with music today. This is most obvious in cases of hardware and software that orbit around the purchase and sale of recordings, as Jeremy Morris has documented.[8] But so far the scholarship has tended toward considering music as a subset of digital media industries. Scholars interested in the proliferation of recording and dissemination technologies for music will have to go beyond digital industries to consider new manufacturing techniques and standardized shipping that allow for cheap and easy outsourcing. They will have to consider the materials industries and changing politics of materials acquisition and disposal, which today shape the markets for musical instruments in countless ways. Ableton's new plastic controller for the company's widely used Live music-making software comes with a lengthy disquisition on proper disposal, alongside the other mandatory regulatory language in its manual. Meanwhile, speaker manufacturers, musicians, architects, and people involved in sound reinforcement have taken an unusually keen interest in the price of neodymium, a lightweight element that is replacing ceramic magnets in speakers, making them considerably lighter and more portable. Neodymium supply mainly comes from China, and price increases have affected the global market (a story that echoes the switchover during World War I from oil and wax to shellac finishes on disc records because of supply shortages). And those examples are drawn only from musical instruments industries. Imagine the construction of a city's new concert hall, opera house, or entertainment district as a media industries problem; or the materials inside of a smartphone; or the role of music education in musicians' and companies' online self-promotion (and not only music companies per se: Energy beverage manufacturer Red Bull has been a major player in international electronic music culture).[9]

For scholars interested in music as a media industries issue, our first analytical step must be a simple subtraction. When we go looking for unity inside a music industry, we should instead assume a polymorphous set of relations among radically different industries and concerns, especially when we analyze economic activity around or through music. There is no "music industry." There are many industries with many relationships to music.

---

[1] Pierre Bourdieu, Jean-Claude Chamboredon, and Jean-Claude Passeron, *The Craft of Sociology: Epistemological Preliminaries*, trans. Richard Nice (New York: Walter de Gruyter, 1991), 33-55.

[2] Siva Vaidhyanathan, *Copyrights and Copywrongs: The Rise of Intellectual Property and How It Threatens Creativity* (New York: New York University Press, 2001); Kembrew

McLeod, *Freedom of Expression: Tales from the Dark Side of Intellectual Property Law* (New York: Doubleday, 2005); Kembrew McLeod and Rudolf Kuenzli, eds., *Cutting across Media: Appropriation Art, Interventionist Collage and Copyright Law* (Durham: Duke University Press, 2011).

3 LeRoi Jones(Amiri Baraka), *Blues People: Negro Music in White America* (New York: William Morrow and Company, 1963); Alan Merriam, *The Anthropology of Music* (Evanston: Northwestern University Press, 1964); Charles Keil and Steven Feld, *Music Grooves* (Chicago: University of Chicago Press, 1996); Christopher Small, *Music-Society-Education* (London: John Calder, 1977); Ivan Illich, *Tools for Conviviality* (New York: Harper and Row, 1973).

4 Christopher Small, *Musicking: The Meanings of Performing and Listening* (Hanover: Wesleyan University Press, 1998), 8.

5 Louise Meintjes, *Sound of Africa! Making Music Zulu in a South African Studio* (Durham: Duke University Press, 2003).

6 Paul Théberge, *Any Sound You Can Imagine: Making Music/Consuming Technology* (Hanover: Wesleyan University Press, 1997), 62.

7 On vintage instruments, see H. Stith Bennett, *On Becoming a Rock Musician* (Amherst: University of Massachusetts Press, 1980); Tom Wilder, ed., *The Conservation, Restoration, and Repair of Stringed Instruments and Their Bows* (Montreal: IPCI-Canada, 2010).

8 Jeremy Morris, "Sounds in the Cloud: Cloud Computing and the Digital Music Commodity," *First Monday* 16, no. 5 (2011); Jeremy Morris, "Making Music Behave: Metadata and the Digital Music Commodity," *New Media and Society* 14, no. 5 (2012).

9 The environmental dimensions of media are especially important for media industries scholarship going forward. Not only do they offer a glimpse of a different valence of the "materiality" of media, a term now widely in fashion, this area is also a political front line for media reform. See Richard Maxwell and Toby Miller, *Greening the Media* (New York: Oxford University Press, 2012).

Bibliography

Bennett, H. Stith. *On Becoming a Rock Musician*. Amherst: University of Massachusetts Press, 1980.

Bourdieu, Pierre, Jean-Claude Chamboredon, and Jean-Claude Passeron. *The Craft of Sociology: Epistemological Preliminaries*. Translated by Richard Nice. New York: Walter de Gruyter, 1991.

Illich, Ivan. *Tools for Conviviality*. New York: Harper and Row, 1973.

Jones, LeRoi (Amiri Baraka). *Blues People: Negro Music in White America*. New York: William Morrow and Company, 1963.

Keil, Charles, and Steven Feld. *Music Grooves*. Chicago: University of Chicago Press, 1996.

Maxwell, Richard, and Toby Miller. *Greening the Media*. New York: Oxford University Press, 2012.

McLeod, Kembrew. *Freedom of Expression: Tales from the Dark Side of Intellectual Property Law*. New York: Doubleday, 2005.

McLeod, Kembrew, and Rudolf Kuenzli, eds. *Cutting across Media: Appropriation Art, Interventionist Collage and Copyright Law*. Durham: Duke University Press, 2011.

Meintjes, Louise. *Sound of Africa! Making Music Zulu in a South African Studio*. Durham: Duke University Press, 2003.

Merriam, Alan. *The Anthropology of Music*. Evanston: Northwestern University Press, 1964.

Morris, Jeremy. "Making Music Behave: Metadata and the Digital Music Commodity."*New Media and Society* 14, no. 5 (2012): 850-66.

Morris, Jeremy. "Sounds in the Cloud: Cloud Computing and the Digital Music Commodity." *First Monday* 16, no. 5 (2011).

Small, Christopher. *Music-Society-Education*. London: John Calder, 1977.

Small, Christopher. *Musicking: The Meanings of Performing and Listening*. Hanover: Wesleyan University Press, 1998.

Théberge, Paul. *Any Sound You Can Imagine: Making Music/Consuming Technology*. Hanover: Wesleyan University Press, 1997.

Vaidhyanathan, Siva. *Copyrights and Copywrongs: The Rise of Intellectual Property and How It Threatens Creativity*. New York: New York University Press, 2001.

Wilder, Tom, ed. *The Conservation, Restoration, and Repair of Stringed Instruments and Their Bows*. Montreal: IPCI-Canada, 2010.

29.

Globalization through the Eyes of Runners: Student Interns as Ethnographers on Runaway Productions in Prague

PETR SZCZEPANIK

In 2012 and 2013, approximately 100 Czech Republic-based students were given the opportunity to work as assistants on the set of domestic and international film and television productions, in production offices, or in cultural policy institutions.[1] While on the job, they conducted participant observations, and kept field diaries. By way of preparation, they were taught about production studies to ensure that they were sensitive to the key dynamics of production cultures; this would allow for a comparative analysis of their field notes as well as providing them with the basics of general ethnographic methods.[2] They also received a living allowance and were assigned a paid supervisor to ensure that the educational purposes of job shadowing were fulfilled and the students were not mistreated.[3] In follow-up seminars, they developed coding schemas and analyzed the field notes in order to identify important issues related to the mediation processes that take place in globalized production cultures: tensions and inequalities within transnational production teams,[4] knowledge transfers and the distribution of creativity, changing career patterns, and so on.

Twenty-four years after the end of the Cold War, the media industries of East-Central Europe are struggling to respond to the dissolution of both the state-controlled economies and their previous organizational structures, and to develop strategies in order to compete internationally. The profession of the producer, in particular, needed to be re-established because from 1945 to 1990 the state itself functioned as the head producer, which is to say that often, untrained personnel improvised their role based on knowledge they captured from visiting professionals. Today, local production companies still lack long-term strategies and medium-term script development plans; they live a hand-to-mouth existence made possible by the revenues that each production generates.[5]

Both private and public television channels have underestimated the importance of developing or adapting new formats, especially in the entertainment field.[6] Nevertheless, regional productions have attracted significant domestic audiences, especially in the Czech Republic and Poland, and some local facilities, such as those in Prague and in Budapest, have attracted US, Western European, Russian, and Asian productions.

In the mid-to-late 1990s, Prague earned a reputation for production quality rather than affordability. Larger projects were attracted by the prospect of experienced crews, the fourteen-stage Barrandov Studios, and historical locations that could seemingly stand in for any city or period in European history. A decade-long boom ended in 2004 when a right-wing government refused to match the new financial incentives that were being offered by competitors such as Hungary. In 2003, Prague generated 178 million dollars from foreign productions, twenty times more than domestic productions. By 2004, however, foreign investment had dropped to an estimated 60 million dollars.[7] In 2009, a new law offering a 20 percent rebate was passed. This brought Prague in line with neighboring countries and thereby initiated a new wave of international productions, with projected spending of 200 million dollars in 2013. Since 1990, around 140 foreign feature films and TV series have been shot at Barrandov Studios.[8] Of these 140, sixty were US productions, including *Mission: Impossible* (1995), *The Chronicles of Narnia: Prince Caspian* (2007), and *Child 44* (2014).

Local production-service companies have helped to attract foreign productions to the Czech Republic. As go-betweens seeking to develop Hollywood-like working conditions within a culturally alien environment, these firms became key channels for knowledge transfer. Interviews that I conducted show that these exchanges mainly involved organizational knowledge relating to the division of labor, pacing, problem-solving, ethics, and communication; even below-the-line workers stressed that they learned managerial, rather than technical, skills.[9] Production managers function as cultural mediators of these transfers. As David Minkowski, the American-born head of film production at Prague's largest production-service company, Stillking, stated:

It's easier to take somebody who is young, flexible and speaks English and train them than it is to retrain or reeducate the older generation. [...] In the areas of accounting, production management, coordination, assistant directors, [...] locations, you can train people who don't have any experience and you can put them in positions of authority and if they are the right personality and have the right internal skills, they can learn it quickly. That's what was really missing. Essentially it was the management layer, because that's so important. Financial, organizational, all that stuff. That's probably eighty percent of what we do. [...] Now, after twelve years, my job is easy, because basically Czech production managers do everything, because they have those skills.[10]

Minkowski's account of generational and cultural change illustrates the kind of volatile, learning-centered multinational environment that our interns enter. Their immediate superiors are usually Czech production managers in their late twenties or early thirties who have been trained by experienced American producers and crews rather than at film school. If older Czechs with experience from state-socialist times are indeed present, they usually occupy marginal positions, with the notable exceptions of those in costume departments and art departments. This generation was either pushed out of the business in the late 1990s or had to to adapt to the dynamics of what's now called a "boundaryless career," moving from one project to another. Department heads within international production teams are mostly American and British; those on non-American productions may be from other countries. Lower-level crewmembers are usually Czech.

The production-service business is distinct from domestic production in that it involves bigger budgets, higher salaries, and better technology. Impacting runaway production, however, are distant external decision-making centers; a changing Czech rebate program; overseas studio heads and financiers; and competition from cities like Budapest and Berlin. For this reason, information flows between groups and individuals in highly fragmented fashion, making it difficult for interns to ascertain the real reasons why decisions are made and who is making them. In the absence of industrial macro-analysis skills and supplementary field research in the form of interviews with mid- and high-level players, students struggled to see past the social rituals and power relations of individual departments and thus found it difficult to "cross scales" between micro- and macro-structures of global media production. They also failed to identify significant distinctions and hierarchies in the apparent chaos of this environment.

The former was typically experienced by interns placed in costume departments, probably the most spatially enclosed, feminized, and, in terms of symbolic and economic capital, marginal of departments. Minkowski contends that this is the hardest department for him to deal with; it is the only one that has not transformed and is still staffed by the older generation.[11] Students tended to immerse themselves in a peculiar social micro-world populated by costume supervisors and makers struggling with personal anxieties and professional insecurities. The students' diaries focused on this department's internal dynamics and its members' views of others. Here, globalization was seen to have underscored the sense of exploitation, segregation, and discrimination that this department had historically seen itself encountering.[12] The isolated nature of the costume workshops regularly became a site of nationally-based mistrust, and of secrets, misunderstandings, and humiliations. Costumers submit to a strict spatial politics. Members are assigned a restricted area in the department, and are granted limited access to the set. In contrast, an intern working on a prestigious Asian production reported that higher-ranking crew members would drop by whenever they felt like it, and would even demand to have their everyday clothing altered free of charge. In response, Czech costumers complained, gossiped, quietly mocked, and even circumvented their American superiors while at the same time sought to confirm their status as hardworking but underappreciated creative professionals. Interns in costume departments tended to present the gloomiest pictures of transnational production and often lost sense of the broader industrial and creative contexts of the project. Nevertheless, they demonstrated the greatest insight into the cultural specificities of a professional subgroup.

The opposite was true of runners. Their work life oscillated between scurrying across departments, offices, and production sites, and experiencing periods of enforced idleness and listening on walkie-talkies to the incessant flow of communication. They oversaw numerous spatial and social boundaries and monitored the movement of key personnel across them. Unlike costume department interns, their long days were filled with ever-changing social interactions and unpredictable tasks. From the outset, their job description and status (which involved changing between total outsiders and regular team members) were unclear; they were forced to demonstrate their indispensability by requesting work, anticipating crew members' needs, and by responding in a swift and flexible manner. They usually accepted that they were paying their dues in a culture of "deferred career gratification."[13] In principle, it was much easier for these interns to access higher-level team members, including assistant directors and foreign producers; however, the more introverted interns quickly felt marginalized or excluded. Consequently, several quit. Interns who worked as runners were not immersed in a single workspace characterized by internal politics. Instead, they developed loose alliances that crossed professional and national boundaries, thereby confirming this position's reputation as a temporary entry-level role, one that might lead to other professions but which offered few guarantees of career development. Their field notes tended to be vague and scattered, reflecting both their manifold experience and uncertain professional status. Transnational teams gave interns a fast track to the top international professionals,[14] albeit to ones who perhaps would never return to Prague and would therefore not provide their mentees ongoing and much-needed support.

Overall, the project has shown that group-based ethnography offers innovative opportunities for academic-industry collaboration, and for teaching students about media industries. The project is nonetheless an ethically and methodologically risky undertaking insomuch as it is reliant upon untrained collaborators and an ethnographic authority that is split between interns in the field and an analyst in the classroom. Thus, it challenges traditional concepts of fieldwork, allowing for multi-focal descriptions of global media production. Consequently, the project facilitates the development of a revisionist, "provincial" perspective on global capital's interaction with local creative labor. Last but not least, given that it also involves job shadowing, this kind of collective ethnography may well help media studies to survive in a time of austerity towards the humanities.

---

1 Those companies and institutions were not accustomed to offering unpaid internships.

2 A core group of interns also took part in a seminar on the ethnography of media production held by Georgina Born at Masaryk University in fall 2012.

3 The project team is always conscious of the ethical and political implications of internships, and tries to be sensitive to the needs of both interns and media professionals. For recent criticism of the exploitative aspects of internships see Ross Perlin, *Intern Nation: How to Earn Nothing and Learn Little in the Brave New Economy* (New York: Verso Publishing, 2011). For examples of anti-internship activism, and attempts to articulate principles for ethical internship in cultural industries, see *Carrotworkers' Collective* (blog), accessed September 5, 2013.

4 The term "transnational" is used here in the sense of "opportunistic transnationalism" as defined by Mette Hjort, "On the Plurality of Cinematic Transnationalism," in *World Cinemas, Transnational Perspectives*, eds. Nataša Ďurovičová and Kathleen Newman (New York and London: Routledge, 2010), 19-20.

5 See Petr Szczepanik, "Začínáme pořád od nuly," *Iluminace* 25, no. 1 (2013): 89-98.

6 See Blog.Respekt.Cz, last modified July 25, 2013.

7 See Olsberg SPI, *Studie ekonomického vlivu filmového průmyslu v České republice* (London, 2006).

8 See "Barrandov Studios," accessed September 5, 2013.

9 Between 2009 and 2011, I conducted twenty semi-structured interviews with producers, production managers, art directors, and other professionals involved in international production in Prague. This research was funded by the Czech Science Foundation (grant no. P409/10/1361) and the Fulbright Foundation.

10 Interview conducted at Barrandov Studios, May 15, 2009.

11 Ibid.

¹² See Miranda Banks, "Bodies of Work: Rituals of Doubling and the Erasure of Film/TV Production Labor" (PhD diss., University of California, Los Angeles, 2006).

¹³ Erin Hill, "Distributed Assistanthood: Dues-Paying Apprentices and 'Desk Slaves,'" in *The International Encyclopedia of Media Studies, Volume II: Media Production*, ed. Vicki Mayer (Malden: Wiley-Blackwell, 2013), 9-15.

¹⁴ Several interns have been hired on international productions.

Bibliography

Banks, Miranda. "Bodies of Work: Rituals of Doubling and the Erasure of Film/TV Production Labor." PhD dissertation, University of California, Los Angeles, 2006.

Carrotworkers' Collective (blog). Accessed September 5, 2013.

Hill, Erin. "Distributed Assistanthood: Dues-Paying Apprentices and 'Desk Slaves'." In *The International Encyclopedia of Media Studies, Volume II: Media Production*, edited by Vicki Mayer, 9-15. Malden: Wiley-Blackwell, 2013.

Hjort, Mette. "On the Plurality of Cinematic Transnationalism." In *World Cinemas, Transnational Perspectives*, edited by Nataša Ďurovičová and Kathleen Newman, 19-20. New York and London: Routledge, 2010.

Olsberg SPI. *Studie ekonomického vlivu filmového průmyslu v České republice*. London, 2006.

Perlin, Ross. *Intern Nation: How to Earn Nothing and Learn Little in the Brave New Economy*. New York: Verso Publishing, 2011.

Szczepanik, Petr. "Začínáme pořád od nuly." *Iluminace* 25, no. 1 (2013): 89-98.

30.

Where in the World is *Orphan Black*? Change and Continuity in Global TV Production and Distribution

SERRA TINIC

The proliferation of digital windows, specialty channels, and fragmented audiences compels global media scholars to reassess the increasingly complex cultural negotiations that underpin new forms of transnational financing and the distribution of television dramas. Despite two decades of scholarship that has insightfully questioned the stability of the nation as the primary arbiter of a unified sense of cultural identity (or singular site of cultural production), the literature tends to remain somewhat polarized into homogenization and hybridity perspectives on global media texts. Under the former, we see the standardization of cultural expression with global media conglomeration, global formats, and international joint ventures (IJVs) that target transnational audience markets. Hybridity theories, conversely, highlight the ways that global narratives are adapted or reconstructed such that they speak to local cultures and industry assumptions about domestic audience categorizations. Consequently, this essay moves beyond these dichotomies to examine the contradictions and disjunctures that characterize contemporary global television production partnerships through a brief case study of the Canadian series *Orphan Black* (2013–), produced for the specialty channels Space (Canada) and BBC America. The production and distribution contexts of this series exemplify the changes in a transnational environment of evolving post-network structures, increased competition for content, and a renewed emphasis on national as well as channel branding. The success of the series illustrates the necessity of sustained attention to the policies and funding structures that continue to enable producers in small-market countries to develop programs that speak to the specificities of the cultural geographies of space and place.

Since the early days of broadcasting, Canada and other countries with perceivably small audience-advertising markets (relative to population size) have sought to foster and protect a space for national television production through domestic content regulations and the establishment of public service broadcasting systems, as well as preferential labor and production-location tax credits. Government intervention in the cultural sphere was seen as integral to the maintenance of what is referred to as "shelf space" for domestic storytelling, given Hollywood's dominance in the global mediascape. These measures were further seen as a means to address concerns over "market failure": namely, that without regulatory oversight, commercial broadcasting networks would have little incentive to invest in locally specific programming that might translate into a "cultural discount" in global sales and distribution agreements.[1] However, today's new media environment of expanded channel capacity and multiplatform delivery systems has revitalized debates about the continued relevance and legitimacy of public investment in the transition from the high, or classic, network era to an age of digital spectrum surplus. Georgina Born astutely describes such arguments as "projection" or "abstractions and future-oriented discourses" that are strategically invoked in favor of deregulation, particularly by large media conglomerates and neoliberal governments, in ways that elide the persistence of conventional industry practices and constraints in a digital, multiplatform world.[2] Similarly, two consecutive research task forces on the future of Canadian cultural production (the Juneau Report, 1996, and the Standing Committee on Canadian Heritage, 2003) both cautioned against liberal pluralist visions of a new millennium with free-flowing domestic production premised on the exponential growth of windows for televisual content. Indeed, both task force reports concluded that divestment of funding, tax credits, and content regulations would merely negate any incentives for the country's largest media corporations to support the independent production sector as they would, instead, focus on generating greater profit margins through less expensive international content acquisitions, especially from American networks and cable channels. The circuitous route from production to distribution of the series *Orphan Black* appears to confirm the prognostications of both task force committees.

Creating and Selling *Orphan Black*

Orphan Black is a science fiction dystopia in which the lead actor,

Tatiana Maslany, plays several characters of various nationalities who eventually meet and discover that they are clones being hunted by both their creators and religious groups opposed to genetic experimentation. The premise explicitly invokes both Orwell's *1984* and Huxley's *Brave New World* as all of the clones were "born" in 1984 and the scientist who developed them is named Aldous Leekie (while a central train depot is called Huxley Station). The series was conceived and created by Graeme Manson and John Fawcett (who would continue as head writer and director, respectively) through the independent production company Temple Street Productions during a residency with the Prime Time TV Program at the Canadian Film Centre (CFC) in Toronto. The CFC was established in 1988 by filmmaker Norman Jewison and has since grown to be a significant national training and mentoring program for all facets of television and film development from writing to financing and developing domestic and international distribution strategies. Manson, Fawcett, and the production executives at Toronto's Temple Street were no strangers to the North American television market as all partners had proven successes in Canada-US IJVs as well as programs produced independently in each country (*The Secret Circle 2011-12, Flashpoint 2008-12, Lost Girl 2010-*, and *Being Erica 2009-11*, to name but a few).

Despite the track records of the creative team and the initial positive responses to the premise of the series, *Orphan Black* was destined to face the customary challenges of most Canadian productions: piecemeal financing and risk-averse network executives.[3] Unable to secure a commitment from any Canadian broadcaster or cable channel (including Space), Temple Street decided to pursue distribution deals in the United States. It was only after BBC America, in search of original programming, agreed to an acquisition agreement that *Orphan Black* was able to find its way home. Once BBC Worldwide (the commercial arm of the British public service broadcaster) guaranteed financing and international distribution, Space's parent company Bell Media moved quickly to purchase the series.[4] *Orphan Black* eventually debuted in March 2013 with 513,000 viewers, making it the highest-rated original series premiere for Space.[5] Its simultaneous launch on BBC America garnered 680,000 viewers.[6] The series rapidly grew audience ratings in both countries after being widely praised by American television critics and fans' word of mouth across social media sites.

Consequently, despite the fact that Space had originally passed on the project, Bell Media's vice president of specialty channels proudly announced: "This joint-Canadian production demonstrates our commitment to produce original, world-class content in Canada while simultaneously showcasing our amazing homegrown talent."[7] The fact that *Orphan Black* also helped the specialty channel fulfill its mandated Canadian content (CanCon) requirements remained unstated.

In this regard, *Orphan Black*'s current global success needs to be understood within the larger cultural and financial contexts of the contemporary transnational production ecology. Perhaps ironically, Canada's comparative advantage in the global television arena lies in the domestic content regulations and concomitant public production funding that have acted as an integral component of growing the media industries in a small-market nation. In brief, Canadian producers are attractive to IJV partners due to the tax credits and financial grants that they bring to project development. With over fifty official coproduction treaties, Canada has become the world leader in IJVs. This has not been without opportunity costs on a cultural level. Until recently, Canadian producers and their coproduction partners tended to erase culturally specific markers and follow the grammar of American network formulas and genres. These type of generic or "industry" productions were commonly seen as the hallmarks of the culturally homogenizing impact of capital interests in the quest to access one of the most restrictive television import markets: American broadcast networks and basic cable channels.

Orphan Black presents a departure from this model to the extent that, while not made overly specific, there is no erasure of its cultural spatiality or domestic reference points. Nevertheless, some American television critics "read" the series as a British story set in the United States.[8] Although *Orphan Black* is not "British," despite being acquired by BBC America, the fact that it may be perceived as such aligns with BBC Worldwide's current objective to build the BBC brand globally through investing in and developing coproductions with culturally proximate industry partners.[9] Canadian producers have long been seen as favorable international coproduction partners due to the perception that they are cultural intermediaries who are conversant with the American television industry yet bring a slightly "European sensibility" to their projects.[10] Moreover, *Orphan Black* fulfilled the channel's goal to purchase content that would complement and expand its genre-based brand recognition in the US market beyond the landmark *Doctor Who*.

This very brief sketch of the industrial context of *Orphan Black* should not be seen as primarily a coming-of-age story for Canadian television. Given the historic structural constraints of domestic drama production, Canadian production companies merely had a head start in developing global strategies that other nations are now adopting as well. In fact, prior to the establishment of BBC Worldwide in 1996, Canada did not even have an official coproduction treaty with the United Kingdom despite their Commonwealth ties. By 2001, the United Kingdom had become the country's largest production partner and contributed to 57 percent of Canada's treaty coproductions. While financial concerns are paramount, shared industrial histories of public service broadcasting have also led to affinities in storytelling styles that have enabled Canadian and UK producers to negotiate cultural specificity in ways that are not always possible with every transnational partner.[11] *Orphan Black* is instructive to the extent that it illustrates the necessity of avoiding both generalized depictions of cultural homogenization and optimistic "projection" discourses in mapping the complexities of transnational television financing and distribution.

Case studies of specific international joint ventures allow us to see continuity amid change in global television production. New platforms and specialty channels have increased opportunities for producers in small-market nations to sell their programs globally.

Yet concomitant audience fragmentation and ever-increasing production budgets have resulted in intensified competition for content in an era that simultaneously requires unique brand differentiation and nuanced cultural negotiations between transnational creative partners. At the same time, differential power structures between national television markets persist—namely, the enduring importance of access to the American audience market on the part of Anglo-production communities.[12] Indeed, the popularity of *Orphan Black* in the United States facilitated BBC Worldwide and Bell Media's ability to further monetize the series, in a seemingly reverse flow, through sales to their respective national broadcast networks (BBC Three and CTV, Canada's largest private broadcaster) several months after the series had completed its first season in Canada and the United States.

Consequently, the example of *Orphan Black* compels those of us working within global media industries research to reconceptualize our analyses of international coproductions to include nuanced studies of television distribution and, in particular, branding. The series is not a treaty coproduction (it is completely written and produced in Toronto), nor does it fall under the very productive category that Michele Hilmes identifies as transnational coproduction, where "national interests must be combined and reconciled."[13] The questions of distribution, acquisition, and branding are both old and new again in transnational television studies as we ponder the future and where the contradictions of both national specificity and structural histories of "broadcasting" are now significant selling points for select TV series globally.

---

[1] Colin Hoskins, Stuart McFadyen, and Adam Finn, "The Environment in Which Cultural Industries Operate and Some Implications," *Canadian Journal of Communication* 19 (1994): 353–75.

[2] Georgina Born, "Strategy and Projection in Digital Television: Channel Four and the Commercialization of Public Broadcasting in the UK," *Media, Culture, and Society* 25 (2013): 773–99.

[3] The production house would eventually patch together financing through several provincial and national programs including the Cogeco Program Development Fund, the Canadian Film or Video Production Tax Credit program, the Ontario Media Development Corporation Film and Television Tax Credit, and the Rogers Cable Network.

[4] Mark Dillon, "Space: Boldly Going Where No Channel Had Gone Before at 15," *Playback* (fall 2012).

[5] Debra Yeo, "*Orphan Black* Gets Second Season on Space," *The Star*, May 3, 2013.

[6] Nellie Andreeva, "BBC America's '*Orphan Black*' Renewed for Second Season," *Deadline Hollywood*, May 2, 2013.

7 Bell Media, "Seeing Double: Space Orders Second Season of Hit Original Drama *Orphan Black*," last modified May 2, 2013.

8 Linda Stasi, "Identity Thief," *New York Post*, March 21, 2013.

9 Tim Davie, "BBC Worldwide Annual Review 2012/13 — CEO Review," BBC Worldwide.

10 Serra Tinic, *On Location: Canada's Television Industry in a Global Market* (Toronto: University of Toronto Press, 2005).

11 Serra Tinic, "Between the Public and the Private: Television Drama and Global Partnerships in the Neo-Network Era," in *Television Studies after TV: Understanding Television in the Post-Broadcast Era*, ed. Graeme Turner and Jinna Tay (New York: Routledge, 2009), 74.

12 Both Temple Street Productions and BBC Worldwide acknowledge the imperative to maintain production offices within the United States for access to industry partners and to pursue the most lucrative production and distribution agreements. Competition from large-budget series such as *Game of Thrones* and *Mad Men* are cited as setting a new threshold for evolving financial partnerships via specialty channel distribution windows. Jordan Twiss, "Best of the Year: Temple Street," *Playback*, December 13, 2012; BBC Worldwide, "Annual Review 2012/13 — Market Context."

13 Michele Hilmes, "Transnational TV: What Do We Mean by 'Coproduction' Anymore?" *Media Industries Journal* 1, no. 2 (2014): 10–15.

Bibliography

Andreeva, Nellie. "BBC America's '*Orphan Black*' Renewed for Second Season." *Deadline Hollywood*. May 2, 2013.

BBC Worldwide. "Annual Review 2012/13 — Market Context."

Bell Media. "Seeing Double: Space Orders Second Season of Hit Original Drama *Orphan Black*." May 2, 2013.

Born, Georgina. "Strategy and Projection in Digital Television: Channel Four and the Commercialization of Public Broadcasting in the UK." *Media, Culture, and Society* 25 (2013): 773–99.

Davie, Tim. BBC Worldwide. "BBC Worldwide Annual Review 2012/13 – CEO Review."

Dillon, Mark "Space: Boldly Going Where No Channel Had Gone Before." *Playback* (fall 2012).

Hoskins, Colin, Stuart McFadyen, and Adam Finn. "The Environment in Which Cultural Industries Operate and Some Implications." *Canadian Journal of Communication* 19 (1994): 353–75.

Lederman, Marsha. "How Canada Is Becoming the Sci-Fi Nation." *Global Mail*, April 13, 2013.

Stasi, Linda. "Identity Thief." *New York Post*, March 21, 2013.

Tinic, Serra. "Between the Public and the Private: Television Drama and Global Partnerships in the Neo-Network Era." In *Television Studies after TV: Understanding Television in the Post-Broadcast Era*, edited by Graeme Turner and Jinna Tay, 65–74. New York: Routledge, 2009.

Tinic, Serra. *On Location: Canada's Television Industry in a Global Market*. Toronto: University of Toronto Press, 2005.

Twiss, Jordan. "Best of the Year: Temple Street." *Playback*, December 13, 2012.

Yeo, Debra. "*Orphan Black* Gets Second Season on Space." *The Star*, May 3, 2013.

31.

The Case for Studying In-Store Media

JOSEPH TUROW

An Overlooked Landscape

It has become a truism within communication studies and related fields that the rise of digital technologies is reshaping media industries. Researchers have fixed their sights on the profound changes taking place in the television, recorded music, movie, book, magazine, advertising, and newspaper industries.[1] Academics with an industry bent have also turned their attention toward the internet and mobile businesses to explore ways executives from those "legacy" industries use the new technologies to investigate more independent areas of the media economy. Scholarship from only the past decade has ignited important discussions of topics that hardly, if ever, came up in previous writings on media industries: privacy;[2] surveillance;[3] security;[4] piracy and fair use;[5] the audience as both producer and consumer of media materials;[6] the increasing quantification of data about audiences;[7] the implications of changing brand strategies and media subsidies;[8] and how in the face of new digital competition and capacities companies are redefining the scope, qualifications, and compensation terms of media labor.[9]

This research has led to a growing body of exciting work on the processes of media creation and distribution not seen since the 1970s and early 1980s, a major period for research on media industries. At the same time, researchers have shown almost no interest in activities, such as shopping, that take place outside businesses we typically think of centrally as "media." Retail venues have long presented visitors with a cavalcade of patterned materials about goods and services—product packaging, circulars, store-sponsored magazines, coupons, posters, shelf notices, floor ads, ceiling attention grabbers, shopping-cart advertising cards, end-cap display fixtures, video monitors, audio programming and announcements, computer kiosks, and more. Yet consider in-store media's infinitesimal footprint at the annual International

Communication Association and the National Communication Association conferences from 2008 through 2012: Of the more than 2,500 presentations at ICA and NCA during that half decade, only eighteen papers included the words *supermarket, mall, retail,* or *outdoor* in the title. Moreover, only five of the presentations had title terms that evoked the more specialized, mobile-related aspects of retail: *GPS, geolocation,* or *geo-location.*[10]

The Social Importance of In-Store Media

This scant attention has led communication researchers to miss out on fascinating developments with potentially important social implications. Online sellers are becoming adept at tailoring product, price, and lifestyle offers to prospects based on what they have learned about them. Executives in physical ("brick and mortar") stores are also implementing strategic changes involving segmentation and personalization as they face down threats from digital competition that result not only from shopping conducted at home but also from contestations taking place within their own walls.

In the physical establishments, the aisle is the locus of much struggle. Before the digital age, retailers, manufacturers, and distributors negotiated the products, descriptions, offers, and prices customers would confront in store aisles. The smartphone has given customers new ways to see the aisle that have stoked store executives' fears as well as their sense of opportunity. One of their concerns is that mobile-equipped visitors can check websites and comparative-shopping applications (apps) for prices the physical store must match if it doesn't want to lose business. Executives also worry about "showrooming": when people enter physical stores to assess products and then, often after checking handset reviews and prices, buy the goods from virtual competitors. Despite these threats, many retailers quoted in the trade literature agree with an app executive who predicted the handset would become "the number-one marketing tool [in the service of physical] retailers and brands."[11] They contend that a properly designed mobile-phone application will help a store tailor offers to desirable customers in the aisle via the handset, thereby creating a high chance of purchase.

Most retailers with a brick-and-mortar legacy have by now built a virtual presence. For them, getting to know the customer well means linking data from an individuals' purchases in the physical store to activities (product views as well as purchases) on the store's app, mobile website, and desktop/laptop website. It may also mean paying third parties such as Axciom or Experian for a customer's income, age, and other information that will help calculate the person's long-term value to the store. These activities are part of a larger galaxy of retail work using myriad technologies of data extraction, analysis, and implementation with the aim, in one consultant's words, to "significantly manage customer relationships in this environment."[12] "Frequent shopper" programs, for example, provide a valuable way to discriminate among customers. In addition, the desire to discern the best prospects may lead a store to pay for a person's Klout or similar score that calculates the individual's influence with peers, an indication, providers claim, of the person's value regarding spreading the word about the retailer.

In an age when marketers try to follow prospects wherever they go, shining a light on in-store media also provides a neglected context for understanding challenges media industries face from far outside their typical boundaries. Observers suggest, for example, that the growing use of smartphones is hurting the magazine industry: customers in checkout lines are so busy with their mobile devices that they are not looking at, and therefore not buying, the magazines alongside them.[13] While it can be a source of distraction, the phone can, on the other hand, play a significant role in reaching prospects *prior to* checkout. Procter and Gamble executives have long termed the confrontation between a person and a product in the aisle as "the first moment of truth" for an advertising campaign.[14] The mobile handset and various digital shelf technologies provide unprecedented opportunities for seduction and negotiation in that "moment." Indeed, advertisers might in coming years re-route substantial portions of their traditional-media subsidies to increasingly persuasive in-store media modes instead.

The Need for a Media Industries Perspective

Perhaps media researchers haven't explored these developments in the retail arena because they are unaware of them. A second explanation may be communication studies' historical tendency to focus on industries that centrally aim to create and circulate media content, not industries that generate content as subsidiary to selling other products. It's also tempting to propose the seemingly pedestrian nature of shopping as another reason the media studies scholars have paid this area little attention. Cents-off coupons, noisy audio announcements, mercenary electronic and printed signs, social media for collectivizing decisions about clothing purchases–these may not signal political or cultural importance to academics as straightforwardly as news and entertainment materials do.

Yet decades of academic writings underscore that phenomena – which at first glance appear to be mere cacophonies of textual, visual, audio, audiovisual, and olfactory stimuli – can, with appropriate scholarly lenses, be seen as having patterned social relevance. The challenge for researchers is to move away from their historically comfortable world of clearly defined media industries. The goal should instead be to take a media industries *perspective*. This lens focuses on the industrialized production, distribution, and exhibition of messages in whatever social institutions the process takes place. *Industrial* refers to a conglomeration of for-profit or nonprofit organizations that interact regularly (though not necessarily harmoniously) to create and circulate products, which can include messages. A social institution is a conglomeration of collectivities (advocacy organizations, government entities, industries, individuals) that interact regularly (though not necessarily harmoniously) to direct key areas of collective life. Think of health care, education, the military, the media—and retailing.

The guiding proposition of the media industries perspective is that when message production and circulation is industrialized within an institution, it takes on features that distinguish it from mediated interpersonal activities, such as friends or acquaintances exchanging emails, texting one another, or sharing their shopping lists electronically. That is because the industrial production and distribution of messages inevitably links to large-scale power dynamics that course through the institution. So, for example, when supermarkets, banks, and airlines work with market research firms to define target audiences and create messages to attract them, the resulting activities have implications both for individuals who are selected as targets and those who are not. Personalized websites, coupons, and advertisements tell shoppers where stores place them

242

in the customer hierarchy. Loyalty programs for the "right" people signal that they can achieve protection from discomfort and bad service. Different prices that stores offer valued versus non-valued prospects signal customers' disparate statuses. So do the different treatments they experience from store representatives who rate customers' value based on information gathered from check-in and check-out technologies.

Sometimes sellers want shoppers to know they are winners or losers so that customers will change their habits to benefit the sellers. People who are treated well algorithmically live in very different symbolic and material worlds than those who are not. Yet retailers embed even valued people in information systems that sometimes work against these valued buyers' best interests.[15] For example, retailers build apps linked to their own discounts and loyalty programs with the aim of discouraging people from accessing information from competitors or neutral sources. Retailers expect that shoppers' desire to accumulate loyalty points will lead them to spend more money than they otherwise would. And retailers hope loyalty-program members will even compromise on products they purchase in order to stay within the fold. The success of such tactics depends on how valued shoppers respond to the selling environment—for example, whether they engage loyalty programs or tire of those regimens and turn to showrooming. Also crucial to retailers' success are the instruments they use to counter wayward actions of shoppers they covet, and how and how long this potentially iterative process continues.

All these activities point to a wide gamut of research possibilities. The data-led treatment of customers raises important questions about when and how retail-based media reinforce, extend, and shape anti-pluralistic, even anti-democratic, processes and perceptions. Some readers may object that studying peripheral media is unnecessary because industries that centrally produce and circulate news, entertainment, and advertising materials also engage in audience constructions, targeted depictions, and the prejudices linked to them.[16] Yet these dynamics may manifest themselves in substantially different ways across different social institutions. Moreover, today's relatively minor media environment may well be tomorrow's dominant one. Retailing, which intersects profoundly with people's daily needs and their most pervasive communication technologies, is moving toward dominance. Interrogating it from a media industries viewpoint will undoubtedly yield absorbing new insights and questions about communication and power in society.

[1] See, for example, Amanda Lotz, *The Television Will Be Revolutionized* (New York: NYU Press, 2007); Mark Deuze, *Media Work* (Cambridge: Polity Press, 2007); David Hesmondhalgh, *The Cultural Industries*, 3rd ed. (Thousand Oaks: Sage Publications, 2012); Robert McChesney and Victor Pickard, *Will the Last Reporter Please Turn Out the Lights? The Collapse of Journalism and What Can Be Done to Fix It* (Washington: New Press, 2011); Pablo Boczkowski and Eugenia Mitchelstein, *The News Gap: When the Information Preferences of the Media and Public Diverge* (New Haven: Yale University Press, 2013); Brooke E. Duffy, *Remake, Remodel: Women's Magazines in the Digital Age* (Champaign: University of Illinois Press, 2013); Joseph Turow, *Breaking Up America: Advertising and the New Media Age* (Chicago: University of Chicago Press, 1997); and Joseph Turow, *Niche Envy: Marketing Discrimination in the Digital Age* (Cambridge: MIT Press, 2006).

[2] Helen Nissenbaum, *Privacy in Context: Technology, Policy, and the Integrity of Social Life* (Stanford: Stanford Law Books, 2009); Daniel J. Solove, *Nothing to Hide: The False Tradeoff between Privacy and Security* (New Haven: Yale University Press, 2010); Joseph Turow, *The Daily You: How the New Advertising Industry is Defining Your Identity and Your Worth* (New Haven: Yale University Press, 2012).

[3] Mark Andrejevic, *iSpy: Surveillance and Power in the Interactive Era* (College Station: University Press of Kansas, 2007); David Lyon, *Surveillance Studies: An Overview* (London: Polity, 2007); Rebecca MacKinnon, *Consent of the Networked: The Worldwide Struggle for Internet Freedom* (New York: Basic Books, 2012).

[4] Daniel Solove, *Understanding Privacy* (Cambridge: Harvard University Press, 2013).

5 Peter Decherney, *Hollywood's Copyright Wars* (New York: Columbia University Press, 2012); Adrian Johns, *Piracy* (Chicago: University of Chicago Press, 2011); Lawrence Lessig, *Free Culture: The Nature and Future of Creativity* (New York: Penguin Books, 2005).

6 Yochai Benkler, *The Wealth of Networks: How Social Production Transforms Markets and Freedom* (New Haven: Yale University Press, 2007); Henry Jenkins, *Convergence Culture: Where Old and New Media Collide* (New York: NYU Press, 2008).

7 Turow, *The Daily You*; Vicki Mayer, *Below the Line: Producers and Production Studies in the New Television Economy* (Durham: Duke University Press, 2011).

8 Henry Jenkins, *Spreadable Media: Creating Value and Meaning in a Networked Culture* (New York: NYU Press, 2013); Sarah Banet-Weiser, *Authentic ™: The Politics of Ambivalence in a Brand Culture* (New York: NYU Press, 2012).

9 Mark Deuze, ed., *Managing Media Work* (Thousand Oaks: Sage Publications, 2010); Mayer, *Below the Line*.

10 Thanks to Bo Mai, a doctoral student at Penn's Annenberg School, for these findings.

11 Patricia Orsini, "Millennials in Aisle 2.0," *eMarketer*, November 2012.

12 Ibid.

13 Martin Gicheru, "Mobile Phones in Supermarkets are Killing Magazine Business," *Techweez*, February 12, 2013.

14 Procter and Gamble, "Annual Report: 2006," accessed September 2, 2013.

15 Thanks to Annenberg doctoral student Lee McGuigan for helping me think through this point.

16 Turow, *The Daily You*.

Bibliography

Andrejevic, Mark. *iSpy: Surveillance and Power in the Interactive Era.* College Station: University Press of Kansas, 2007.

Benkler, Yochai. *The Wealth of Networks: How Social Production Transforms Markets and Freedoms*. New Haven: Yale University Press, 2007.

Banet-Weiser, Sarah. *Authentic ™: The Politics of Ambivalence in a Brand Culture*. New York: NYU Press, 2012.

Boczkowski, Pablo, and Eugenia Mitchelstein. *The News Gap: When the Information Preferences of the Media and Public Diverge*. New Haven: Yale University Press, 2013.

Decherney, Peter. *Hollywood's Copyright Wars: From Edison to the Internet*. New York: Columbia University Press, 2012.

Deuze, Mark, ed. *Managing Media Work*. Thousand Oaks: Sage Publications, 2010.

Deuze, Mark. *Media Work*. Cambridge: Polity Press, 2007.

Duffy, Brooke E. *Remake, Remodel: Women's Magazines in the Digital Age*. Champaign: University of Illinois Press, 2013.

Gicheru, Martin. "Mobile Phones in Supermarkets are Killing Magazine Business." *Techweez*. Last modified February 12, 2013.

Hesmondhalgh, David. *The Cultural Industries*. 3rd edition. Thousand Oaks: Sage Publications, 2012.

Jenkins, Henry. *Convergence Culture: Where Old and New Media Collide*. New York: NYU Press, 2008.

Jenkins, Henry. *Spreadable Media: Creating Value and Meaning in a Networked Culture*. New York: NYU Press, 2013.

Johns Adrian. *Piracy: The Intellectual Property Wars from Gutenberg to Gates*. Chicago: University of Chicago Press, 2011.

Lessig, Lawrence. *Free Culture: The Nature and Future of Creativity*. New York: Penguin Books, 2005.

Lotz, Amanda. *The Television Will Be Revolutionized*. New York: NYU Press, 2007.

Lyon, David. *Surveillance Studies: An Overview*. London: Polity Press, 2007.

MacKinnon, Rebecca. *Consent of the Networked: The Worldwide Struggle for Internet Freedom*. New York: Basic Books, 2012.

Mayer, Vicki. *Below the Line: Producers and Production Studies in the New Television Economy*. Durham: Duke University Press, 2011.

McChesney, Robert, and Victor Pickard. *Will the Last Reporter Please Turn Out the Lights? The Collapse of Journalism and What Can Be Done to Fix It*. Washington: New Press, 2011.

Nissenbaum, Helen. *Privacy in Context: Technology, Policy, and the Integrity of Social Life*. Stanford: Stanford Law Books, 2009.

Orsini, Patria. "Millennials in Aisle 2.0." *eMarketer*. November 2012.

Procter and Gamble. "Annual Report: 2006." Accessed September 2, 2013.

Solove, Daniel. *Nothing to Hide: The False Tradeoff between Privacy and Security*. New Haven: Yale University Press, 2010.

Solove, Daniel. *Understanding Privacy*. Cambridge: Harvard University Press, 2013.

Turow, Joseph. *Breaking Up America: Advertising and the New Media Age*. Chicago: University of Chicago Press, 1997.

Turow, Joseph. *Niche Envy: Marketing Discrimination in the Digital Age*. Cambridge: MIT Press, 2006.

Turow, Joseph. *The Daily You: How the New Advertising Industry is Defining Your Identity and Your Worth*. New Haven: Yale University Press, 2012.

32.

Industry Proximity

PATRICK VONDERAU

Opening his keynote speech at the 2013 International Association for Media and Communication Research (IAMCR) conference in Dublin, noted political economist of media Richard Maxwell came up with what he had found to be an "interesting" statistic: "Did you know that 90 percent of all of the data that exist today were created in the last two years? [...] Like, 'OMG.' It makes you think that since Gutenberg we were twittering on our fingers [sic]."[1] Pointing to the many different ways political economy could make use of such statistical evidence, Maxwell invoked surveillance issues and the security state before turning to the actual topic of his talk: the environmental consequences that arguably follow our uses of digital media technology. Focusing on mobile computing whose "dirty business" he dissected from an "eco-materialist point of view," Maxwell invited us to rethink the very foundations of media and communication studies, an imperative articulated more fully in his and Toby Miller's recent book, *Greening the Media* (2012). Media studies, the diagnosis reads, abstains from deep analysis of technology's materiality due to its humanist and scientist bias, a bias to be overcome if we ever are to understand where our media originate.

However, a viable starting point for such an endeavor could actually be Maxwell's talk itself. Where does that statistic come from? Any Internet search relates its claim to the executive summary of an IBM report widely quoted online since 2011, entitled *The IBM CMO Study*.[2] This report is based on data collected from 2008 to 2010, through interviews with 1,700 chief marketing officers worldwide, in order to assess if marketing organizations are prepared to manage media change, with the barely concealed aim of advertising IBM's own data mining services. Even the full, internal version of the original report does not contain any data itself; it merely adds that "we now create as much information every two days as we did from the dawn of civilization to 2003."[3] As a source for the latter statement, the IBM report footnotes a 2010 *TechCrunch* interview with Google's then executive chairman, Eric Schmidt.

Whatever its original source, it is difficult to understand what such a statistical finding is supposed to tell us. Given that large private IT (information technology) corporations are notoriously secretive about the actual volume of data traffic, any "big data" estimations can hardly be verified. And what data are we speaking about? Data initially appear unstructured and useless, as chaotic or repetitive noise. Once data are turned into exploitable information, that information still would need to travel through different pipelines, with widely varying implications for the world's economies or ecologies. While Maxwell and Miller rightfully criticize Facebook and Google for their staggering electricity consumption as much as the "YouTubers, bloggers, and other volunteers in the digital congregation,"[4] Maxwell's talk is made accessible via YouTube and also linked to Facebook, where Miller and Maxwell advertise both their book and brand of political economy in separate (and rather popular) profiles. According to the Schmidt statement quoted by IBM, it is exactly such user-generated content that makes for the five exabytes of data every second day or, what Miller and Maxwell have referred to as "the irony of exemplary ironies."[5]

But does it matter? My point here is not to devalue critical research on media ecologies; indeed, such research is certainly needed. Nor am I aiming to expose political economy's "data bias" or putative weaknesses in Maxwell's (and Miller's) widely discussed argument. Rather, my question is this: If science is in the business of producing objectivity, how does this production relate to the objectivities produced by the business? Where to locate the politics today given that we arguably have come to live in, rather than with, media?[6] Media industry scholars always face the dilemma that quantitative analyses are put at the core of analyzing industries,[7] while simultaneously taking part in the very production of "the industry" itself, with statistics serving as an industry mechanism for managerial efficiency and centralized control.[8] This holds especially true for IT-based industries and services whose operations are essentially invisible and subject to representation in infographics, telecom maps and metrics, data center imageries, marketing taglines, and the like. How are we ever to get out of what John Thornton Caldwell aptly describes as "contact zones that media industries stage carefully around us as we study them?"[9]

In my current research on Sweden's digital media infrastructure, I am confronted with an excess of visibility when it comes to new servicing platforms, to internet service providers, or the people using them, while the more complex technological, material, or social dimensions remain hidden, or in engineering terms, "blackboxed."[10] Rephrasing my question above, how are we ever to get "close" to these industries? While today's content providers, delivery pipelines, and data centers arguably have become what telecommunication networks once were to communication scholars, macro-political institutional analysis seems barely suited to cope with this development. "Who owns the physical infrastructure that we use and need? The layer upon where all of our communication is based," a Swedish blogger worried recently. He continued, "The Internet is no longer just a playground, it's not just for entertainment. It's for real, we're totally dependent on it." In another ironic twist, these are the words of Peter Sunde, co-founder of The Pirate Bay, a website that facilitates peer-to-peer file sharing.[11]

Media industries constitute a zone where agency is permanently subverted, undermined, blackboxed, and distributed. Research on media industries thus necessitates an awareness of the politics of our own data gathering and of what Langdon Winner called the "politics of artifacts," an acknowledgment that technologies mediate the relation between us and our world so thoroughly that our ability to understand "subjectivity" and "objectivity" comes to depend upon our ability to grasp how these artifacts amplify the "forms of contact" that relate us to one another and our environment.[12] If even cyberlibertarianism's "smart kids" like Sunde can't acknowledge that our media ecologies are beyond grasp then we need to follow Maxwell's and Miller's call for studying these ecologies. For that, however, we do not need to reinvent media and communication studies.

By evoking a schism between humanism and scientism, a study of media that deals with numbers and another dealing with qualities, and the old debate between naturalistic versus interpretative forms of scientific work, *Greening the Media* questions the contribution of "orthodox histories" to media industries scholarship. I would like to argue, however, that decades of historical, philosophical, and other "humanist" research have been vital in providing both the documentation and methods for the most pertinent research on media industries today. Rather than creating another divide between humanities and social sciences, online and offline, "old" and "new" media, or in-between the very disciplinary fields involved in media industries research, we need to make their inherent tensions productive. Infrastructure studies and media archeology offer two examples for approaches that are productive in this sense. Sociologist Susan Leigh Star, for instance, asks us to go beyond any a priori idea of what infrastructures are (i.e., a means of control over information) in order to understand how they work. Instead of assuming that control is always already contained in, and guaranteed by, some form of ownership over pipelines or internet protocols, she suggests seeing infrastructure as a specific outcome of "distributions" between the social/technical and global/local, an outcome that reflects everyday decisions in infrastructure design, development, or enactment.[13] Media archeology, in turn, has long engaged in the study of the material, non-representational dimensions of media that Miller and Maxwell now request, with the explicit aim of identifying structures of power through technology and policy analysis.[14]

Such "reverse engineering" that builds on insights outside of media industries' own orthodox methodologies may even lead to new, interventionist formats of research. If it holds true that capitalist media industries manage to "colonize any new public good," turning any "subversion into profit,"[15] then it might be high time to turn subversion into a research strategy and the industry's contact zones into zones of experiment and play. Together with Swedish internet activists Rasmus Fleischer and Christopher Kullenberg, who hold doctoral degrees in musicology and philosophy/theory of science, respectively, along with ethnologist Anna Johansson and my cinema studies colleague Pelle Snickars, I am currently preparing a research project that sets out to investigate music distribution and aggregation services. This project's methodological innovation consists of following digital files rather than those involved in making, using, or collecting them. After initial talks with Spotify's management, we asked how we would be able to get "close" or "into" its music distribution engine. Instead of being content with the study of the industry's extensive self-representations, we decided to "unbox" online music aggregation by creating a non-profit digital record label that would allow access to the industry through its very own distribution platforms. "Following the thing"[16] allows us to study "the digital" with the same tools that organize information, and to get beyond interview answers to questions about unexpected file "behavior," aggregation platform strategies, processes of (de)valuation, and the infrastructures that make all these possible. While certainly not intending to "rethink" the field as such, this project design allows us to bring politics back in an interventionist form reminiscent of what ethnomethodologist Harold Garfinkel once called "breaching experiments": by breaking the rules of unstated social roles in order to study them.[17] Whatever data our media have become, we still may metaphorically "hack" ourselves into the material infrastructures providing them, shedding light on their built-in political values and our own.

1 Richard Maxwell, "IAMCR 2013 Plenary No. 3 – Conference video," DCU School of Communications, June 27, 2013, published June 28, 2013.

2 "From Stretched to Strengthened: Insights from the Global Chief Marketing Officer Study," IBM, 2011.

3 Ibid.

4 Richard Maxwell and Toby Miller, Greening the Media (Oxford: Oxford University Press, 2012), 29, 161.

5 Maxwell and Miller, Greening the Media, commenting on how Manuel Castells had overlooked IT's polluting side while detailing the reliance on such technology, 13

6 See, e.g., Mark Deuze, Media Life (Cambridge: Polity Press, 2012).

7 Toby Miller, "Can Natural Luddites Make Things Explode or Travel Faster? The New Humanities, Cultural Policy Studies, and Creative Industries," in Media Industries: History, Theory, and Method, eds. Jennifer Holt and Alisa Perren (Malden: Blackwell, 2009), 192.

8 Nitin Govil, "Recognizing 'Industry,'" Cinema Journal 52, no. 3 (Spring 2013): 175.

9 John T. Caldwell, "Para-Industry: Researching Hollywood's Blackwaters," Cinema Journal 52, no. 3 (Spring 2013): 165.

[10] Bruno Latour, *Science in Action: How to Follow Scientists and Engineers through Society* (Cambridge: Harvard University Press, 1987). See also Jennifer Holt and Patrick Vonderau, "Where the Internet Lives: Data Centers as Digital Media Infrastructure," in *Signal Traffic: Critical Studies of Media Infrastructures*, eds. Lisa Parks and Nicole Starosielski (University of Illinois Press, forthcoming 2014).

[11] Peter Sunde (brokep), "Intertubes," *Copy me happy* (blog), May 26, 2013.

[12] Langdon Winner, *The Whale and the Reactor* (Chicago: University of Chicago Press, 1986); see also Peter-Paul Verbeek, *What Things Do: Philosophical Reflections on Technology, Agency, and Design* (Pennsylvania: The Pennsylvania State University Press, 2005) and Josh Braun, "Over the Top: Online Television Distribution as Sociotechnical System," *Communication, Culture & Critique* 6 (2013): 438.

[13] See, e.g., *Standards and Their Stories: How Quantifying, Classifying, and Formalizing Practices Shape Everyday Life*, eds. Martha Lampland and Susan Leigh Star (Ithaca/London: Cornell University Press, 2009), and Geoffrey Bowker et al., "Toward Information Infrastructure Studies: Ways of Knowing in a Networked Environment," in *The International Handbook of Internet Research*, eds. Jeremy Hunsinger, Lisbeth Klastrup, and Matthew Allen (Heidelberg/London: Springer, 2010), 101.

[14] Jussi Parikka, *What Is Media Archeology* (Malden: Polity Press, 2012), 164.

[15] Sean Cubitt, "The Political Economy of Cosmopolis," in *Digital Labor: The Internet as Playground and Factory*, ed. Trebor Scholz (New York: Routledge, 2013), 59-60.

[16] George Marcus, "Ethnography in/of the World System: The Emergence of Multi-sited Ethnography," *Annual Review of Anthropology* 24 (1995): 95-117.

[17] Harold Garfinkel, *Studies in Ethnomethodology* (Malden: Polity Press, 1991).

Bibliography

Bowker, Geoffrey, Karen Baker, Florence Millerand, and David Ribes. "Toward Information Infrastructure Studies: Ways of Knowing in a Networked Environment." In *The International Handbook of Internet Research*, edited by Jeremy Hunsinger, Lisbeth Klastrup, and Matthew Allen, 97-117. Heidelberg/London: Springer, 2010.

Braun, Josh. "Over the Top: Online Television Distribution as Sociotechnical System." *Communication, Culture & Critique* 6 (2013): 432-438.

Caldwell, John T. "Para-Industry: Researching Hollywood's Blackwaters." *Cinema Journal* 52, no. 3 (2013): 157-165.

Cubitt, Sean. "The Political Economy of Cosmopolis." In *Digital Labor: The Internet as Playground and Factory*, edited by Trebor Scholz, 58-68. New York: Routledge, 2013.

Deuze, Mark. *Media Life*. Cambridge: Polity Press, 2012.

Govil, Nitin. "Recognizing 'Industry.'"*Cinema Journal* 52, no. 3 (2013): 172 - 176.

Holt, Jennifer, and Patrick Vonderau. "Where the Internet Lives. Data Centers as Digital Media Infrastructure." In *Signal Traffic: Critical Studies of Media Infrastructures*, edited by Lisa Parks and Nicole Starosielski. Forthcoming, 2014. Champaign: University of Illinois Press.

IBM, "From Stretched to Strengthened: Insights from the Global Chief Marketing Officer Study." 2011.

Lampland, Martha, and Susan Leigh Star, eds. *Standards and their Stories: How Quantifying, Classifying, and Formalizing Practices Shape Everyday Life*. Ithaca/London: Cornell University Press, 2009.

Latour, Bruno. *Science in Action: How to Follow Scientists and Engineers through Society*. Cambridge: Harvard University Press, 1987.

Marcus, George. "Ethnography in/of the World System: The Emergence of Multi-sited Ethnography." *Annual Review of Anthropology* 24 (1995): 95-117.

Maxwell, Richard. "IAMCR 2013 Plenary No. 3 – Conference video." *DCU School of Communications*, June 27, 2013. Published June 28, 2013.

Maxwell, Richard, and Toby Miller. *Greening the Media*. Oxford: Oxford University Press, 2012.

Miller, Toby. "Can Natural Luddites Make Things Explode or Travel Faster? The New Humanities, Cultural Policy Studies, and Creative Industries." In *Media Industries: History, Theory, and Method*, edited by Jennifer Holt and Alisa Perren, 184-198. Malden: Blackwell, 2009.

Parikka, Jussi. *What Is Media Archaeology*. Malden: Polity Press, 2012.

Sunde, Peter. "Intertubes." *Copy me happy* (blog). May 26, 2013.

Verbeek, Peter-Paul. *What Things Do: Philosophical Reflections on Technology, Agency, and Design*. Pennsylvania: The Pennsylvania State University Press, 2005.

Winner, Langdon. *The Whale and the Reactor*. Chicago: University of Chicago Press, 1986.

33.

TV, Digital, and Social: A Debate

JING WANG

One of the most important debates in the digital era centers on the future of TV. This question seems as urgent as the crumbling of the old journalism establishment.[1] If, as Jeff Bezos avows, "The Internet is transforming almost every element of the news business,"[2] what is happening to the TV business, where content is also undergoing digitization?

This question is crucial to a class I teach every spring at MIT, Advertising and Media: Comparative Perspective, which examines the changing fortunes of media outlets from the perspective of advertising research. When I first offered this course a decade ago, I focused on how advertising and marketing operated in the old media environment in which TV dominated as *the* most favored medium for branding a product or service. Back then, media placement was an afterthought for advertisers. Parasitically embedded in the big holding companies of Adland, media service primarily involved channel planning and media buying. This division sat at the very end of the workflow of branding. Not anymore. Advertising companies WPP, Omnicom, Publicis, and Interpublic have all unbundled media from their full-service agencies. Business clients now dictate that their media investments include digital strategies. Indeed, a silent revolution has triggered an overhaul of traditional media agencies. New ad formats such as Twitter and Facebook marketing, mobile marketing, and online word-of-mouth have all emerged as critical components of the marketing mix, keeping step with client demands for "seamlessly integrating digital into all media plans" which is now a performance measure that advertisers rank as second in importance to "research on consumer insights."[3]

Three years ago, I started restructuring my class, giving 50 percent of our time to digital. My real challenge, however, has involved interweaving discussions of broadcast and new media into each other's domain instead of treating them separately. To set us on the right course, I emphasize from the start the importance, and even the necessity, of studying media through advertising. The fact is, media and advertising are codependent: advertisers buy media spots to place advertisements and, equally important, media companies need advertisers to support content. Changing advertising paradigms — from TV-centric to digital and mobile and on to social TV — can account for the instability of some media platforms vis-à-vis others. The close relationship between content and advertising can never be overstated. After all (with a few exceptions such as premium pay TV), the ecosystem of television stands on three legs: networks, *advertisers*, and viewers.

This think piece reflects on the future of TV through a critical review of my advertising course. In my opening lecture to students taking Advertising and Media, I begin with this statement: TV as a medium is still relevant, and the rise of social TV as a new sector will create synergies between old media and social media that can be game changing to the industry as a whole. One crucial pedagogical task I take up in my class is to find ways of deconstructing the dichotomy between TV and digital (of which social marketing is a major component). There is a huge difference between brand building on TV and using social media to create buzz about a brand. In the contemporary context, we need both: brand building and brand extension. There is a dual danger of prioritizing one medium at the expense of the other. First, in advertisers' mad rush to be digital, they often lose sight of the importance of brand-building skills. Second, driving the train while laying the tracks (as it goes with all things digital), the clients risk forgetting that with television, a brand's infrastructure is built over time. Clients' hurried dive into digital may result in the disintegration of a brand's core values.

How best can we structure a class that treats TV and digital as two complementary media that deliver different benefits for brands? I place emphasis on teaching the basics about "brand positioning," the rationale for which is closely tied to TV as an ad medium. At the same time, I discuss recent digital campaigns by megabrands (e.g., Pepsi's "Refresh", Nike's "#findgreatness" social campaign, and Coca-Cola's "Coke Chase" and "China Beat") side by side with their earlier classic TV commercials. This creates a set of comparisons that drives home the mutual dependency of TV and digital in shaping a brand's presence. Nobody knows better than Coke, Pepsi, and Nike—veteran TV advertisers—that TV and digital are complementary. This is the case not because these two media reach different audiences but because each engages consumers in its own way(s).

Most excitingly, I juxtapose the well-celebrated cases noted above with brands with fewer financial resources whose experimentation with digital and social is especially energizing. In comparison with the megabrands mentioned above, these brands are less hampered by the history of a long and successful affair with old media. Many of their daring innovations have triggered sustained viral effects. For example, Hewlett Packard's China campaign, "My Computer My Stage" (2007-2009) ran three seasons. Tipp-Ex's lighthearted "Hunter and Bear," (2010-2014), an old interactive campaign, enjoyed a renewed round of applause with several funny but thoughtful sequels. The Old Spice guy and his personalized video sequence, "The Man Your Man Could Smell Like," ruled the social media realm for the greater part of 2010. Finally, Wendy's groundbreaking, but ultimately unsuccessful, Red Wig campaign (2007-2008) pushed to the fore a central question for those jumping on the new bandwagon: are digital tactics and social reach good enough to boost sales?

Coca-Cola's answer would probably be a resounding no. Burger King's should also be a no since the King ditched Crispin, [4] its agency partner for seven years and the genius behind the Subservient Chicken viral campaign (2004-), one of the most celebrated interactive campaigns in recent advertising history. Though a widely lauded campaign, the Subservient Chicken ultimately failed to boost sales. Burger King's 2011 severance from Crispin was a sure sign that the digital game itself was changing: just going viral and altering how we think about creative is no longer sufficient. Today, interactivity for its own sake no longer moves the sales needle fast enough. Advertisers need to do more.

They have to shift from treating new media as mere eye candy to focusing on making digital/social the core driver of the brand's strategic breakthroughs that transform branding practices, retail models, and, more fundamentally, business models from the inside out. Marc Speichert, the CMO of L'Oreal USA, hit the nail on the head when he observed, "Suddenly, digital becomes the catalyst for thinking differently about marketing." [5]

As a means of further contextualizing and complicating our ideas regarding the digital and the social, my class scrutinizes the biggest social media blunders of recent history. This involves diving into the culture of the "always-on generation," tying demographic changes to larger media technological trends, and thinking about the social media revolution that has impacted the entertainment industry. Surely, all those interactive (and crowdsourced) ad campaigns conveyed one message loud and clear: we are witnessing a sea change in viewer demographics. Millennials want to party with brands—but on their own terms.

So how does TV withstand the unstoppable dual trend of decentralization and personalization of both content and messaging? This is one of the problematics that students in my class are asked to unravel during the semester. They are put to the test with one final class assignment for the semester where they are asked to critique the meanings of "social" at the same time that they remake an interactive marketing campaign for a brand of their choice.

Students make several important discoveries during the course. They learn, for example, that the thirty-second spot is not "on its last leg"[6] despite such repeated proclamations by the press. They also find out that although the internet is the fastest-growing medium, TV continues to offer a unique scale of reach. In short, the impact that a creative television commercial has in driving brand awareness remains unsurpassed. Even Google sometimes bows to TV advertising: for example, the appearance of its commercial "Parisian Love" in the 2010 Super Bowl was a big surprise to all. Few students knew that the company, whose CEO once called marketing "unacceptable spending,"[7] had created many lackluster

TV ads before this one became a hit. Despite proclamations to the contrary, TV has continued to figure prominently in Google's strategies. Such lessons prompt me to ask the class: "Why TV?"

Where Social Meets TV

One can narrow down all the problems that television faces to one sentence: the medium does not work for narrowcasting in an age that fetishizes the micro-niche. We can also summarize the medium's longevity in an equally shorthand fashion: TV is the "last bastion of cheap, broad reach in an age of media fragmentation."[8] So what if TV were to remain intact and online were to become "TV" too? That scenario is already happening as viewership on tablets and smartphones continues to increase dramatically. There is much journalistic and industry fanfare about the dual-screen experience. But in fact, we should be talking about a triple-, or even quadruple-, screen reality. For example, imagine this scenario: I am watching the popular Chinese TV drama "The New *Romance of the Three Kingdoms*" (2010) on my video player while debating on my Mac with Facebook friends the superiority of this remake to the 1994 original, even as I am checking a video snippet on my iPad that reenacts the death of a minor character killed by the archvillain Cao Cao. At the same time, I could be tuning in to my iPhone to communicate with my Beijing WeChat friends about John Woo's *Red Cliff*, a 2008 Hollywood remake of the *Three Kingdoms*. And of course, I have also downloaded the original novel to my Kindle, just in case I need to read episodes that were left out of those TV and film adaptations.

As more viewers are multitasking and splintering their attention across multiple screens, TV is no longer bound to any piece of hardware. Indeed, once we realize that TV is just a state of mind, its longevity needs no further questioning and the logic behind the emergence of social TV becomes obvious. But what does social TV do? Second-screen apps like Snappy TV and tvtag allow us to watch TV while sharing our thoughts on smartphones or tablets about plot, characters, or indeed anything we watch. By making live streams and TV broadcasts social, mobile, and viral, these apps turn us into *active audiences*. Some optimists even opine that social chatter generated on second-screen services and apps will prompt more young viewers to watch TV in real-time again. [9]

For the broadcast networks, TV conversations on social media have generated data to help them adjust their programming and enabled them to produce more engaging content. Most importantly, having the knowledge of who has "checked in" to programs helps the networks shape a more personalized relationship with target viewers. A much-debated issue is whether social buzz gooses ratings. [10] Perhaps such buzz does increase ratings, but more often than not, social-TV metrics are inconsistent and should not be taken as a solution to the challenges faced by those involved in audience measurement. But all that is beside the point. Marketers who have belittled the new phenomenon and called it hype are missing the bigger picture: social TV gets consumers to engage with content and brands far beyond the broadcast window. This point takes us back to my earlier discussion about "brand extensions" of digital vis-à-vis TV. With the arrival of social TV technologies, a brand crosses over multiple platforms and drives multimedia storytelling. Moreover, social TV goes in tandem with the most obvious payoff: endorsements of brands from fans to their friends. Small wonder that Nielsen rolled out its Cross-Platform Online Campaign Ratings in October 2012!

Eventually, the real question for advertisers is a practical one: "Is it better to advertise on the first screen (TV), second screen (digital devices), or both?" [11] For now, the safest option is a mixed-media strategy, not least because turning the second-screen experience into a mainstream activity is a challenge. On the one hand, there are relatively few users of social TV apps and platforms. On the other hand, we know that there will not be any massive exodus of TV ad dollars until media buyers stop showing up at the Big TV upfronts—the place where networks sell the bulk of their inventory to advertisers for the coming fall season. A quick look at the ongoing debates in the digital marketing sector may help illuminate the mixed view about the viability of digital. Among the much-debated issues, industry observers wonder whether the Web needs a TV-style hit to get the attention of TV advertisers and why it has been so hard to prove return on investment (ROI) when digital data and metrics are so abundant.

I will end my reflection on the relationship between "old television" and "digital media" with two conflicting quotes, each proclaiming that one medium outperforms the other. Leslie Moonves, the CEO of CBS Corporation, made the first statement: "The 'first screen' comes first, and there's no 'second screen' without it."[12] A second, more nuanced, pronouncement comes from Omnicom President-CEO John Wren: "We believe that 2011 was the year in which the historical distinction between so-called traditional and digital media disappeared, as we had always said it would."[13] He continues: "everything we do has a digital component to it." So it seems that

TV's tango with things digital takes on an unforeseen turn, thanks to the development of social TV. In this case, *synergy*, rather than *dual*, is the new catchword.

At the end of the semester, my students in "Advertising and Media" showcase the media strategies they design for a brand-repositioning campaign. I am always pleased to find that no teams choose to invest their budget exclusively in any single media outlet. A usual mix includes TV, social, radio, and billboards. Those teams that do lean heavily on TV are smart enough to develop multistation, multichannel, and multidevice strategies. Wary of underdeveloped social media metrics, most teams that work on brand luxury goods decide to give up Facebook in favor of younger platforms such as Pinterest and Vine. This move rightfully warns us of the ephemeral appeals of all digital and social platforms.

The pedagogical approach described here provides a few clues about my agenda for media industry scholarship. Apart from emphasizing the *continuum* of broadcast, digital, and social media and thus prioritizing the necessity of examining the media ecosystem as a whole, I believe that any thorough research on such an ecosystem has to include studies of the impact of advertising and marketing on media.

---

[1] In August 2013, the NEW YORK TIMES announced that it sold the 141-year-old *Boston Globe* to Boston Red Sox owner John Henry for a mere $70 million. Almost simultaneously, the Graham family sold the *Washington Post* to Jeff Bezos, the founder of Amazon.com.

[2] Laura Norton Amico, "The Great Improvisation: Jeff Bezos, Duke Ellington, and the Washington Post," *Jazz & Journalism*, accessed August 7, 2013.

[3] Julie Lisse, "What Clients Want," *Advertising Age*, April 30, 2012, C4.

[4] Maureen Morrison, "Crispin's Breakup with the King Results in $300 Million Whopper Sacrifice," *Advertising Age*, March 21, 2011.

[5] Jack Neff, "L'Oreal Boosted Digital Spending, and It's Paying Off Big Time," *Advertising Age*, September 17, 2012.

⁶ Joseph Jaffe argued in his *Life after the 30-Second Spot* (Hoboken, NJ: John Wiley & Sons, 2005) that the thirty-second commercial was dying. His was an influential view in the mid-2000s.

⁷ Google's Eric Schmidt once called advertising "the last bastion of unaccountable spending in corporate America." See Michael Learmonth, "Why Anti-marketer Google Has Embraced Marketing," *Advertising Age*, November 7, 2011.

⁸ Matthew Creamer, "Why 'Advanced' TV Ads Haven't Spawned a Marketing Utopia," *Advertising Age*, April 16, 2012.

⁹ Kip Cassino, "Media's Millenial Myth: 'They'll Grow into It,'" *Advertising Age*, February 14, 2014.

¹⁰ Simon Dumenco, "Believe the Hype? Four Things Social TV Can Actually Do," *Advertising Age*, April 13, 2012.

¹¹ Shawndra Hill, "Social TV: Linking Content, Buzz and Sale," *Think Insights with Google*, last modified September 2012.

¹² Brian Steinberg, "TV's Upfront Pitch: Our Shows Offer Best Social-Media Traction," *Advertising Age*, May 21, 2012.

¹³ Bradley Johnson, "With 16.4% Growth, Digital Is Adland's Star Performer," *Advertising Age*, April 30, 2012.

Bibliography

Amico, Laura Norton. "The Great Improvisation: Jeff Bezos, Duke Ellington, and the *Washington Post.*" *Jazz & Journalism.* Accessed August 7, 2013.

Cassino, Kip, "Media's Millenial Myth: 'They'll Grow into It,'" *Advertising Age*, February 14, 2014.

Creamer, Matthew. "Why 'Advanced' TV Ads Haven't Spawned a Marketing Utopia." *Advertising Age*, April 16, 2012.

Dumenco, Simon. "Believe the Hype? Four Things Social TV Can Actually Do," *Advertising Age*, April 13, 2012

Hill, Shawndra. "Social TV: Linking Content, Buzz and Sale." Think Insights with Google. Last modified September 2012.

Jaffe, Joseph. *Life after the 30-Second Spot*. Hoboken, NJ: John Wiley & Sons, 2005.

Johnson, Bradley. "With 16.4% Growth, Digital Is Adland's Star Performer." *Advertising Age*, April 30, 2012.

Learmonth, Michael. "Why Anti-marketer Google Has Embraced Marketing." *Advertising Age*, November 7, 2011.

Lisse, Julie. "What Clients Want." *Advertising Age*, April 30, 2012, C4.

Morrison, Maureen. "Crispin's Breakup with the King Results in $300 Million Whopper Sacrifice." *Advertising Age*, March 21, 2011.

Neff, Jack. "L'Oreal Boosted Digital Spending, and It's Paying Off Big Time." *Advertising Age*, September 7, 2012.

Steinberg, Brian. "TV's Upfront Pitch: Our Shows Offer Best Social-Media Traction." *Advertising Age*, May 21, 2012.

34.

Learning from the History of the Field

JANET WASKO

Once upon a time, it was rare to find much interest from cinema scholars in research on the film or media industries. Indeed, times have changed. Media industry studies has been recognized as a viable and somewhat popular approach to the study of media, despite lingering issues relating to its definitions, scope, and motivations. The large number of Society for Cinema and Media Studies (SCMS) scholars who identified with the Media Industries Scholarly Interest Group when it was formed in 2011-2012 is just one indication. But the proliferation of studies that fit under this umbrella is another encouraging sign. While not necessarily in the "mainstream" of cinema or media research, the number of studies related to media industries has increased consistently over the last few decades.

This is not to say that the field of media industry studies is new. Indeed, a great deal of work has been done in the past that also fits under the media industry studies umbrella. One may not know that, however, when reading much of the recent research or many theoretical discussions of this approach. In fact, it is rare to see references to a number of classic studies that might be considered predecessors of current media industry studies.

It might be useful to provide a few examples. While the focus here is on the US film industry, similar examples could be cited for other media and other countries. A number of classic studies of film production, distribution, and exhibition in the United States emerged during the 1930s and 1940s. Howard T. Lewis's work in *The Motion Picture Industry* (1933) and Mae Huettig's excellent research in *The Economic Control of the Film Industry*[1] focus mostly on economic factors motivating Hollywood, including trends such as concentration and monopolistic practices. Written by an industry insider, Benjamin Hampton's *History of the American Film Industry from Its Beginnings to 1931*[2] provides interesting behind-the-scenes stories of the emerging film business. Peter Bächlin's *Histoire Economique du Cinema*[3] is another example of economic analysis of film conducted during this period.

Moving into the 1950s, Michael Conant's *Antitrust in the Motion Picture Industry*[4] is a clear and insightful analysis of the details and consequences of the Paramount decrees for the industry in the years following the 1948 Supreme Court decision. Meanwhile, Hortense Powdermaker's *Hollywood, the Dream Factory*[5] looks at Hollywood from an anthropological perspective, revealing quite a lot about the business of film in the United States. A key text from the 1960s is Thomas Guback's *The International Film Industry*.[6] This was one of the first studies of film by a media scholar employing a political economic perspective; it drew attention to the role of the state in Hollywood's international activities, clearly showing us that globalization of the US film industry is certainly not new.

Guback's work in particular could be helpful in responding to one of the questions posed to board members by the *Media Industries* editors when they solicited these essays: "Media production, distribution, and consumption are increasingly an international affair. What are the ramifications of this globalization process for the study and practices of the media industries?" We know that global markets are vitally important to the current transnational entertainment conglomerates that dominate the US film industry, which have been enticed even further into foreign markets during the last few decades. Guided by neoliberal economic policies, the ongoing deregulation and privatization of media operations have opened up new commercial channels and greatly expanded programming and advertising markets. A thorough accounting of these developments may benefit from some of the earlier studies mentioned above.

For instance, the international distribution of US cultural products, especially films, extends back to the early twentieth century. Hollywood has nearly always looked beyond the United States to expand its markets and increase profits from its products. And at least since the 1920s, the US film industry dominated much of the global film business (even though the US may not have been the first global force in the world cinema business). The development and proliferation of technologies such as television, both satellite and cable, as well as video technology such as VCRs and DVDs, enhanced and expanded international film markets. As discussed below, different types of experts, from academics to industry analysts, have offered widely differing explanations for this dominance. Indeed, Hollywood's power is a complex mix of historical, economic, political, and cultural factors.

Beyond cultural explanations, historical analysis reveals Hollywood's initial commercial orientation. While other countries may have been developing film as art or propaganda, from early in its history the American motion picture industry developed as a profit-oriented, commodity-based enterprise. Several scholars have documented the US film industry's rise in global markets during WWI and the maintenance of that dominant position through the mid-1930s.[7] Kristin Thompson points out that not only was the US film industry able to export films during and after the war: new distribution procedures also led to the establishment of offices in various countries.[8] World War II, which decimated European industries, strongly reinforced the US dominance of global film markets because, again, US products were plentiful. In addition, through its activities after the war, the US government assured the industry's continued power. Guback's study provides information specifically on how that process worked in Western Europe. Overall, the US film industry benefited immeasurably from the historical circumstances that allowed for the continued American production and distribution of films during these global conflicts; being tied to a conquering nation that became *the* world economic and political power also contributed. Previous work on the international markets for film thus provides an essential foundation for considering the contemporary globalization process.

Of course, other studies could be cited as providing important foundations for the study of the film industry today. Interestingly, most of the studies before the 1960s cited above were not conducted by media scholars. As cinema and media studies grew in the 1970s and 1980s, scholars such as Thomas Schatz, Tino Balio, Douglas Gomery, Gorham Kindem, and others gave more attention to the industrial policies and structures of the film industry. All of these scholars have provided a historical context that could contribute valuable insights for future media industries research. We need to be sure that we introduce these studies — along with other work that explores the history of media industries—to graduate students working in this area and acknowledge them more often in our own research and theoretical discussions. In other words, we need to be aware of the history of our field as well as the history of the media industries.

---

1 Mae D. Huettig, *Economic Control of the Motion Picture Industry* (Philadelphia: University of Pennsylvania Press, 1944).

2 Benjamin Hampton, *History of the American Film Industry from Its Beginnings to 1931* (1931; New York: Dover Press, 1970).

3 Peter Bächlin, *Histoire Economique du Cinema* (Paris: La Nouvelle Edition, 1947).

4 Michael Conant, *Antitrust in the Motion Picture Industry* (Berkeley: University of California Press, 1960).

5 Hortense Powdermaker, *Hollywood, the Dream Factory* (Boston: Little, Brown, 1950).

6 Thomas Guback, *The International Film Industry: Western Europe and America Since 1945* (Bloomington: Indiana University Press, 1969).

7 For instance, see Kerry Segrave, *American Films Abroad: Hollywood's Domination of the World's Movie Screens from the 1890s to the Present* (Jefferson: McFarland, 1997) and Jørgen Ulff-Møller, *Hollywood's Film Wars with France: Film-Trade Diplomacy and the Emergence of the French Film Quota Policy* (Rochester, NY: University of Rochester Press, 2001).

8 Kristen Thompson, *Exporting Entertainment: America in the World Film Market 1907–1934* (London: British Film Institute, 1985).

Bibliography

Bächlin, Peter. *Histoire Economique du Cinema*. Paris: La Nouvelle Edition, 1947.

Conant, Michael. *Antitrust in the Motion Picture Industry*. Berkeley: University of California Press, 1960.

Guback, Thomas H. *The International Film Industry: Western Europe and America Since 1945.* Bloomington: Indiana University Press, 1969.

Hampton, Benjamin. *History of the American Film Industry from Its Beginnings to 1931.* 1931. New York: Dover Press, 1970.

Huettig, Mae D. *Economic Control of the Motion Picture Industry.* Philadelphia: University of Pennsylvania Press, 1944.

Lewis, Howard T. *The Motion Picture Industry.* New York: D. Van Nostrand, 1933.

Powdermaker, Hortense. *Hollywood, the Dream Factory.* Boston: Little, Brown, 1950.

Segrave, Kerry. *American Films Abroad: Hollywood's Domination of the World's Movie Screens from the 1890s to the Present.* Jefferson: McFarland, 1997.

Thompson, Kristen. *Exporting Entertainment: America in the World Film Market 1907–1934.* London: British Film Institute, 1985.

Ulff-Møller, Jørgen. *Hollywood's Film Wars with France: Film-Trade Diplomacy and the Emergence of the French Film Quota Policy.* Rochester, NY: University of Rochester Press, 2001.

35.

The Ramifications of Media Globalization in the Global South for the Study of Media Industries

HERMAN WASSERMAN

Media industries worldwide are affected by the globalization of production, distribution, and consumption. The widening reach of global media is the most visible consequence of these processes. It is no longer considered unusual to receive Sky News, BBC, or Al Jazeera in locations around the world or to receive news from far-flung places in one's living room on a daily basis. Social media are ubiquitous and have not only given rise to new constructions of subjectivity (the infamous "selfie" is a case in point) and new forms of political engagement (of which the so-called Arab Spring has now become a popular, if much debated, example) but have also posed challenges to beleaguered traditional media industries (especially newspapers) that now have to adapt business models in response to audiences who migrate online and who increasingly become media producers themselves. Jay Rosen's notion of "the people formerly known as the audience" has become a well-known description of these consumer-producers.[1] But although these processes are by their very nature global in scope, they play out in different ways and have different social and political implications in various parts of the world. While big media conglomerates have global reach, the political economy of communication and historical legacies of news production mean that news discourses are still dominated by perspectives from the global North (although channels like Al Jazeera and Al Arabiya provide some contraflow). Access to new media technologies is also asymmetrical; and while social media platforms on mobile phones may have contributed to the Arab Spring uprisings (although the extent to which this was a "new media revolution" has also been disputed),[2] Facebook and Twitter remain blocked in China, and mainstream media are under state control.

More attention needs to be paid to how the dynamics of media globalization play out in various parts of the world, especially in the global South. Too often there is an implicit assumption that the changes that media industries in media-saturated countries of the North are undergoing have implications for the future of media — the imminent demise of newspapers or the political power of social media via smartphones, for example, are universally true. Yet the flows and contraflows of global media, and the shifts that media industries undergo as a result, require a more nuanced social reading informed by a study of the contextual factors and dynamics. For instance, while the demise of newspapers in the global North is widely believed to be merely a question of time, the newspaper industry is still vibrant in many regions in the South.[3]

One example that may illustrate the complexity of global media flows and contraflows and their effect on media industries in the global South is that of South Africa.

Perhaps the most significant contextual aspects of the South African media industry are that it operates within a "new democracy"[4] — and therefore in a political climate that is still transitional — and that it is located in a society that is among the most socially and economically unequal in the world and marked by continued political protest and conflict.[5] These sociopolitical factors may at first glance not have direct implications for a study of media industries and technological change. A study of media industries in the South in particular should, however, not be divorced from social, political, and historical developments. At the very least, the inequalities in South Africa have a bearing on the levels of access to media and especially new technologies, while the political and social dimensions have important implications for the role that media industries can play in society, civic participation and engagement, and political change. Access to media in South Africa is unequal, and the skewing of mainstream media's audience has implications for the way media industries develop and seek to cater to a market that rhetorically presents itself as "the public" in political discourse but in fact represents a tiny sliver of society.

The fragmentation and differentiation of audiences in South Africa also has implications for how media industries are globalized, localized, and "glocalized." The opening up of the South African media landscape in the 1990s to the forces of global capital — with international media companies investing in South Africa and South African companies moving outward into the continent and further — coincided with the democratization of the country. Independent News and Media, an Irish publishing group formerly owned by Tony O'Reilly, bought a major South African newspaper company, the Argus Group, in 1994, while the South African media conglomerate Naspers continued to spread its wings on the continent and around the world. The latest and most profitable among the outward moves by this company has been its investment in the online platform Tencent in China.[6]

Although it could be argued that the globalization of media ownership has political implications elsewhere as well (for instance, Rupert Murdoch's changing political allegiances in the UK), the globalization of the media industry in South Africa has been particularly controversial politically. On the one hand, the arrival of the Independent newspaper group in the country in the year that South Africa became a democracy was seen as signaling an attempt by the African National Congress-led government to gain an ally in the press (the deal with Tony O'Reilly was said to have been brokered by Nelson Mandela); and when this group was again sold to the South African Sekunjalo consortium in 2013, the close ties between the latter's chairman, Iqbal Survé, and the government, as well as the inclusion of a Chinese partner, raised concerns about editorial independence at the group. On the other hand, the Naspers media group, a global conglomerate that was built on Afrikaner capital during apartheid, has seen considerable success as a result of its investment in China. This achievement is often celebrated as an indication of CEO Koos Bekker's business acumen, even if the transnationalization of South African media across the African continent has raised questions of expansionism and media imperialism.[7] These controversies underscore how important it is that studies of media globalization in contexts such as South Africa and other transitional democracies in the global South take heed of the political and historical specificities of the local contexts within which these processes play out.

The opportunities to branch out into the continent and internationally afforded South African media companies as a result of the ending of the country's isolation did not, however, mean an immediate, radical transformation of South African media internally. Debates about racial representation in the media industry and the industry's transformation of ownership and control started soon after democratization and continue twenty years into democracy;[8] the South African media industry remains characterized by an "elite continuity."[9] The media continue to be criticized for presenting a "view from the suburbs"[10] — catering to the small percentage of the population that represents lucrative audiences for advertisers. That section of the population has benefited most from media globalization, as its members have access to the broad array of media consumption and production opportunities offered by the influx of international media as well as the cornucopia of social media and online platforms that are now within their reach. Globalization of content has, however, not only been limited to the exchange of media capital and content for the elite. Interesting manifestations of glocalization in platforms and formats — for instance, the adoption of the red-top tabloid newspaper format for a mass readership consisting of black working-class readers that continue to be marginalized by mainstream newspapers[11] — have made their mark on the South African media industry.

The South African example — which has been discussed only very briefly here — illustrates how media globalization is a multi-levelled process that plays out within specific social and political contexts. When flows and contraflows in global media industries are studied, it remains important to pay attention to these contextual specificities, especially within the global South, where patterns often look very different from those in the media-saturated global North. Moreover, globalization of media industries should not only be seen in terms of flows and contraflows between countries and regions, but should also telescope down to domestic contestations that play out internally in local media industries but are a result of global processes. The study of media industries can therefore benefit from greater attention to those regions of the "Rest"[12] that are too often neglected in contemporary debates about the changes impacting on media industries as a result of globalization.

1 Jay Rosen, "The People Formerly Known as the Audience," Press Think: Ghost of *Democracy in the Media Marchine* (blog), last modified June 27, 2006.
2 Martin Hirst, "One Tweet Does Not a Revolution Make: Technological Determinism, Media, and Social Change," *Global Media Journal* 12, no. 2 (2012): 1–29. See also Herman Wasserman, "Mobile Phones, Popular Media, and Everyday African Democracy: Transmissions and Transgressions," *Popular Communication* 9, no. 2 (2011): 146–58.
3 Conway-Smith, Erin. "Read All About It: Newspapers Are Thriving!" *Global Post*, October 20, 2012.
4 Katrin Voltmer, *The Media in Transitional Democracies* (Cambridge: Polity, 2013); Herman Wasserman, "Freedom's Just Another Word? Perspectives on Media Freedom and Responsibility in South Africa and Nambia," *International Communication Gazette* 72, no. 7 (2010): 567–88.
5 See, for instance, Hein Marais, *South Africa Pushed to the Limit* (Cape Town: UCT Press, 2011); Patrick Heller, "Democratic Deepening in India and South Africa," *Journal of Asian and African Studies* 44, no. 1 (2009): 123–49; Edgar Pieterse and Mirjam Van Donk, "Local Government and Poverty Reduction," in *State of the Nation, 2012–2013*, ed. Udesh Pillay et al. (Cape Town: HSRC Press, 2013), 98–123.
6 Herman Wasserman, "South Africa and China as BRICS partners: Media Perspectives on Geopolitical Shifts," *Journal of Asian and African Studies*, published electronically December 16, 2013, doi:10.1177/0021909613514191.
7 Fackson Banda, "The Media in Africa," in *Media Studies*, vol. 1, ed. Pieter J. Fourie (Cape Town: Juta, 2007), 59–86.
8 See Nelson Mandela, "Address to the International Press Institute's Congress" (speech, February 14, 1994); "Report on the Transformation of Print and Digital Media," Print and Digital Media Task Team, last modified September 2013.
9 Colin Sparks, "South African Media in Transition," *Journal of African Media Studies* 1, no. 2(2009): 195–220.

[10] Steven Friedman, "Whose Freedom? South Africa's Press, Middle-Class Bias and the Threat of Control," *Ecquid Novi: African Journalism Studies* 32, no. 2 (2011): 106–21.

[11] Herman Wasserman, *Tabloid Journalism in South Africa: True Story!* (Bloomington: Indiana University Press, 2010).

[12] Fareed Zakaria, *The Post-American World*, updated and expanded ed. (New York: W. W. Norton, 2011).

Bibliography

Banda, Fackson. "The Media in Africa." In *Media Studies*, vol. 1, edited by Pieter J. Fourie, 59–86. Cape Town: Juta, 2007.

Conway-Smith, Erin. "Read All About It: Newspapers Are Thriving!" *Global Post*, October 20, 2012.

Friedman, Steven. "Whose Freedom? South Africa's Press, Middle-Class Bias and the Threat of Control." *Ecquid Novi: African Journalism Studies* 32, no. 2 (2011): 106–21.

Heller, Patrick. "Democratic Deepening in India and South Africa." *Journal of Asian and African Studies* 44, no. 1 (2009): 123–49.

Hirst, Martin. "One Tweet Does Not a Revolution Make: Technological Determinism, Media and Social Change." *Global Media Journal* 12, no. 2 (2012): 1–29.

Mandela, Nelson. Speech, February 14, 1994.

Marais, Hein. *South Africa Pushed to the Limit*. Cape Town: UCT Press, 2011.

Pieterse, Edgar, and Mirjam Van Donk. "Local Government and Poverty Reduction." In *State of the Nation, 2012–2013*, edited by Udesh Pillay, Gerard Hagg, Francis Nyamnjoh, and Johnathan Jansen, 98–123. Cape Town: HSRC Press, 2013.

Print and Digital Media Task Team. "Report on the Transformation of Print and Digital Media." Last modified September 2013.

Sparks, Colin. "South African Media in Transition." *Journal of African Media Studies* 1, no. 2 (2009): 195–220.

Voltmer, Katrin. *The Media in Transitional Democracies*. Cambridge: Polity, 2013.

Wasserman, Herman. "Freedom's Just Another Word? Perspectives on Media Freedom and Responsibility in South Africa and Nambia." *International Communication Gazette* 72, no. 7 (2010): 567–88.

———. "Mobile Phones, Popular Media, and Everyday African Democracy: Transmissions and Transgressions." *Popular Communication* 9, no. 2 (2011): 146–58.

———. "South Africa and China as BRICS Partners: Media Perspectives on Geopolitical Shifts." *Journal of Asian and African Studies*. Published electronically December 16, 2013. doi:10.1177/0021909613514191.

———. *Tabloid Journalism in South Africa: True Story!* Bloomington: Indiana University Press, 2010.

Zakaria, Fareed. *The Post-American World*. Updated and expanded ed. New York: W. W. Norton, 2011.

36.

Home Is Where Hollywood Isn't: Recasting East Asian Film Industries

EMILIE YUEH-YU YEH

In *East Asian Screen Industries*, Darrell Davis and I introduced the notion of "new localism" to emphasize the rise of modestly budgeted comedies, romance, action, and even sex pictures that worked like sleepers, helping to regenerate East Asian filmmaking and film viewing.[1] By *new localism*, we mean films made with distinct local ingredients that allow the audience a sense of recognition and empowerment. New localism is different from previous local productions shielded by protectionism and the limited distribution of foreign products. New localism is a strategic move, a shrewd way that East Asian filmmakers handle commercial challenges. Though theirs were films without much transnational ambition, made to recoup their costs within a small market, they found significant contemporary resonance among local viewers. Films like *The Ring* (1997), *Christmas in August* (1998), *Needing You* (2000), *Love on a Diet* (2000), *Shaolin Soccer* (2001), *Double Vision* (2002), and *Cell Phone* (2003) were made close by, using local talent and local "premises." The producers of these films did not react against Hollywood; rather, they registered Hollywood's potency and tried to carve out a niche for their products in the local market, and possibly beyond. By distinguishing themselves from imported blockbusters, they offer a communal experience that affirms local affiliation.

Two especially hot stories simmered in 2011. According to Hong Kong's official film classification, Category III refers to adult films restricted to viewers over eighteen years of age. One particular restricted "Category III" picture, *Sex and Zen: Extreme Ecstasy*, lured Chinese mainlanders across the border to Hong Kong with the promise of something racy and novel. Screening for over two months, this independent film made over US$5.5 million and injected a rare energy into the local industry at a time when most Hong Kong filmmakers had already decamped to the new film capital, Beijing.[2] The 3-D gimmick helped break the record set by Ang Lee's 2007 adult feature, *Lust, Caution*. In the 1990s, when Hong Kong cinema was robust, Category III was a recognized local genre on par with action, horror, and martial arts.[3] By revisiting this familiar if outré formula, bringing it up to date with enhanced exhibition, 3-D Category III films could compete with A-list pictures.

You Are the Apple of My Eye (2011) was the first film directed by Taiwan's internet writer Giddens Ko. This low-budget (US$300,000) youth film set new records in four territories: Taiwan, Hong Kong, mainland China, and Singapore. Most surprisingly, it surpassed Stephen Chow's *Kung Fu Hustle* (2004) to become Hong Kong's top-grossing Chinese film. This was unprecedented, as the Hong Kong market is known for picky viewers resistant to mainland and Taiwanese pictures. In China, *Apple* took in US$10 million against strong competition from *Mission: Impossible—Ghost Protocol* (2011) and Zhang Yimou's war epic, *Flowers of War* (2011). Gory eroticism might have been the major (guilty) pleasure of the sex pictures, but *Apple* combined word of mouth with a repackaged sentimentality to successfully attract local viewers.[4] Between sex and nostalgia, local producers in East Asia actively reengaged with local audiences. A resurgence of new localism was on the way.

Since 2009, domestic films in Japan, South Korea, and China have enjoyed 50 percent of overall market share (see table 1). Compared to figures from France (41.6 percent in 2011),[5] Germany (22.8 percent in 2011),[6] and Brazil (11.8 percent in 2011),[7] these East Asian figures demonstrate Hollywood is not as global as is often assumed. Except for in 2012, domestic films have garnered over 50 percent of China's box office.

Similarly, in Taiwan, local productions have surged since 2008, representing 18.65 percent in 2011 and 11.9 percent in 2012. Domestically produced Taiwanese films increased in number from around twenty per year to forty-five in 2012.[8]

The popularity of these local pictures was not a short-lived, fleeting thing. In 2012 and 2013, the momentum continued. In the PRC, *Lost in Thailand* (2012), *Journey to the West* (2013), *So Young* (2013), and *Tiny Times* (2013) set new records; and Japan's *Thermae Roma* (2012, earning US$50 million), South Korea's *Thieves* (2012), Taiwan's *Din*

Tao: Leader of the Parade (2012), and gangster comedy *David Loman* (2013, "Big-assed thug" in local dialect) all played well. This is a highly varied crop of pictures, not easy to generalize. In addition to the new localism and Hong Kong eroticism, we also see government protectionism and a growing awareness of integrated distribution and marketing contributing to the high sales of East Asian pictures.

Table 1: Percent Market Share of Domestically Produced Films			
Year	China %	Japan %	S. Korea %
2013	58.65	60.6	59.7
2012	48.46	65.7	58.8
2011	53.6	54.9	51.9
2010	56.37	53.6	46.6
2009	56.6	56.9	48.8
2008	60	59.5	42.1

Sources: Data from China Film Press, Chinese Film Review (Beijing: CFP, 2008–2012); *Korean Cinema 2013* (Busan: Korean Film Council, 2013), 23; "Statistics of Film Industry in Japan: 2000–2013" (Tokyo: Motion Picture Producers Association of Japan, 2013).

It is well known that the government regulates the market share of imported films in China. The box office of imported films is assumed to be capped at around 50 percent of total box office. This means that the distributors must cautiously monitor the overall performance of foreign imports. When foreign-film box office revenues approach this 50 percent mark, blackouts and delays on Hollywood releases are activated. Occasionally, Hollywood pictures may also be pulled from screens while demand is still high. This regulation has shielded Chinese pictures for many years, and the preferred domestic big-budget pictures have enjoyed a near monopoly of screens.⁹ Policy, both explicit and unwritten, is a key factor in the high performance of contemporary PRC cinema.

However, in 2012, as a result of China's agreement to deliver on its WTO promise, the quota for Hollywood imports increased by fourteen IMAX films, raising the limit to thirty-four. This change wrought a slightly higher permissible market share for Hollywood pictures (see table 1) and directly impacted the performance of high-budget costumers. This shift is a result of state protectionism submitting to global trade pressure. But, just when the Chinese industry began to worry about foreign incursions into its playing field, smaller pictures performed surprisingly well. It is almost as if the local players stepped up to slay the giant, though the reality is more complex.

Consider the pictures *Lost in Thailand* (2012), *So Young* (2013), and *Tiny Times 1.0* (2013), which had no special effects, no monsters, and no big stars. What is the reason for their huge success? *Lost in Thailand* (box office: US$200 million), a modest comedy, actually rivaled the box office of *Avatar* (2009). Given its cost (US$10 million) and scale, *Thailand* can be seen as decisively trouncing Cameron's 3-D leviathan. The party line explaining this victory held that a story and characters focused on common people entranced Chinese viewers. This is a veiled comment not just on Hollywood blockbusters but also on China's *dapian*, the domestic high-budget visual effects extravaganzas that have dominated Chinese screens since 2002, such as Zhang Yimou's *Hero* (2002) and its descendants. The image of *Lost in Thailand* is again David versus Goliath: humble human interest defeats the foreign - and domestic - colossus. This is another proven instance of localism, where the stress of coping with rapid economic growth was made into a journey of self-discovery.

Vicky Zhao Wei's MFA thesis, *So Young* (2013), earned a final box office total of US$110 million. For years, college students have voted Zhao as China's most popular female star, and her broad fan base directly contributed to the film's earning power. *Tiny Times 1.0* (2013, US$112 million) was the directorial debut of Guo Jingming, a Shanghai-based celebrity who made his fortune from internet fiction. Like *So Young* and *You Are the Apple of My Eye*, *Tiny Times*

1.0 was a presold[10] project that capitalized on the writer-filmmaker's fame and bankability.

Both *Tiny Times 1.0* and *You Are the Apple of My Eye* were adapted from popular works of fiction distributed on the internet. These digital roots promise more involvement in film production by webzines, web agencies, portals, service providers, and e-commerce facilitators. Le Vision, for example, is an internet viewing platform that invested in *Tiny Times*. Social networks — aligned with various internet companies as investors, technical checkpoints, aggregators, and game designers — are becoming an essential marketing channel for movies, audience feedback, and film criticism. It is crucial to note that a hit movie does not necessarily entail shifts in audience tastes. It is also important to trace the way a film is branded, advertised, distributed, and sold to specific market segments. Audience tastes can be shaped by canny attention to both online and offline hooks. *People's Daily* criticized *Tiny Times 1.0* for its ardent materialism (featuring rich and beautiful protagonists) and commodity fetishism (its celebration of high fashion and product placement) that exceeded the socialist norm.[11] Despite the criticism, *Tiny Times* has raised the benchmark for Chinese cinema, bringing local products closer to an ideal commodity form capable of being exploited in ancillary markets.

The title of this article, "Home Is Where Hollywood Isn't," refers to the limitations of media imperialism approaches. However, these rising limitations do not translate into a revival of media nationalism. Far from it: recent hits in East Asia indicate that nationalism is less a factor in the growth of domestic pictures than are changing patterns in distribution, marketing, and consumption. To many young consumers, home is where their favorite social networks reside. Whether local or global, home is where the tiny smartphone is.

---

[1] See Darrell Davis and Emilie Yeh, "The New Localism: Alternatives to Blockbuster Benchmarks," chap. 2 in *East Asian Screen Industries* (London: BFI, 2008).

[2] Michael Curtin, "Media Capital: Towards the Study of Spatial Flows," *Journal of International Cultural Studies* 6, no. 2 (2003): 202–28.

3 Darrell William Davis and Emilie Yeh, "Warning! Category III: The Other Hong Kong Cinema," *Film Quarterly* 54 no. 4 (2001): 12–26.

4 Darrell William Davis, "Second Coming: The Legacy of Taiwan New Cinema," in *A Companion to Chinese Cinema*, ed. Yingjin Zhan (London: Blackwell, 2012), 133–50.

5 Melanie Goodfellow, "French Cinema Admissions Hit 45-Year, 215 Million High in 2011, *Screendaily*, January 4, 2012. http://www.screendaily.com/french-cinema-admissions-hit-45-year-215-million-high-in-2011/5036125.article.

6 Bénédicte Prot, "More Cinema-Goers in 2011 Thanks to German Films," *Cinerupa*, March 5, 2012. http://cineuropa.org/nw.aspx?t=newsdetail&l=en&did=2 16965.

7 Elaine Guneri, "Brazilian Box Office Climbs for Third Year; Local Titles Falter," *Screendaily*, January 13, 2012. http://www.screendaily.com/news/box-office/brazilian-box-office-climbs-for-third-year-local-titles-falter/5036454.article.

8 "Statistics of Films Passed by Censorship Board (1996–2011)," TaiwanCinema.com, January 16, 2012. http://www.taiwancinema.com/ct_50897_144

9 Emilie Yeh and Darrell William Davis, "Re-nationalizing China's Film Industry: Case Study on the China Film Group and Film Marketization," *Journal of Chinese Cinemas* 2, no. 1 (2008): 37–51.

10 *Presold* refers to the adaption of a preexisting literary work.

11 Liu Qiong, "*Tiny Times 2* and *Tiny Times 3* Must Not Be Coddled without Warnings," *People's Daily*, July 15, 2013, p. 24.

Bibliography

Association of Chinese Film Distributers and Exhibitors. *2008–2009 Chinese Film Review*. Beijing: ACFDE, 2008, 2009.

Curtin, Michael. "Media Capital: Towards the Study of Spatial Flows." *Journal of International Cultural Studies* 6, no. 2 (2003): 202–28.

— — —. *Playing to the World's Biggest Audience: the Globalization of Chinese Film and Television.* Berkeley: University of California Press, 2007.

Davis, Darrell William. "Second Coming: the Legacy of Taiwan New Cinema." In *A Companion to Chinese Cinema*, edited by Yingjin Zhang, 133–50. London: Blackwell, 2012.

Davis, Darrell William, and Emilie Yeh. *East Asian Screen Industries.* London: BFI, 2008.

— — —. "Warning! Category III: The Other Hong Kong Cinema." *Film Quarterly* 54, no. 4 (2001): 12–26.

Goodfellow, Melanie. "French Cinema Admissions Hit 45-Year, 215 Million High in 2011." *Screendaily*, January 4, 2012. http://www.screendaily.com/french-cinema-admissions-hit-45-year-215-million-high-in-2011/5036125.article.

Guneri, Elaine. "Brazilian Box Office Climbs for Third Year; Local Titles Falter," *Screendaily*, January 13, 2012. http://www.screendaily.com/news/box-office/brazilian-box-office-climbs-for-third-year-local-titles-falter/5036454.article.

Liu, Qiong. "*Tiny Times* 2 and *Tiny Times* 3 Must Not Be Coddled Without Warnings." *People's Daily*, July 15, 2013, p. 24.

Keane, Michael. "Once Were Peripheral: Creating Media Capacity in East Asia." *Media, Culture, and Society* 28 (2006): 835–55.

Prot, Bénédicte. "More Cinema-Goers in 2011 Thanks to German Films." *Cineuropa.* May 3, 2012. http://cineuropa.org/nw.aspx?t=newsdetail&l=en&did=216965.

"Statistics of Films Passed by Censorship Board (1996–2011)." TaiwanCinema.com, January 16, 2012.

Yeh, Emilie, and Darrell William Davis. "Re-nationalizing China's Film Industry: Case Study on the China Film Group and Film Marketization." *Journal of Chinese Cinemas* 2, no. 1 (2008): 37.

Contributors

CHARLES R. ACLAND is Professor of Communication Studies at Concordia University, Montreal. His books include *Screen Traffic: Movies, Multiplexes, and Global Culture* (2003), *Swift Viewing: The Popular Life of Subliminal Influence* (2012), and *Useful Cinema* (2011), co-edited with Haidee Wasson (all Duke University Press).

MARK DEUZE is Professor of Media Studies, specializing in journalism, in the University of Amsterdam's Faculty of Humanities. From 2004 to 2013, he worked at Indiana University's Department of Telecommunications in Bloomington, United States. Publications of his work include over fifty articles in academic journals and seven books, including *Media Work* (Polity, 2007), *Managing Media Work* (Sage, 2011), and *Media Life* (Polity, 2012).

DES FREEDMAN is Professor of Media and Communications in the Department of Media and Communications at Goldsmiths, University of London. He is the author of *The Contradictions of Media Power* (2016), *The Politics of Media Policy* (Polity, 2008), and co-author with James Curran and Natalie Fenton of *Misunderstanding the Internet* (Routledge, 2016). He is an editor of the journal *Global Media and Communication*, former chair of the Media Reform Coalition and project lead for the Inquiry into the Future of Public Service Television chaired by Lord Puttnam.

TEJASWINI GANTI is a visual anthropologist specializing in South Asia. Her research interests include Indian cinema, anthropology of media, production cultures, visual culture, cultural policy, nationalism, neoliberalism, capitalism, ideologies of development, and theories of globalization. She has been conducting ethnographic research about the social world and filmmaking practices of the Hindi film industry since 1996 and is the author of *Producing Bollywood: Inside the Contemporary Hindi Film Industry* (Duke University Press, 2012) and *Bollywood: A Guidebook to Popular Hindi Cinema* (Routledge, 2004; 2nd ed., 2013).

288

NITIN GOVIL is Associate Professor of Cinema & Media Studies in the School of Cinematic Arts at the University of Southern California. He is the author of *Orienting Hollywood: Film Culture Between Los Angeles and Bombay* and coauthor of *Global Hollywood* and *Global Hollywood 2*. He is currently completing a coauthored book on the Indian film industries and a coauthored book on global media.

TIMOTHY HAVENS is Professor of Communication Studies, African American Studies, and International Studies at the University of Iowa. He is the author of *Black Television Travels: African American Media Around the Globe* (NYU Press, 2013) and *Global Television Marketplace* (BFI Publishing, 2006); the co-author with Amanda D. Lotz of Understanding Media Industries (Oxford University Press, 2011, 2016); the co-editor with Aniko Imre and Katalin Lustyik of Popular Television in Eastern Europe During and Since Socialism (Routledge, 2012); and a former Senior Fulbright Scholar to Hungary. His research has also appeared in numerous scholarly journals in media and cultural studies and anthologies on media globalization and television studies.

DAVID HESMONDHALGH is Professor of Media, Music and Culture in the School of Media and Communication at the University of Leeds. He is the author of *Culture, Economy and Politics: The Case of New Labour* (Palgrave, 2015, co-written with Oakley, Lee and Nisbett); *Why Music Matters* (Wiley-Blackwell, 2013), *Creative Labour: Media Work in Three Cultural Industries* (Routledge, 2011, co-written with Sarah Baker), and *The Cultural Industries*, now in its third edition (Sage, 2012). He is also editor or co-editor of five other books and, with Anamik Saha, a special issue of the journal *Popular Communication* on "Race, Ethnicity and Cultural Production."

MICHELE HILMES is Professor Emerita of Media and Cultural Studies at the University of Wisconsin–Madison. Her work focuses on media history and historiography, particularly in the areas of transnational media and sound studies. She is the author or editor of several books in this field, including *Radio Voices: American Broadcasting 1922–1952* (1997), *Network Nations: A Transnational*

History of British and American Broadcasting (2011), *Only Connect: A Cultural History of Broadcasting in the United States* (4th ed., 2013), and *Radio's New Wave: Global Sound in the Digital Era* (2013), coedited with Jason Loviglio.

DINA IORDANOVA has published over fifteen books dealing with matters of global film circulation, film festivals, and transnational cinema. Having conceived and realised books about the global film festival circuit, about festivals and activism, and about film festivals in East Asia and the Middle East, she is the conceptual leader and editor of the *Film Festival Yearbook* series, which triggered a buoyant new strand of research into film festivals. Dina is an acknowledged authority on European cinema (with focus on Eastern Europe and the Balkans), migration, global film, and media. She is Professor and Director of the Institute of Global Cinema and Creative Cultures at the University of St Andrews in Scotland. Her work is translated in numerous languages. Her most recent edited volume (with Jean-Michel Frodon) *Cinemas of Paris* (2016).

APHRA KERR is a senior lecturer in the Department of Sociology at NUI Maynooth, Ireland. She has extensive research experience with a focus on the international digital games, animation, and television industries. She has previously been a visiting professor at the Annenberg School for Communication at the University of Pennsylvania and worked as a full-time researcher in the UK and the Netherlands. She has consulted for the European Commission and the Organization for Economic Co-operation and Development (OECD). For more, http://www.nuim.ie/sociology/our-people/aphra-kerr.

MARWAN M. KRAIDY is the Anthony Shadid Chair in Global Media, Politics and Culture and Director of the Project for Advanced Research in Global Communication, at the Annenberg School, University of Pennsylvania. He has been the Edward Said Chair in American Studies at the American University of Beirut, the Dupront Chair at CELSA Université-Sorbonne, and the Bonnier Professor at Stockholm University. The recipient of Guggenheim, ACLS, NEH, Woodrow Wilson and NIAS fellowships, Kraidy has published 120+ essays and 8 books, including *Hybridity, or the Cultural Logic of Globalization* (Temple, 2005), and *Reality Television and Arab Politics* (Cambridge, 2010), which won three major prizes. On May 9, 2016, Harvard University Press will release Kraidy's *The Naked Blogger of Cairo: Creative Insurgency in the Arab World*. Also forthcoming in 2016: *Global Media Studies* (co-author, Toby Miller, Polity, October), and *American Studies Encounters the Middle East* (co-editor, Alex Lubin, University of North Carolina Press, October). Kraidy tweets at @MKraidy.

SHIN DONG KIM is a Professor at the School of Media and Communication, Hallym University, Korea, and also a Founding Director of the Institute for Communication Arts and Technology. He has taught and conducted research in the areas of political economy of communication, media policy, global communication, and mobile communication for the past two decades. He is now leading a National Research Foundation's multi-year project on the ICT development models in Korea and other countries. Dr. Kim served many visiting positions including the Korean Studies Chair Professor at Sciences Po, Paris, Visiting Professor at Peking University, and at Dartmouth College among others.

SHANTI KUMAR is Associate Professor in the Department of Radio-Television-Film at the University of Texas, Austin. He is the author of *Gandhi Meets Primetime: Globalization and Nationalism in Indian Television* (University of Illinois Press, 2006), and the coeditor of *Global Communication: New Agendas in Communication* (2014), *Television at Large in South Asia* (Routledge, 2012) and *Planet TV: A Global Television Reader* (NYU Press, 2003). He has also published book chapters in edited anthologies and articles in journals such as *BioScope, Jump Cut, Popular Communication, South Asian Popular Culture, Quarterly Review of Film and Video,* and *Television and New Media*.

AMANDA D. LOTZ is Professor of Communication Studies and Screen Arts and Cultures at the University of Michigan. She is the author of *Cable Guys: Television and American Masculinities in the 21st Century* (New York University Press, 2014), *The Television Will Be Revolutionized* (New York University Press, 2007, 2014) and *Redesigning Women: Television after the Network Era* (University of Illinois Press, 2006) and editor of *Beyond Prime Time: Television Programming in the Post-Network Era* (Routledge, 2009). She is coauthor, with Timothy Havens, of *Understanding Media Industries* (Oxford University Press, 2011, 2015) and, with Jonathan Gray, of *Television Studies* (Polity, 2011).

DENISE MANN is an associate professor in the UCLA School of Theater, Film, and Television and head of the UCLA Producers Program (1996–present). Mann is the editor of *Wired TV: Laboring over an Interactive Future* (2014); the author of *Hollywood Independents: The Postwar Talent Takeover* (2008); and the co-editor of *Private Screenings: Television & the Female Consumer* (1992). She served as an associate editor on *Camera Obscura: A Journal of Feminism and Film Theory* (1986–1992). With Professor Henry Jenkins, Mann co-chairs the annual "Transmedia, Hollywood" conference (2010–present), which brings together cutting-edge scholars, industry professionals, and creators to debate the future of entertainment.

RICHARD MAXWELL is Professor and Chair of Media Studies at Queens College, City University of New York. He has published widely on a range of topics: media and the environment; broadcast reform during Spain's democratic transition; Hollywood's international dominance; media politics in the post-9/11 era; marketing research and the surveillance society; and the impact of political economic forces in daily life and culture.

VICKI MAYER is Professor of Communication at Tulane University. She is author or editor of four books and numerous other publications about media production. She edits the journal *Television & New Media* (SAGE Publications) and directs the digital humanities project MediaNOLA. This piece is drawn from her most recent work on the cultural impacts of runaway film economies.

RANJANI MAZUMDAR is Professor of Cinema Studies at the School of Arts and Aesthetics, Jawaharlal Nehru University. Her publications focus on urban cultures, popular cinema, gender, and the cinematic city. She is the author of *Bombay Cinema: An Archive of the City* (2007) and co-author with Nitin Govil of the forthcoming *The Indian Film Industry*. She has also worked as a documentary filmmaker, and her productions include *Delhi Diary*

2001 and *The Power of the Image* (codirected). Her current research focuses on globalization and film culture, and the intersection of technology, travel, design, and color in 1960s Bombay cinema.

TOBY MILLER is Emeritus Distinguished Professor, University of California, Riverside; Sir Walter Murdoch Professor of Cultural Policy Studies, Murdoch University (40%); Profesor Invitado, Escuela de Comunicación Social, Universidad del Norte (25%); Professor of Journalism, Media and Cultural Studies, Cardiff University/Prifysgol Caerdydd (20%); and Director of the Institute of Media and Creative Industries, Loughborough University London (100%). The author and editor of over forty books, his work has been translated into Spanish, Chinese, Portuguese, Japanese, Turkish, German, Italian, Farsi, and Swedish. His most recent volumes are *The Sage Companion to Television Studies* (edited with Manuel Alvarado, Milly Buonanno, and Herman Gray, 2015), *The Routledge Companion to Global Popular Culture* (edited, 2015), *Greening the Media* (with Richard Maxwell, 2012) and *Blow Up the Humanities* (2012). He can be contacted at tobym69@icloud.com and his adventures scrutinized at www.tobymiller.org.

PHILIP M. NAPOLI (Ph.D., Northwestern University) is Professor of Journalism and Media Studies in the School of Communication and Information at Rutgers University and a Media Policy Fellow with the New America Foundation. His books include *Audience Economics: Media Institutions and the Audience Marketplace* (Columbia University Press, 2003) and *Audience Evolution: New Technologies and the Transformation of Media Audiences* (Columbia University Press, 2011).

PHIL OPPENHEIM is the Chief Curator and Pop Culture Officer for the Comic-Con/Lionsgate Subscription Video-on-Demand service (launching in Spring 2016). Oppenheim previously serviced as Senior Vice President of Programming and Scheduling for TNT and TBS, overseeing programming, scheduling, and acquisition selection strategies for the two linear networks and their digital extensions. He also currently consults for KXRY/XRAY.FM and KFFP/Freeform Portland, two public-radio stations based in Portland, Oregon.

YEIDY M. RIVERO is Professor in the Department of Screen Arts and Cultures at the University of Michigan. Her research centers on television history, media and globalization, and race and ethnic representations in media. She is the author of *Tuning Out Blackness: Race and Nation in the History of Puerto Rican Television* (Duke University Press, 2005), *Broadcasting Modernity: Cuban Commercial Television, 1950–1960* (Duke University Press, 2015), and coeditor (with Arlene Dávila) of *Contemporary Latina/o Media: Production, Circulation, Politics* (New York University Press, 2014).

THOMAS SCHATZ is Professor of Film and Media Studies in the Radio-Television-Film Department at the University of Texas at Austin. He has written four books (and edited many others) about Hollywood films and filmmaking, including *Hollywood Genres* (New York: McGraw-Hill, 1981); *Boom and Bust: American Cinema in the 1940s* (Berkeley: University of California Press, 1999); and *The Genius of the System: Hollywood Filmmaking in the Studio Era* (Minneapolis: University of Minnesota Press, 2010).

JAMES SCHWOCH is Professor in the Department of Communication Studies at Northwestern University. His research explores a nexus of global media, media history, international studies, and global security. His most recent books are *Down to Earth: Satellite Technologies, Industries, and Cultures*, co-edited with Lisa Parks (Rutgers University Press, 2012), and *Global TV: New Media and the Cold War, 1946–69* (University of Illinois Press, 2009).

JOHN SINCLAIR is Honorary Professorial Fellow in the School of Historical and Philosophical Studies at the University of Melbourne. His published work covers various aspects of the internationalization of the media and communication industries, with a special emphasis on Asia and Latin America. His recent books include *Latin American Television Industries*, co-authored with Joe Straubhaar; and two co-edited works: *Consumer Culture in Latin America* and *Media and Communication in the Chinese Diaspora*. He has held visiting professorships at leading universities in Europe and the United States, is on the editorial advisory boards of various international journals, and is active in professional organisations.

JEANETTE STEEMERS, Ph.D, is Professor of Media and Communications and Co- Research Director of the School of Media, Arts and Design at the University of Westminster in London. She has worked as an industry analyst (CIT Research) and Research Manager (HIT Entertainment). Her books include *Global Media and National Policies (*2016 with T. Flew and P. Iosifidis*), European Media in Crisis (*2015 with J. Trappel and B. Thomass*), Creating Preschool Television (2010), Regaining the Initiative for Public Service Media* (co-editor with G.F. Lowe, 2012), *Media in Europe* (Co-editor, 2011), *Selling Television* (2004) and *European Television Industries* (2005 with P. Iosifidis and M. Wheeler). She is European Editor of *Convergence*. Her work has been funded by the Leverhulme Trust, the British Academy and the Arts and Humanities Research Council.

JONATHAN STERNE is Professor and James McGill Chair in Culture and Technology in the Department of Art History and Communication Studies at McGill University. He is author of *MP3: The Meaning of a Format* (Duke 2012), *The Audible Past: Cultural Origins of Sound Reproduction* (Duke, 2003); and numerous articles on media, technologies and the politics of culture. He is also editor of *The Sound Studies Reader* (Routledge, 2012). His new projects consider instruments and instrumentalities; mail by cruise missile; and the intersections of disability, technology and perception. Visit his website at http://sterneworks.org.

JOE STRAUBHAAR is Amon G. Carter Sr. Centennial Professor of Communications in the Radio-Television-Film Department of the University of Texas. He is also Director of the Latino and Latin American Media Studies Program in the College of Communications. He has held visiting professor positions in Asian, Europe and Latin America. He regularly publishes on Brazilian television and digital media, U.S. and Brazilian digital inclusion, Latin American television, BRICS as emerging media powers, and global television. He is Co-editor of *Comparative Approaches to the Digital Age Revolution in Europe and Latin America* (IGI, 2015); coauthor of *Latin American Television Industries* (BFI/Palgrave, 2013); and author of *World Television: from Global to Local* (Sage, 2007), among others.

PETR SZCZEPANIK is an Associate Professor at Charles University, Prague; and editor of the Czech film journal *Iluminace*. His current research focuses on the Czech (post)socialist production system, some of the results of which were published in *Behind the Screen. Inside European Production Culture* (Palgrave, 2013, co-edited with Patrick Vonderau). In 2015, he published (with a team of collaborators) an extensive report on film development practices in Czech Republic, commissioned by the Czech State Film Fund. He was also the main coordinator of an EU-funded project, "FIND" (www.projectfind.cz), which used student internships in production companies to combine job shadowing with ethnographic research of production cultures.

SERRA TINIC is Associate Professor of Media Studies at the University of Alberta. Her research focuses on critical television studies and media globalization. She is the author of *On Location: Canada's Television Industry in a Global Market* (University of Toronto Press). Her work has been published in a range of scholarly anthologies and journals, including *Television and New Media, The Journal of Communication, Social Epistemology, Velvet Light Trap, Popular Communication: The International Journal of Media and Culture,* and *Communication, Culture, and Critique.*

JOSEPH TUROW is the Robert Lewis Shayon Professor of Communication at the University of Pennsylvania's Annenberg School for Communication. He has authored nine books, edited five books, and written over 150 articles on media industries. Among his authored books are *Getting Books to Children: An Exploration of Publisher-Market Relation* (American Library Association, 1981), *Media Systems in Society* (Addison Wesley, two editions), *Media Today* (Routledge, five editions), *Playing Doctor: Television, Storytelling and Medical Power* (Oxford University Press and University of Michigan Press, two editions), *Breaking Up America* (University of Chicago Press, 1998), *Niche Envy* (MIT Press, 2006), and *The Daily You* (Yale University Press, 2012). He is an elected Fellow of the International Communication Association and has received a Distinguished Scholar Award by the National Communication Association.

PATRICK VONDERAU is Professor in the Department for Media Studies, Stockholm University. His most recent book publications include *Films that Sell: Moving Images and Advertising* (2016, with Nico de Klerk & Bo Florin), *Behind the Screen: Inside European Production Cultures* (2013, with Petr Szczepanik), and *Moving Data: The iPhone and the Future of Media* (Columbia University Press, 2012). Patrick is a co-editor of Germany's leading media studies journal, *Montage*, and a cofounder of NECS - European Network for Cinema and Media Studies (http://www.necs.org/).

JING WANG is Professor of Chinese Media and Cultural studies at MIT. She is the author of *Brand New China: Advertising, Media, and Commercial Culture* (2008) [http://www.amazon.com/Brand-New-China-Advertising-Commercial/dp/0674047087]. Her coedited special issue (with Winnie Wong) *Reconsidering the MIT Visualizing Cultures Controversy* (2015) [http://positions.dukejournals.org/content/23/1.toc] won the Council of Editors of Learned Journals Award [http://www.celj.org] for Best Special Issue of the year. Wang has a dual research interest: the impact of social media on both commercial and civic communications. She is also the Director of NGO2.0 [http://www.ngo20.org/?lang=en], a China-based activist project that advocates the development of a new brand of public-interest sector that utilizes social media and nonprofit technology to build a better society. She is currently working on a book manuscript titled *The Other Digital China: NGOs and Activism 2.0.*

JANET WASKO is Knight Chair Communication Research at University of Oregon in Eugene. She is the author, coauthor, or editor of nineteen books, including *Understanding Disney: The Manufacture of Fantasy and How Hollywood Works*. Her research and teaching focuses on the political economy of media, especially the political economy of film, as well as issues relating to democracy and media. She currently serves as President of the International Association for Media and Communication Research.

HERMAN WASSERMAN is Professor of Media Studies in the Centre for Film and Media Studies, University of Cape Town, South Africa. He has published widely on media in post-apartheid South Africa, including the monograph *Tabloid Journalism in South Africa:*

True Story! (Indiana University Press, 2010) and the edited collections *Popular Media, Democracy, and Development in Africa* and *Press Freedom in Africa: Comparative Perspectives* (Routledge, 2010 and 2012). He edits the journal *Ecquid Novi: African Journalism Studies.*

EMILIE YUEH-YU YEH is Professor and Director of the Academy of Film at Hong Kong Baptist University. Her publications include: *Staging Memories: Hou Hsiao-hsien's A City Of Sadness* (with Markus Nornes, Michigan Publishing, 2015), *Rethinking Chinese Film Industry: New Methods, New Histories* (Beijing University Press, 2011), *East Asian Screen Industries* (with Darrell Davis, British Film Institute, 2008), *Taiwan Film Directors: A Treasure Island* (with Darrell Davis, Columbia University Press, 2005), *Chinese-Language Film: Historiography, Poetics, Politics* (with Sheldon Lu, University of Hawaii Press, 2005), and more than 50 articles. Some of her publications have been translated to Japanese, Hungarian, Spanish and Chinese. Her two forthcoming books are on newspaper data and early cinema practices in Chinese cities.

298

AMELIA ARSENAULT is an Assistant Professor of Communication at Georgia State University. Her scholarly work has appeared in the *International Journal of Communication, International Sociology, The ANNALS of the American Academy of Political and Social Science,* and *Information, Communication, and Society.* She is currently working on a book project that explores the nascent industry of digital "information warriors" who provide contract propaganda services to political actors seeking to influence the online media agenda. She teaches courses in new media, network theory, and communication and power. She was previously a non-resident fellow at the USC Center on Public Diplomacy at the Annenberg School for Communication (2012 – 2014) and a resident fellow at the Center for Media, Data, and Society and the Institute for Advanced Studies at Central European University (Fall 2014). She holds a B.A. in Film and History from Dartmouth College and an MSc in Global Media and Communication from the London School of Economics and Political Science, and a PhD from the University of Southern California Annenberg School.

ALISA PERREN is Associate Professor in the Department of Radio-TV-Film at The University of Texas at Austin. She is co-editor of *Media Industries: History, Theory, and Method* (Wiley-Blackwell, 2009) and author of *Indie, Inc.: Miramax and the Transformation of Hollywood in the 1990s* (University of Texas Press, 2012). Her work has appeared in a range of publications, including *Film Quarterly, Journal of Film and Video, Journal of Popular Film & Television, Managing Media Work,* and *Moving Data.* From 2010 to 2013, she served as Coordinating Editor for *In Media Res,* an online project experimenting with collaborative, multi-modal forms of scholarship. Her current book project is *The American Comic Book Industry and Hollywood,* co-authored with Gregory Steirer for BFI's International Screen Industries series.

Editorial Collective

STUART CUNNINGHAM is Distinguished Professor of Media and Communications, Queensland University of Technology. His most recent books are *Digital Disruption: Cinema Moves Online* (edited with Dina Iordanova, 2012), *Key Concepts in Creative Industries* (with John Hartley, Jason Potts, Terry Flew, John Banks and Michael Keane, 2013), *Hidden Innovation: Policy, Industry and the Creative Sector* (2014), *Screen Distribution and the New King Kongs of the Online World* (with Jon Silver, 2013), *The Media and Communications in Australia* (edited with Sue Turnbull) and *Media Economics* (with Terry Flew and Adam Swift, 2015). His most recent honours include admission into the fellowship of the UK-based Academy of Social Sciences in 2013, the award of a Fulbright Senior Scholarship for 2014-15, and investiture as a Member of the Order of Australia in 2015 for 'significant service to higher education, particularly to the study of media and communications, as an academic and researcher'.

MICHAEL CURTIN is the Duncan and Suzanne Mellichamp Professor in the Department of Film and Media Studies at the University of California, Santa Barbara. He is lead professor of the Mellichamp Global Dynamics cluster and is co-founder and former director of the Media Industries Project at the Carsey-Wolf Center. His books include *Playing to the World's Biggest Audience: The Globalization of Chinese Film and TV*, *Distribution Revolution: Conversations about the Digital Future of Film and* Television, and *Precarious Creativity: Global Media, Local* Labor. Curtin is currently at work on *Media Capital: The Cultural Geography of Globalization* and is co-editor of the *Chinese Journal of Communication* and the International Screen Industries book series of the British Film Institute.

ELIZABETH EVANS is Assistant Professor in Film and Television Studies at the University of Nottingham. She is the author of *Transmedia Television: Audiences, New Media and Daily Life* (2011) and has published articles in a number of journals including *Media, Culture and Society, Participations, The International Journal of Communication Studies* , and the *Journal of Pervasive Ubiquitous Computing*. Her research explores the relationship between audiences, technology, and the screen industries with particular emphasis on interrogating the notion of "engagement" and transmedia content.

TERRY FLEW is Professor of Media and Communications in the Creative Industries Faculty at the Queensland University of Technology (QUT). His books include *Media Economics* (Palgrave, 2015, with Stuart Cunningham and Adam Swift), *Global Creative Industries* (Polity, 2013), *The Creative Industries, Culture and Policy* (Sage, 2012), *Creative Industries and Urban Development: Creative Cities in the 21st Century* (Routledge, 2012), *Key Concepts in Creative Industries* (Sage, 2012), and *Understanding Global Media* (Palgrave, 2007), and *New Media: An Introduction* (Oxford, 20082014). He is also Chief Investigator with the ARC Centre of Excellence for Creative Industries and Innovation (CCI), and the Digital Media Research Centre (DMRC) at QUT.

ANTHONY Y.H. FUNG is Director and Professor in the School of Journalism and Communication at the Chinese University of Hong Kong. His research interests and teaching focus on popular culture and cultural studies, gender and youth identity, cultural industries and policy, and new media studies. He is currently working on a project on Asian creative and game industries and cultural policy with a focus on China and Hong Kong. He has authored and edited more than 10 Chinese and English books. His recent books are *New Television Globalization and East Asian Cultural Imaginations* (Hong Kong University Press, 2007) (with Keane and Moran), *Global Capital, Local Culture: Transnational Media Corporations in China* (Peter Lang, 2008), *Riding a Melodic Tide: The Development of Cantopop in Hong Kong* (Subculture Press, 2009) (in Chinese), *Policies for the Sustainable Development of the Hong Kong Film Industry* (Chinese University Press, 2009) (with Chan and Ng), *Imagining Chinese Communication Studies* (Hong Kong Institute of Asia-Pacific Studies, 2012) (in Chinese) (with Huang), *Melodic Memories: The Historical Development of Music Industry in Hong Kong* (2012) (Subculture Press, in Chinese), and *Asian Popular Culture: the Global (Dis)continuity* (Routledge, 2013).

JENNIFER HOLT is Associate Professor of Film and Media Studies at the University of California, Santa Barbara and a Faculty Associate of the Berkman Center for Internet & Society at Harvard University. She is the author of *Empires of Entertainment* (2010) and co-editor of *Distribution Revolution* (2014); *Connected Viewing: Selling, Sharing, and Streaming Media in the Digital Era* (2013); and *Media Industries: History, Theory, and Method* (2009). Her work has appeared in journals and anthologies including the *Journal of Information Policy, Moving Data,* and *Signal Traffic: Critical Studies of Media Infrastructures.* She is former Director of the Carsey Wolf Center's Media Industries Project. Her current book project examines the political and cultural stakes of digital media policy.

PAUL MCDONALD is Professor of Cultural and Creative Industries in the Department of Culture, Media and Creative Industries at King's College London. Publications include *Video and DVD Industries* (BFI, 2007) and *Hollywood Stardom* (Wiley-Blackwell, 2013), and co-editing *Hollywood and the Law* (BFI, 2015) and *The Contemporary Hollywood Film Industry* (Blackwell, 2008). Since 2001 he has co-edited the *International Screen Industries* series from BFI Publishing. He founded, and is now co-chair of, the Media Industries Scholarly Interest Group of the Society for Cinema and Media Studies (SCMS), and founded and co-ordinates the Screen Industries Work Group in the European Network for Cinema and Media Studies (NECS).

BRIAN MCNAIR is Professor of Journalism, Media and Communication at Queensland University of Technology. He is the author of twelve books and many scholarly essays on topics including news and journalism, political communication, the media in post-Soviet Russia, and mediated sexuality. His most recent books are *An Introduction To Political Communication* (5th edition, 2011), *Journalists In Film* (2010), and *Porno? Chic!* (2013). His books have been widely translated, and are standard reading on media and communication courses across the world. He sits on the editorial boards of *Journalism Studies, Journalism Practice, Journalism: theory, practice and criticism, International Journal of Press/Politics,* and

Sexualities. He is currently working on an ARC-funded study of Australian political media.

KEVIN SANSON is Lecturer of Entertainment Industries in the Creative Industries Faculty at Queensland University of Technology. Previously, he was Research Director of the Carsey-Wolf Center's Media Industries Project at the University of California, Santa Barbara. His current book project examines the spatial dynamics of international film and television production, focusing especially on shifting working conditions and practices in global production hubs. He is co-editor of *Precarious Creativity: Global Media, Local Labor* (UC Press 2016), *Connected Viewing: Selling, Streaming, & Sharing Media in the Digital Era* (Routledge 2014) and *Distribution Revolution: Conversations about the Digital Future of Film and Television* (UC Press 2014). He earned his Ph.D. from the University of Texas at Austin.

Editorial Staff

LAURA E. FELSCHOW is a PhD candidate in the department of Radio-Television-Film at the University of Texas at Austin. She holds an MA in Media Studies from the State University of New York at Buffalo and a BFA in Film with a minor in Animation from Syracuse University. Her published work includes "'Hey, check it out, there's actually fans': (Dis)empowerment and (mis)representation of cult fandom in *Supernatural*" in *Transformative Works and Culture* and a chapter in *TV Goes to Hell: An Unofficial Road Map to Supernatural*. Her dissertation project considers gender and production in the superhero genre from an industrial perspective.

CHARLOTTE E. HOWELL is a doctoral candidate in the Department of Radio-Television-Film at The University of Texas-Austin, set to receive her PhD in 2016 before joining the faculty at Boston University as an Assistant Professor in the Department of Film and Television. Her research interests include: religion and television, genre studies, media history, and media industry studies.

AALEEYAH PRINGLE is a graduate student at Georgia State University pursuing a Masters in Communication and a Public Health Certificate. She ranked among the top 10% of her incoming cohort and was awarded a graduate assistantship. Aaleeyah graduated with a Bachelor of Science in Communication in 2014.

KYLE WRATHER is a PhD student in the department of Radio-Television-Film at the University of Texas at Austin. He holds an MA from Georgia State University. His master's thesis, "Comparitive Modalities of Network Neutrality" examines how different forms of regulation have affected network neutrality policy. He holds a BA in English and a BA in Communication with a focus on journalism from Mississippi State University. While at Mississippi State, he served as the Editor in Chief of *The Reflector*, the university's independent student newspaper. His research interests include media industries, new media technologies, podcasting, and streaming television.

Media Industries would also like to thank Georgia State University Graduate Student Assistants, **Nicole Worthington** and **Kiara Clark**.

CPSIA information can be obtained
at www.ICGtesting.com
Printed in the USA
BVOW06s0844211217
503376BV00011B/419/P

9 781522 991830